Spirit Cure

Spirit Cure

A History of Pentecostal Healing

JOSEPH W. WILLIAMS

OXFORD
UNIVERSITY PRESS

OXFORD

UNIVERSITY PRESS

Oxford University Press is a department of the University of Oxford. It furthers the University's objective of excellence in research, scholarship, and education by publishing worldwide.

Oxford New York
Auckland Cape Town Dar es Salaam Hong Kong Karachi
Kuala Lumpur Madrid Melbourne Mexico City Nairobi
New Delhi Shanghai Taipei Toronto

With offices in
Argentina Austria Brazil Chile Czech Republic France Greece
Guatemala Hungary Italy Japan Poland Portugal Singapore
South Korea Switzerland Thailand Turkey Ukraine Vietnam

Oxford is a registered trade mark of Oxford University Press in the UK and certain other countries.

Published in the United States of America by
Oxford University Press
198 Madison Avenue, New York, NY 10016

Library of Congress Cataloging-in-Publication Data
Williams, Joseph W.
Spirit cure : a history of pentecostal healing / Joseph W. Williams.
p. cm.
Includes bibliographical references and index.
ISBN 978-0-19-976567-6 (alk. paper)
1. Healing—Religious aspects—Pentecostal churches—History. 2. Spiritual healing—Pentecostal churches—History. 3. Pentecostal churches—United States—History. I. Title.
BT732.W54 2013
234'.13108828994—dc23
2012020495

9780199765676

1 3 5 7 9 8 6 4 2

Printed in the United States of America on acid-free paper

For Karen

CONTENTS

ACKNOWLEDGMENTS

While my name may appear by itself on the front cover of this book, this hardly does justice to the numerous mentors, colleagues, friends, and family who contributed in a wide variety of ways to its completion. I wish first to express my gratitude to Amanda Porterfield. A course she taught on religious healing spurred my initial interest in the subject, and at every stage of the project since then I have benefited immensely from her sage advice and constant encouragement. I owe a similar debt to John Corrigan, Mark Noll, and Grant Wacker. Their discerning recommendations regarding the manuscript and on a host of other issues modeled a level of intellectual generosity that I hope to emulate in my own career.

I am also very grateful for the generous support I have received from Rutgers University, and especially from my colleagues in the Religion Department, including Edwin Bryant, Tao Jiang, James T. Johnson, James W. Jones, Tia Kolbaba, Jawid Mojaddedi, and Emma Wasserman. James Johnson in particular deserves a special thank you for all the times he stopped by my office to offer a word of encouragement and inquire regarding my progress. I could not ask for a more stimulating or congenial environment in which to conduct my research and teaching.

At Oxford University Press, Theo Calderara provided expert guidance at every stage of the process, and the superb suggestions made by the press's readers strengthened the manuscript in crucial areas. When the project was still very much in incipient form, Frederick Davis, Curtis Evans, Martin Kavka, and Amy Koehlinger offered helpful feedback, while Ruth Schwartz Cowan, David Daniels, Kathleen Flake, Bill Buker, and Sean McCloud responded to conference papers that formed the basis of different chapters. Much of my argument took shape during my time in the Religion Department at Florida State University, where I benefited greatly from the camaraderie that developed among the graduate students in the program, many of whom shared my interest in American religious history. I am especially thankful for the continued friendship of Kelly Baker,

Betsy Barre, Todd Brenneman, Laura Brock, Cara Burnidge, Michael Gueno, Katie Hladky, Gene Mills, Michael Pasquier, Molly Reed, Art Remillard, Brooke Sherrard, and Howell Williams.

In the course of my research I had the good fortune to work with dedicated archivists and librarians who went out of their way to help me track down materials related to my research. Special thanks go to Mark Roberts and the staff at the Holy Spirit Research Center in Tulsa, Oklahoma; to Darrin Rodgers, Glenn Gohr, and the staff of the Flower Pentecostal Heritage Center in Springfield, Missouri; to David Roebuck and Susan Fletcher at the Dixon Pentecostal Research Center in Cleveland, Tennessee; to Harold Hunter and the staff at the archives of the International Pentecostal Holiness Church in Bethany, Oklahoma; to Robert Sivigny and Donald Gantz at Regent University Library in Virginia Beach, Virginia; to Robert Shuster and Paul Erickson at the Billy Graham Center Archives in Wheaton, Illinois; and to Nurah-Rosalie Jeter at the Schomburg Center for Research in Black Culture in New York City. Financial assistance provided by Professor Ralph Berry and the selection committee for the Edward H. and Marie C. Kingsbury Award and a research grant provided by the Florida State Office of Graduate Studies helped fund much of my research. I am also indebted to the interlibrary loan departments at both Florida State University and Rutgers University for tracking down what must have seemed like an endless number of requests. The generous support of the Byrne Summer Research Program, and Michael Pazzani, Vice President for Research and Graduate and Professional Education at Rutgers University, allowed me to hire a research assistant, Shumaila Chishti, who did an excellent job helping me wrap up the final details for this project. To the staff at the Bunnvale branch of the Hunterdon County Library, including Wendy Harding, Eileen Lebida, Joan Lucas, and Ada Roth: thank you for allowing me to claim the table downstairs as my own on so many occasions!

Friends and family have also provided crucial support at various points, whether it involved rummaging through their personal libraries or memories for relevant titles and information, pressing me to think carefully about the relationship between my Christian commitments and my scholarly pursuits, or simply reminding me that I should in fact venture out beyond the cloistered walls of academia from time to time. For these and numerous other kindnesses I owe a special thank you to Ruth and Thomas Atkinson, Debbie and Josh Booth, Thom Cochran and HRH Tracey Rajack Cochran, John Fawcett, Jason and Sarah Furrow, Don and Nina Helms, Stephen and Christi Layman, Aunt Joyce and Uncle Karl, Grandma Leora, Grandma Maria, Larry Perry, Evelyn Russell, Luther and Jeane Sherman, "Aunt" Valerie, Jim and Shauna Williams, and Mary Jo Williams. In many respects my grandfather Ward Williams's commitment to higher education paved the way for my current endeavors. More than anyone else my brother David Williams has worked to keep me humble, repeatedly reminding me that while I may have a Ph.D. after my name, I still am not a "real" doctor. My parents, Paul and Sofia Williams, and my in-laws, Paul and Shirley Furrow, provided a steady stream of love and encouragement, not to mention several extended babysitting visits that freed up big chunks of time to conduct research and to write. Both of my beautiful daughters, Elise and Alexa, were born during the course of this project. Sleepless nights notwithstanding, the level of joy and love in my life has expanded exponentially due to their presence. I love you girls.

Finally, I dedicate *Spirit Cure* to my wife, Karen. More than anyone else, she bore the brunt of my seemingly nonstop writing sessions, and she witnessed firsthand my detachment from the present as I got lost in old pentecostal periodicals and healing tracts. Thank you for loving me through it all. My life simply does not make sense without you.

Spirit Cure

Introduction

On a Thursday in October 1926, a Mrs. T. Mathews Izor of Detroit was suddenly "seized with excruciating pains which grew worse until it seemed to be unbearable." Deeply committed to her pentecostal faith and to prohibitions in the pentecostal movement condemning reliance on medicine, Izor instinctively clung to her Bible, "pressing it against the torturing parts" as she tried to pray. When the pain did not relent, she then called fellow believers who "prayed with laying on of hands." Unable to watch his mother suffer, Izor's son summoned a doctor against her wishes. The physician promptly diagnosed acute appendicitis and insisted that Izor be rushed to the hospital. The news apparently had little impact on Izor's faith. "I told him I would not take any medicine," she recounted, "neither would I be operated on." She had "trusted God for my healing for 17 years and would still trust him." True to her word, Izor refused to take her prescription at the hospital. According to the pentecostal mother, God remained true to his word as well. When astonished nurses and interns checked on her the next day she happily informed them that "the Lord has healed me," hastily adding that she "came for the sake of her son, and this is a dear place to rest."[1]

No doubt Izor would have been astounded if she had lived to see the changes wrought in pentecostal healing by the early twenty-first century: practical medical advice regarding a wide range of maladies littering the pages of pentecostal periodicals; M.D.s, D.O.s, and N.D.s appearing alongside more traditional healing evangelists on pentecostal and charismatic television programming hawking the latest dietary supplements necessary for health and healing; and practitioners of inner healing taking aim at the suffering caused by psychological maladjustments before directing their spiritual weapons at demonic forces. If the healing practices of the faithful are any indication, the nature of pentecostals' engagement with modern U.S. culture changed drastically over the course of the twentieth century.

The history of pentecostals' shifting attitudes toward more scientific and natural healing methods provides a particularly valuable vantage point for assessing pentecostals' evolving relationship to mainstream U.S. culture, due in no small part to the centrality of healing in the pentecostal tradition and its import for pentecostal identity. Ever since the inception of the pentecostal movement in the early 1900s, healing frequently was as significant a marker of pentecostal spirituality as was speaking in tongues or adherents' emphasis on Christ's imminent return. "Modern Pentecostals commonly distinguish themselves from other Protestants by the doctrine and practice of speaking in tongues," writes the historian Grant Wacker. "This represents a certain loss of historical memory, for an overview of the early literature leaves little doubt that in the beginning divine healing was, if not equally distinctive, at least equally important."[2] As a cornerstone of pentecostal practice past and present, divine healing encompassed much more than adherents' attempts to deal with pain and suffering: it confirmed believers' deepest convictions about the nature of reality; it solidified social ties through ritualized expressions of compassion and concern; and it served as a recruiting tool drawing individuals hungry to see—and experience—tangible manifestations of the supernatural.[3]

No matter how important healing was in the pentecostal movement, the history of pentecostals' responses to physical and emotional suffering would be of limited value in determining believers' place in U.S. culture if that culture had little to say on the subject. Such was (and is) not the case. Whereas very few outsiders offered competing versions of tongues, conventional doctors, psychotherapists, alternative practitioners, and other religious healers supplied a steady stream of competing practical solutions to a wide variety of ailments, as well as competing conceptual frameworks for making sense of the nature of illness.[4] The rising prestige of the medical profession, along with a continued obsession with health and fitness in U.S. culture over the course of the twentieth century, likewise ensured that pentecostals repeatedly would need to address how their understanding of divine healing fit with the rapid technological and scientific advances shaping modern health practices in the United States.

The highly competitive nature of the U.S. healing marketplace frequently pushed pentecostals to defend their distinctive brand of faith healing and aggressively distinguish their approach from other available options, yet the encounter with diverse methodologies occasioned by that competition simultaneously opened the door for a significant dialogue between the faithful and their rivals. The ensuing transformation of the pentecostal healing landscape that followed the saints' engagement with their competitors revealed as much about pentecostals' changing understanding of their relationship to modern U.S. society as it did about changes in their specific healing rituals and practices. By the end of the twentieth century, pentecostal healers, discontented with the cultural isolation and marginalization that early believers experienced, opted instead for models of health and healing that satiated adherents' desire for divine intervention while simultaneously satisfying their appetite for cutting-edge tests, procedures, and products backed by the latest scientific studies and thoroughly in tune with the consumer-oriented celebration of perfect health and self-realization characteristic of mainstream U.S. therapeutic culture.

Pentecostal Healing in Historical Context

The underlying assumptions supporting the earliest pentecostals' approach to healing directly grew out of the late-nineteenth-century evangelical divine healing movement. Part of a much wider revolt in U.S. Christianity against Calvinistic forms of determinism that taught believers to patiently endure suffering as an act of submission to God, divine healing advocates called believers to actively lay claim to God's promise of physical health in this life.[5] "Perhaps no objection [to divine healing] is more strongly urged," wrote A. B. Simpson, a well-known divine healing advocate and founder of the Christian and Missionary Alliance, than the claim that glory "rebounds to God from our submission to His will in sickness." To the contrary, Simpson believed divine healing to be "the Divine prescription for disease; and no obedient Christian can safely dispense with it."[6] Though important differences existed among advocates of "faith cure," they all could agree with Simpson that Christians needlessly endured suffering when God had in fact provided a means of deliverance accessible to every believer.

Radical evangelicals' supreme confidence during the late 1800s in God's desire to heal reflected more than changing theological currents. The expanding role of women in U.S. public life and the demands of an increasingly consumer-oriented economy unsettled deeply embedded gender norms linking ideal femininity with submission and sacrifice. The rise of "muscular Christianity" during the period illustrated similar modifications to notions of masculinity that lessened the importance of disciplined self-restraint in favor of virile action. A God who refused to intervene on behalf of the suffering and constantly demanded self-denial of his followers simply did not comport with the shifting expectations of numerous believers, nor could such a God provide much competition for unorthodox religious healers, who often operated outside the bounds of traditional understandings of the Christian faith.[7]

Viewed from the perspective of believers, radical evangelicals' absolute assurance regarding God's readiness to heal ultimately derived from their reading of scripture. Early pentecostals especially were indebted to nineteenth-century healers who focused on specific passages that they believed located healing power squarely in the atonement provided by Christ's death and resurrection. A passage in Isaiah that Christians typically read in reference to the life of Jesus indicated that "he was wounded for our transgressions, he was bruised for our iniquities: the chastisement of our peace was upon him; and with his stripes we are healed." The author of 1 Peter, writing in the first century CE, echoed Isaiah: Jesus "bare our sins in his own body on the tree, that we, being dead to sins, should live unto righteousness: by whose stripes ye were healed."[8] Healers who associated divine healing with the atonement zeroed in on the explicit connection found in 1 Peter and Isaiah between healing and the "stripes" Jesus endured during the crucifixion. If Christians had little trouble agreeing with scripture regarding the ready availability of forgiveness from sins made possible by Jesus's death, adherents asked, why should they question the ready availability of healing also purchased by Christ's sacrifice? Rather, Jesus's crucifixion and resurrection applied equally to sin and sickness. This conviction that healing was "in the atonement" and intimately connected to Christ's death on the cross in turn solidified divine healing advocates'—and later pentecostals'—assurance that healing equaled a failsafe promise, written in black and white for all to see in the very Word of God.

Armed with biblical evidence of God's promise to heal, late-nineteenth-century healers eschewed the reigning orthodoxy regarding passive acquiescence to suffering, admonishing the afflicted instead to activate faith and trust God for healing. Referring to verses in the Gospel of Mark, the Boston-area Baptist minister A. J. Gordon noted Christ's promise that miraculous signs—including divine healing—would "follow them that believe." "It is important to observe," he wrote, "that this rich cluster of miraculous promises all hangs by a single stem, faith."[9] Stubborn symptoms may persist, yet the true believer knew better than to pay them any attention. The saint's job was to "act faith," to get up and get going in full assurance that God would stay true to his Word.[10] When facing his own illness, Simpson recalled making a pledge to God placing his health in God's hands. Immediately afterward Simpson wrote: "It had only been a few moments, but I knew that something was done. Every fibre [sic] of my soul was tingling with a sense of God's presence." Significantly, Simpson remembered that he did "not know whether my body felt better or not—I did not care to feel it—it was so glorious to believe it simply, and to know that henceforth He had it in hand."[11] According to Simpson, God freely offered healing to everyone. All that was required was an utter reliance on God's power and complete confidence that he would fulfill his healing promises as spelled out in scripture. Any other option proved an idolatrous alternative.

For all of their talk of absolute dependence on God's power, those promoting divine healing in the late 1800s also carved out a significant role for the believer in the healing process that went well beyond mere trust in divine assistance. In this regard, the faithful revealed the divine healing movement's indebtedness to the nineteenth-century holiness movement. A byproduct of the revivalistic fervor of the 1820s and 30s, the holiness movement initially centered around Methodists who promoted John Wesley's claims regarding the possibility of Christian perfection (often referred to as entire sanctification) attained by an all-encompassing commitment to follow Christ and his commands in every detail of life.[12] As holiness emphases spread beyond the holiness movement's Wesleyan roots to impact more and more non-Wesleyan Christians in the second half of the nineteenth century, they helped to keep alive perfectionist themes among evangelicals more generally, including individuals in the Reformed Higher Life movement.[13] The divine healing movement, in fact, which attracted individuals from across the spectrum of late-nineteenth-century evangelicalism, can be read as a logical extension of the holiness emphasis on sanctification, wherein teachings regarding the perfectibility of the soul were extrapolated to apply in the physical realm to the human body as well.[14]

The perfectionist legacy of the Wesleyan-holiness brand of Christianity, with its attendant stress on personal discipline and responsibility, shaped evangelical healers' understanding of the connection between bodily disciplines and physical health. This is not to deny, of course, that the standard holiness credo stressed the spiritual benefits of bodily discipline more than its physical benefits. For leaders in the holiness movement such as Phoebe Palmer, who began her "Tuesday Meeting for the Promotion of Holiness" in the 1830s, the route to *spiritual* perfection demanded "an entire and continual reliance on Christ," including careful regulation of the body in everything from dress to speech to diet.[15] Palmer followed Wesley's lead by reserving Fridays for fasting in order to maintain her spiritual zeal. Though her health did "not permit my fasting . . . wholly," she nevertheless found "it well to observe the day in frequent acts of self-denial. Paul says, 'I keep my body under.' I find it helpful to my spiritual health, to do likewise."[16]

Defenders of faith healing later in the nineteenth century never discarded their predecessors' desire for spiritual health. At the same time, physical disciplines such as fasting proved important allies in the pursuit of bodily healing as well, as these defenders sought to cultivate the requisite faith to pray for God's direct intervention. One testimony recorded in 1882 in the evangelical periodical *Triumphs of Faith*, edited by a prominent healer who eventually joined the ranks of pentecostalism, Carrie Judd Montgomery, illustrated the connection: "Within the last two weeks I have been cured of a very severe cold through fasting and the 'prayer of faith, . . . '. I lay considerable stress on fasting; for how can we expect so rich a blessing in answer to prayer if we are unwilling to humble ourselves before God by taking up this cross."[17] Andrew Murray, an influential evangelical proponent of divine healing in Great Britain and South Africa often quoted by pentecostals in the United States, likewise highlighted the importance of fasting in laying the groundwork for the prayer of faith that preceded God's miraculous intervention. In 1887, Murray insisted that *"prayer needs fasting* for its full growth. . . . Prayer is the one hand with which we grasp the invisible; fasting, the other, with which we let loose and cast away the visible." He believed that "only in a life of moderation and temperance and self-denial . . . will be the heart or the strength to pray much."[18]

Even apart from the link between bodily discipline and faith-filled prayers, most late-nineteenth-century evangelical healers would have readily admitted the natural health benefits associated with the careful regulation of the body. Here again the divine healing movement reflected the legacy of John Wesley. One of Wesley's most popular books well into the nineteenth century, *Primitive Physick*, offered wide-ranging practical advice intended to instruct his readers regarding regimens that aided in the maintenance of health. Drawing heavily on the writings of George Cheyne, a seventeenth-century advocate for carefully regulated diets, Wesley offered several principles necessary for individuals "to retain the Health they have recovered." Regarding diet, Wesley instructed readers to "suit the Quality and Quantity of Food to the Strength of our Degestion." For "studious Persons," this generally worked out to "about eight Ounces of Animal Food, and twelve of Vegetable in twenty-four Hours." Water also quickens "the Appetite and strengthens the Digestion," he said, and a "due Degree of Exercise is indispensably necessary to Health and long Life." For exercise, Wesley recommended two to three hours a day of physical activity ranging from walking to riding horses.[19]

Not surprisingly, given the continued popularity of Wesley's writings and his outsized influence on the development of nineteenth-century U.S. evangelicalism, his spiritual descendants frequently promoted the importance of following the "laws of health" implanted in nature by God. Faith healers in the later decades of the century were no exception, as they joined other nineteenth-century health reformers in promoting "physical Arminianism."[20] A deaconess in John Alexander Dowie's Zion City in Illinois, itself an important precursor of pentecostal trends, confirmed in 1899 that sickness resulted either from "thoughtless disregard of the laws of health or by wilful disobedience."[21] The Reverend Robert Livingston Stanton, a one-time moderator of the Presbyterian General Assembly, warned the faithful in 1883 that healing did not shield believers from the natural consequences associated with neglecting their bodies. Those who experienced healing by the "direct power of God" should not "suppose that all subsequent sickness will be avoided if the person be utterly regardless of the ordinary laws of health." "God's promises do not cover such cases," he stated bluntly. "The continuance of health is placed in large degree under our own care."[22]

Divine healing proponents' utilization of traditional Christian healing rituals recommended in scripture complicated their conceptions of "faith cure" even further. In the Gospel of Mark, Jesus himself promised his followers that they would "lay hands on the sick, and they shall recover," while Christians who read the book of James learned that the sick should call elders in the church not only to pray but also to anoint with oil those suffering from physical ailments.[23] In order to counter accusations that such practices represented blind superstition or a reversion to "magical" Catholic practices, leaders in the late-nineteenth-century divine healing movement typically stressed the symbolic nature of these actions and the way ritualized forms of sacred touch reinforced an individual's faith, yet they never abandoned these biblical directives.[24]

In highlighting the importance of careful ritual observance and of following natural health laws, evangelical healers near the turn of the twentieth century added significant qualifications to their stress on faith in the almighty hand of God. While advocates of divine healing prioritized God's direct, miraculous intervention in their efforts to reinstate divine healing and the restoration of the body as a central aspect of the Christian life, radical evangelicals also cast a significant—if secondary—role for personal discipline, natural processes, and ritual activity in their healing schema.

Pentecostals and the Evangelical Healing Movement

Specifically regarding pentecostals' relationship to the divine healing movement of the late 1800s, historians rightly highlight the continuities linking believers' healing practices to antecedents in the broader evangelical world.[25] Like a number of their predecessors, pentecostals located the power to heal in the atoning work of Jesus's death on the cross and described their vision of healing utilizing a thoroughly biblical discourse replete with references to faith, prayer, and sin. Several advocates also carried forward holiness assumptions regarding the practical health benefits enjoyed by those who followed the "laws of health" and strictly regulated their bodies.[26] While the basic framework provided by previous evangelicals remained intact, when pentecostalism emerged in the first decade of the twentieth century, the saints also accentuated specific themes that heightened even further the tension between reliance on God and any natural remedies: they frequently blamed demonic powers for all manner of illnesses, for instance, and repeatedly underscored the antimedicine implications of divine healing.

A half century after pentecostalism first appeared on the map of U.S. religion, the distance separating pentecostal healing from the practices employed by fellow evangelicals diminished as the pentecostal healing scene began to change dramatically. Claims of direct divine interventions by no means disappeared, yet the strident denunciations of the medical profession characteristic of early pentecostalism increasingly gave way to an unabashed embrace of healing methods condemned by previous pentecostals, as the faithful commingled divine healing with the use of medicine, natural substances, and—with quite a bit more hesitancy—forms of psychotherapy.

Two interrelated developments in particular eventually softened the sharp dualism informing early adherents' inclination to rigidly demarcate divine healing from natural pathways to health. First, the rising socioeconomic status of the average pentecostal following World War II lessened the class warfare that helped fuel early pentecostals' antipathy toward physicians even as it supplied pentecostals with greater resources to pay for a variety of new healing procedures, medicines, and products. The formation of groups such as the Full Gospel Business Men's Fellowship International, founded in 1951, graphically illustrated the growing number of professionals in pentecostal circles, and in the ensuing decades pentecostal televangelists such as Oral Roberts, Jimmy Swaggart, and Jim and Tammy Bakker presided over multimillion-dollar media empires. In the words of one observer: "Many Pentecostals enjoyed seeing their own become stars. . . . They took pride in and lavished funds on those who gave them visibility and reshaped their public image." Whereas early pentecostals embraced a holiness ethic that eschewed worldly indulgences, later generations "seemed inclined to revel in possessions and to find appealing emphases that emanated from independent Pentecostal centers urging the reasonableness of health and wealth for believers."[27] In sum, in the second half of the twentieth century pentecostals proved more than ready to shed the strictures of holiness orthodoxy and instead enjoy new forms of spirituality—and healing—in tune simultaneously with the work of the Spirit and with the dictates of U.S. consumer and therapeutic culture.

The second internal catalyst spurring believers to consider new healing rituals involved the appearance of charismatic renewal and the spread of pentecostal emphases among mainline Protestants and Catholics, and in independent congregations. Pentecostals had always stood apart from other U.S. Protestants on the basis of their insistence that every believer should experience a subsequent work of grace following salvation, referred to as the baptism in the Holy Spirit, accompanied by speaking in tongues. Early pentecostal testimonies brimmed with vivid descriptions of the physical and emotional sensations that frequently accompanied their initial experience of speaking in tongues.[28] The Spirit showered a wide array of other spiritual gifts on the saints as well, including the ability to prophesy regarding the future, to supernaturally know things they had no reason to know, and to watch illness retreat as they prayed for themselves and for others. Similar practices appeared at various times throughout the entire history of Christianity, yet the rise of pentecostalism during the twentieth century helped stimulate the growing prominence of these practices in a wide variety of charismatic churches beginning especially in the 1950s and 1960s.[29]

Early on, tensions bubbled to the surface as pentecostals and charismatics learned to relate to one another; many pentecostals saw their denominations as the only true bastions of the "full gospel message," while charismatics frequently resisted identification with pentecostals, who often were perceived as social outcasts.[30] Over time, the strain in the relationship between the two groups increasingly receded into the background, and historians usually classify pentecostalism and the charismatic renewal as closely related movements that share a similar impulse toward experiential, supernatural Christianity.

As various phenomena associated with pentecostal services gained greater prominence in mainline Protestant, evangelical, and Catholic churches, large numbers of individuals hailing from a solidly middle-class background swelled the ranks of the faithful. Whereas early pentecostals were stereotyped as poor, uneducated individuals, charismatics frequently were well educated and economically comfortable. As a sociologist wrote in 1969, it was now clear to her that one of the trademarks of pentecostal spirituality, speaking in tongues, occurred "also among well-educated, socially successful, and well-adjusted personality types."[31] Building on similar assumptions regarding the wide chasm separating pentecostals and charismatics, other chroniclers of the relationship between pentecostals and charismatics, for example Richard Quebedeaux, argued that the differences between the two groups boiled down to basic socio-economic, educational, and racial dissimilarities that produced very different models of the spirit-filled life.[32]

The historian David Edwin Harrell, Jr., drew on similar distinctions to make sense of pentecostals' and charismatics' differing approaches to healing. He outlined the explosive growth of numerous pentecostal healing ministries beginning in the 1940s, and their rapid decline by the end of the 1950s. As these deliverance evangelists garnered smaller and smaller crowds, a few perpetuated healing crusades featuring dramatic deliverances from sickness-causing demons, but others adapted their message to accord with the more subdued middle-class sensibilities represented by charismatics who were warming to pentecostal forms of spirituality. Harrell highlighted figures such as Gordon Lindsay, Morris Cerullo, and especially Oral Roberts as prominent players in the midcentury revivals who successfully adapted their ministries to appeal to the burgeoning charismatic renewal. Though Harrell never suggested that these figures abandoned their pentecostal backers, his work frequently reinforced a sharp differentiation between pentecostals' predilection for flamboyant revivalism when compared with charismatics' desire for intellectually sophisticated articulations of the healing message.[33]

Several factors caution against drawing too sharp of a division between pentecostals and charismatics. For one, recent historical work calls into question just how socially marginalized even the earliest pentecostal believers actually were, and too much of a focus on the distinctions between pentecostals and charismatics overlooks the crucial role played by numerous individuals with pentecostal backgrounds—including several healers highlighted by Harrell—who helped spread their form of spirituality beyond traditional pentecostal denominations.[34] Specifically regarding pentecostals' and charismatics' evolving healing practices, too much of a focus on the distinctions between pentecostals and charismatics misses the way changing demographics among pentecostals themselves, as well as their changing attitudes toward medical science, helped set the stage for the appearance of naturalized divine healing regimens by the end of the twentieth century. All of that said, the influx of so many middle-class charismatic parishioners who lacked pentecostals' antimedicine, antipsychology baggage reinforced this preexisting momentum and functioned in its own right as an important impetus for change in the realm of pentecostal healing.

The subsequent "naturalization" of divine healing that accompanied charismatic renewal and the changing socioeconomic status of many in the pentecostal movement signified a profound shift away from key aspects of the original pentecostal vision of healing. Whereas early pentecostals condemned reliance on everything from medicines to mental healing and to various other unconventional means of healing hawked by alternative practitioners, in the second half of the twentieth century, figures such as Oral Roberts depicted divine healing as a marriage of medicine and spirituality. Other enterprising individuals celebrated God's use of natural substances as they promoted forms of alternative medicine under the banner of divine healing. Still others combined supernatural healing with psychotherapy and an emphasis on the healing power of the mind. In each of these cases, pentecostals and their charismatic successors increasingly stressed the way God's healing power also could flow through humans and nature, even as claims of dramatic divine healing continued to appear. In the process, numerous believers moved well beyond previous figures' stress on following the "laws of health," as they borrowed practices and emphases linked to metaphysical healing traditions in the United States that resisted any sharp differentiations between natural and supernatural realms.

The dramatic transformations in pentecostals' approach to healing by the late twentieth century, and in particular adherents' growing acceptance of metaphysical-style forms of healing, raise important new questions regarding the history of pentecostal healing: Should pentecostals' retooled healing practices that stressed the healing power of medicine, nature, and the mind be read simply as a sign of the increasing "evangelicalization" of the pentecostal tradition wherein the faithful repudiated the most radical claims made by first-generation believers—claims that set them apart from the majority of their fellow healers in the divine healing movement? Or was more at work here? Did aspects of traditional pentecostal spirituality prepare adherents for their eventual embrace of forms of healing tied to metaphysical traditions that thrived on the margins of mainstream U.S. Christianity throughout much of U.S. history? To what degree did rival metaphysical groups help shape the healing choices made by the faithful over the course of the twentieth century? Any adequate answer to questions such as these requires a fresh look at pentecostals' relationship with the numerous nonevangelical healing groups vying for attention in the crowded healing marketplace in the United States over the course of the twentieth century.

Alternative Healing Traditions in the United States

When pentecostals burst on the scene in the early 1900s, they joined a long line of alternative healers and health reformers who also operated on the fringe of orthodox medicine throughout the history of North America.[35] Dating back to the colonial period and early republic, Americans utilized a hodgepodge of healing methodologies ranging from "old-world" practices brought over from Europe that were often connected to astrology (and popularized via the ubiquitous almanac), to Native American and West African healing practices such as the use of botanical drugs and the art of conjure, to "regular" doctors' use of purgatives, bleeding, and blistering.[36] With the growing professionalization of conventional medicine during the 1800s, what was frequently a hit-or-miss, shotgun approach to curing illness increasingly gave way to alternative healing *systems* that provided rival paradigms challenging conventional doctors' confidence in their "heroic therapies."[37]

By all accounts, mainstream physicians' rudimentary prescriptions often created considerable suffering and left the door wide open for competitors to hawk their healing alternatives to the U.S. public. Fed by eighteenth-century Enlightenment trends that lauded the power of reason, traditional doctors represented a developing medical orthodoxy during the first half of the nineteenth century that struggled to assert itself at first but eventually monopolized the U.S. healing marketplace by the early twentieth century.[38] Their approach placed healing in the hands of an all-knowing physician trained in the medical sciences who wielded his expertise to fight disease. Medical schooling during the early nineteenth century typically armed doctors with weapons such as calomel (a widely used cathartic with less than desirable side effects, including the loss of teeth), blistering, and bloodletting. Emetics, diuretics, and the like facilitated physicians' manipulation of patients' interactions with their environment as physicians sought to "regulate the secretions" and establish what was believed to be an ideal equilibrium between the body and its surroundings.[39]

Dissidents dubbed traditional medicine "allopathy" (literally "other than the disease"), a derogatory term intended to highlight mainstream doctors' application of methods unrelated to the actual problem at hand. (Despite the origins of the term "allopathy," orthodox practitioners eventually accepted the label, ignoring its negative connotations.) While rival practitioners formulated a variety of alternatives to the medical establishment's heroics, they all could agree that the medical establishment's methods ignored the *vis medicatrix naturae* (the healing power of nature) to the detriment of all who suffered physically.[40] In a formula that unorthodox healers would return to time and time again throughout the nineteenth, twentieth, and early twenty-first centuries, they distinguished their "natural" approaches to healing from the "invasive," "synthetic," and "technological" substances and practices employed by orthodox physicians.

As a historian of alternative medicine notes, just what constituted a "natural" remedy or way of life was by no means a self-evident concept. As evidenced by alternative practitioners' widely disparate prescriptions, the term "natural" is "pliable, a value-laden concept capable of being stretched to encompass all manner of subjective notions of purity, beauty, and truth."[41] Unorthodox doctors nevertheless knew an unnatural approach when they saw it, and medical doctors' surgeries and medicines served as exhibit A.

By the second half of the nineteenth century, regular physicians increasingly acknowledged how important the body's natural ability to resist disease was to the healing process—influenced in no small part no doubt by the success of alternative practitioners. By that time, however, distinctive healing systems predicated on the *vis medicatrix naturae* had already taken root, producing the deeply entrenched rivalry between the orthodox mainstream and so-called quackery that would only begin to dissolve toward the end of the twentieth century.[42]

Representative of alternative healers' vigorous critique of the "synthetic" and "invasive" methods employed by conventional doctors, in the early decades of the nineteenth century Samuel Thomson heralded the power of botanical treatments that he discovered in the backwoods of New Hampshire. Thomson focused in particular on restoring the body's natural production of heat, which he identified as the root of true health. Not for the faint of heart, Thomsonian medicine made liberal use of lobelia, the "Emetic Herb," and various other substances and procedures, including cayenne enemas. Though cayenne enemas hardly qualified as a "nonheroic" procedure, Thomsonians vigorously demarcated his recommendation of the use of "vegetable" substances that shared the healing powers of nature from regular physicians' reliance on "mineral" substances (such as calomel, the mercury compound frequently used by regular doctors) that were, according to Thomson, not only devoid of nature's healing power but downright destructive if introduced into the human body.[43]

During the second half of the nineteenth century, homeopathic remedies developed in Germany by Samuel Hahnemann also proved extremely popular in the United States. In offering a variety of mineral, botanical, and animal products believed to initiate healing by producing symptoms identical to those experienced by the sufferer, homeopathic healers sought to cure "likes with likes." Despite skepticism regarding Hahnemann's "doctrine of infinitesimals" wherein practitioners diluted various healing substances into doses of a millionth of a gram and lower, his system nevertheless caught on, and many American socialites made use of homeopathic procedures during the nineteenth century.[44]

Part of homeopathy's success undoubtedly stemmed from the fact that it did not aggravate illness as did much orthodox practice of the time. More important, homeopathy tapped into Americans' confidence—fed by Romantic sensibilities that came to the fore during the middle third of the nineteenth century—in the ability of nature to heal. Hahnemann's approach focused on stimulating "vital forces" that animated the physical universe and the human body. His infinitesimal dilutions were meant to eliminate the material impediments that bound the dynamic healing powers inherent in the substances being used, which in turn stimulated the vital forces within the human body. Simply put, practitioners believed that homeopathy awakened the body's natural healing powers. In testament to Americans' confidence in the healing power of nature, around the same time that pentecostals established their presence in the United States at the turn of the twentieth century, estimates place the number of homeopaths at 10,000, with an additional 10,000 other alternative doctors, and roughly 110,000 mainstream doctors. By the end of the 1920s, researchers estimate these numbers had jumped to around 150,000 conventional physicians and 36,000 rival practitioners.[45]

As these figures suggest, though homeopaths represented the largest alternative healing system challenging conventional medicine at the beginning of the twentieth century, they were by no means alone. Thomson's botanical methods persisted in physio-medical and eclectic groups. The burgeoning fields of chiropractic and osteopathic medicine focused on the healing powers released through careful manipulation of dislocated joints (particularly in the spine). And naturopaths sought to facilitate healing by cleansing the body of inner impurities via dietary choices, baths, herbs, and so forth.[46]

The presence of numerous health reformers in the nineteenth and early twentieth centuries further complicated the picture of the unorthodox healing options available to Americans. Though health crusaders were more narrowly focused than other alternative healers on the achievement of unparalleled health and on the moral implications of individuals' dietary and physical habits, significant commonalities emerged linking these crusaders to the alternative healing systems that emerged during the 1800s. For figures such as the health reformer Sylvester Graham, who initially published his *Lectures on the Science of Human Life* in 1839, overstimulation in the form of too much food or too much sexual intercourse led to all forms of spiritual and physical illness, and he spearheaded a crusade lambasting individuals who failed to strictly regulate their diet and sexuality. "Let every one consider that excessive alimentation is one of the greatest sources of evil to the human family," Graham wrote. "*Every individual should, as a general rule,*" he continued, "*restrain himself to the smallest quantity which he finds from careful investigation and enlightened experience and observation will fully meet the alimentary wants of the vital economy of his system, knowing that whatever is more than this is evil!*"[47]

Quality, not just quantity, also mattered for Graham. He was absolutely convinced that the best foods were natural foods untainted by modern food production. Well before researchers understood the nutritional deficiencies in white flour, he lamented the use of processed light flour devoid of bran; he also promoted a vegetarian diet. Later in the nineteenth century, Seventh-Day Adventists, for example Ellen G. White and the famed cerealist John H. Kellogg, embraced the basic contours of Graham's message.[48]

Because health reformers zeroed in on moralistic concerns and tended to prioritize optimum health as opposed to treating specific diseases, their convictions regarding the benefits of a natural diet did not equate entirely with many unorthodox healers' full-blown confidence in the power of nature to heal. At the same time, nineteenth-century advocates of both health reform and alternative medicine developed a symbiotic relationship that persisted into the twenty-first century.

Mental healers represented yet another significant alternative to the medical mainstream when pentecostalism initially took shape in the early twentieth century. Christian Scientists, inspired by their founder Mary Baker Eddy, employed healing techniques premised on the existence of a divine Mind that formed the foundation of all that was real, including human thought and life. "Christian Science reveals incontrovertibly," Eddy wrote, "that Mind is All-in-all, that the only realities are the divine Mind and idea." Healing in turn required the simple realization that if the divine Mind encompassed *all* that is real, then sickness could be nothing more than an illusion, a mirage generated by a misapprehension of the true nature of reality. Eddy went so far as to claim that the material world itself, and not just illness, derived from faulty thinking and therefore did not truly exist.[49]

New Thought, which initially gained a recognizable identity during the 1890s under the leadership of Julius and Annetta Dresser and their son Horatio Dresser, likewise concentrated on the healing power of the mind. Like Christian Scientists, adherents could trace their practices and teachings back to the healing methodology of Phineas Quimby, a mental healer whose patient-students included Eddy, the elder Dressers, and Warren Felt Evans, the first systematic theologian of the New Thought movement.[50] Leading New Thought figures typically depicted the human mind as a conduit of spiritual insight and energy connecting humans to the Infinite Mind; it functioned as *the* key point of contact between this world and spiritual realms. Ralph Waldo Trine's enormously popular 1897 book *In Tune with the Infinite* provided a quintessential articulation of these themes. Trine instructed his readers to "recognize, working in and through you, the same Infinite Power that creates and governs all things in the universe." In classic New Thought–ese, Trine highlighted the power of a person's thoughts to tap into spiritual resources. "Send out your thought," he wrote; "thought is a force, and it has occult power of unknown proportions when rightly used and wisely directed,—send out your thought that the right situation or the right work will come to you at the right time, in the right way, and that you will recognize it when it comes." Difficult situations in particular called for irrepressible optimism: "When apparent adversity comes, be not cast down by it, but make the best of it, and always look forward for better things, for conditions more prosperous." Again and again the operation of the mind proved key for Trine: "To hold yourself in this attitude of mind is to set into operation subtle, silent, and irresistible forces that sooner or later will actualize in material form that which is today merely an idea. But ideas have occult power, and ideas, when rightly planted and rightly tended, are the seeds that actualize material conditions."[51]

Alternative Medicine as Metaphysical Religion

Despite the evident diversity separating the various unorthodox healing options available during the nineteenth and early twentieth centuries, nearly all of these groups belonged within a broad-based metaphysical tradition within U.S. religion. Their approaches to healing, which derived from or resembled in significant respects magico-religious practices brought to North America from Europe, have been historically categorized as "occultist," "harmonial," "gnostic," or simply "magical." Throughout this book, I will apply the term "metaphysical" to this tradition, as expressed in forms of religion that (1) deemphasized personal conceptions of the divine; (2) stressed the correspondence between supernatural and natural realms governed by discernable laws, collapsing stark distinctions between the two; and (3) by extension underscored the manipulability of spiritual power by adepts for personal—and often quite tangible—ends (such as healing).[52]

Metaphysical practitioners typically assumed an intrinsic connection between physical and spiritual well-being, stressing the central importance of an individual's "rapport with the cosmos," variously conceived as the Divine Mind, Nature, Truth, Idea, and so forth.[53] Emanuel Swedenborg, for example, the Swedish theologian and scientist whose ideas influenced several prominent proponents of metaphysical religion in the United States, denied any sharp division between natural and spiritual worlds, or between visible and invisible spheres of the cosmos. Instead, Swedenborg posited an inherent similitude between these "layers" of reality.[54] While most metaphysical believers did not go so far as Mary Baker Eddy and deny the very existence of a separate natural, material existence, they usually did describe physical and spiritual realms as intrinsically "made of the same stuff," as one historian writes, which in turn allowed for a vision of the natural world as permeated with divine energy.[55] In highlighting the intrinsic similarities uniting the physical and spiritual worlds, advocates of metaphysical religion encouraged a more impersonal notion of the supernatural as a realm of reality that followed predictable laws and patterns that the knowledgeable could manipulate for their own purposes.

The impersonal powers animating the various unorthodox healing systems took on different guises and forms. Starting in the early nineteenth century, mesmerists manipulated a magnetic fluid believed to permeate the entire universe.[56] Likewise, D. D. Palmer, the founder of chiropractic, lectured on the "Innate" power coursing through the human body, a form of "Universal Intelligence" permeating all of creation. According to Palmer, dislocations in various joints, especially in the spinal cord, put pressure on the nerves and limited the flow of Innate. In the words of an early chiropractic manual, "we are well when Innate Intelligence has unhindered freedom to act thru the physical brain, nerves and tissues.... Diseases are caused by a LACK OF CURRENT OF INNATE MENTAL IMPULSES," which in turn led to all manner of illnesses. Manipulating the spine and adjusting subluxated joints offered a drugless source of healing that restored the proper flow of Innate and brought about healing.[57] Similar types of metaphysical powers animated the thoughts of other alternative healers as well, as seen in homeopaths' stress on "vital forces"; early osteopaths' confidence in the power of electricity (touted by founder of osteopathy as the "highest known order of force" placed in the body by God);[58] Christian Scientists and New Thought practitioners' espousal of the "Divine Mind" and "Infinite Intelligence";[59] and other alternative healers' awe before the mysterious, life-giving powers of nature itself.[60]

By learning the nature of the spiritual laws and patterns governing impersonal metaphysical powers, practitioners believed that they could harness these invisible forces in order to heal just as scientists could learn the laws of physics and then exploit them for their own purposes. Metaphysical healers in the United States frequently went so far as cast their theories as a form of science. This explicit combination of scientific claims with overt supernaturalism allowed believers to tap into the cultural authority of scientific knowledge while simultaneously critiquing the thoroughgoing naturalistic and rationalistic assumptions increasingly espoused by mainstream physicians.

Significantly, by the late nineteenth century holistic approaches to healing that took into account environmental, emotional, and spiritual factors in addition to biological ones flourished among alternative healers in the metaphysical tradition even as the medical establishment backed away from such paradigms. Ever since the days of Hippocrates in ancient Greece, physicians had accepted the fact that proper treatment required an understanding of patients' living environments, habits, and temperamental makeup (usually linked to the presence of substances, known as humors, believed to determine a person's disposition). During the second half of the nineteenth century, however, traditional doctors by and large jettisoned these holistic assumptions, and a paradigmatic shift occurred in medical therapeutics as doctors zeroed in on specific diseases and microorganisms that attacked the human body. The emphasis on predictable pathways of disease lessened physicians' focus on each individual's unique experience of an illness, and what came to be known as holism increasingly took a backseat among orthodox physicians.[61] Metaphysical healers happily filled the breach left by the changes in medical orthodoxy as they joined other religious healers in transmitting holistic assumptions to a new generation of Americans.

Pentecostalism and the Metaphysical Tradition

Healers in the metaphysical tradition enjoyed significant success and firmly established various forms of spiritually infused materialism as mainstays in U.S. therapeutic culture as the twentieth century progressed.[62] Such success attracted attention, including the attention of pentecostals; early pentecostals did not hesitate to denounce metaphysical healers with the same verve and vigor that animated their attacks on orthodox physicians. Quite unlike their metaphysically minded healing competitors, the saints drew sharp lines of distinction between supernatural and natural healing agents, rejecting natural remedies of all stripes on principle.

Despite the slash-and-burn rhetoric so frequently employed by the faithful as they excoriated any and all who dared recommend a natural remedy, early pentecostals' relationship with rival healers proved much more complicated than may have appeared at first glance. Not only did some adherents follow their evangelical forebears in stressing the importance of following the "laws of nature," but prominent features of early pentecostal healing and teaching mirrored distinctly metaphysical assumptions as well: Numerous believers insisted that God's healing power could animate and flow through human intercessors and physical objects such as Bibles, prayer cloths, and denominational periodicals (many appeared unconcerned with previous evangelical healers' stress on the strictly symbolic function of the healing rituals prescribed in scripture). Others, especially individuals influenced by the protopentecostal E. W. Kenyon, mimicked the metaphysical philosophy of mental healers in the New Thought tradition by prioritizing the role of the mind and of speech as key conduits of divine power. Of even greater import, early pentecostal depictions of the Holy Spirit frequently approximated metaphysical notions of the universe that tended to treat the supernatural as an impersonal force permeating nature and governed by discernable spiritual laws. A few of the saints went so far as to describe the Spirit's work utilizing the language of science.

Understanding the metaphysical tendencies inherent in the early movement is crucial for making sense of the apparent ease with which many pentecostals later in the century transitioned away from the early rhetoric of pentecostal healing and joined some of their charismatic successors in a full-blown spiritualization of natural healing methods. The eventual metaphysical turn in many pentecostals' approach to disease and illness, with its attendant elevation of impersonal, predictable health-giving pathways linking the activity of the Spirit to natural substances and the mind, paved the way for revised healing practices that proved highly competitive in twentieth- and early-twenty-first-century U.S. culture. Some healers learned that they simultaneously could claim the imprimatur of medical science without relinquishing cherished beliefs in God's supernatural involvement with creation. Other individuals who highlighted the mediating role of the mind in connecting spiritual and natural realms tapped into spiritualized forms of popular psychology in the tradition of New Thought. In a move that resonated with the metaphysical inclination to treat the natural, physical world as a microcosm of a larger spiritual macrocosm, many believers redefined their healing aims to encompass beautiful, perfect bodies and not just disease-free bodies. Those who treated scripture as a kind of Spirit-authorized dietary manual and latched onto the metaphysical-style ideas closely associated with naturopathy soon discovered that predictable forms of healing premised on God's use of natural substances were quite marketable.

Of course, the faithful retained emphases that stood in tension with the rival methodologies that they increasingly emulated, and they still petitioned God for dramatic intervention when necessary. Even so, the transformation of pentecostal healing shines a bright spotlight on the convergence of pentecostalism over the course of the twentieth century with groups and trends often perceived to be at odds with some of the pentecostal movement's core emphases. Much of early pentecostals' rhetoric surrounding healing in particular seemed to place the faithful in direct opposition to mainstream scientific trends, natural reasoning, and metaphysical assumptions. Nonetheless, as the pentecostal movement evolved, and as participants absorbed the influence of charismatics, adherents promoted emphases borrowed from scientific medicine, dietary forms of healing, psychotherapy, and openly metaphysical groups in ever more explicit fashion.

While the growing convergence of pentecostalism with scientific medicine, with dietary forms of healing, with psychotherapy, and in particular with openly metaphysical groups serves as the central storyline in this book, a related convergence interweaves itself throughout the text as well: the integration of pentecostals into the larger evangelical fold. Facilitated in large part by the widespread availability of modern communication technologies such as television and mass-circulation periodicals, a constant exchange of information and ideas regarding healing developed, reinforcing an increasingly dense web of connections linking pentecostals and charismatics to fellow evangelicals.[63] The overlapping healing network that formed as a result of these interconnections ensured that pentecostals and charismatics were not the only conservative Christians incorporating popularized forms of metaphysical healing into their illness-fighting arsenal. Given the prominence of pentecostals and charismatics in the realm of Christian healing, and especially metaphysically inflected forms of Christian healing, however, it is safe to say that the transformation of pentecostal healing in the United States over the course of the twentieth and early twenty-first centuries represented one of the most important factors spurring numerous U.S. Christians' participation in a modern therapeutic culture of spiritually infused materialism that was fully mainstream.

Loose Ends, Caveats, and Disclaimers

This book covers the gamut of U.S. pentecostal and charismatic Christianity throughout the twentieth century, variously addressing developments among individuals in pentecostal denominations, among independent healing evangelists and writers, not to mention charismatic healers associated with mainline Protestant, Catholic, and evangelical churches. Along the way I situate these trends in relation to loosely affiliated movements often lumped together under the banner of holism, metaphysical healing, or alternative medicine. Without denying the ambitious nature of the project, a few caveats and disclaimers are in order.

In stressing the "spirit-friendly materialism" frequently found in the twentieth-century metaphysical tradition in the United States, I do not mean to gloss over the very real differences separating various metaphysical groups, especially in relation to proponents' varying degrees of enthusiasm regarding the importance of the physical realm vis-à-vis spiritual realities. Despite their focus on healing, mind-cure practitioners in the tradition of Christian Science, for example, offered a very different vision of the importance of the body, given their denial of material reality, when compared to those who in describing their healing objectives drew on more conventional assumptions regarding the nature of physical existence. New Thought practitioners did not go so far as Christian Scientists in their rejection of the material world (though several came to New Thought via Christian Science), but here, too, the focus on the mind often translated into a clear hierarchy prioritizing the ethereal mind over the physical body.

If certain factions in the mind-cure movement denied the importance of the body in principle, such ideals often failed to materialize in practice. As the historian R. Marie Griffith concludes, "New Thought writers often seemed to be saying that personal power was accessed by means of mind energy," yet for many "the *body* was the real source of might, site of potential transformation, and basis for revealing the inner truth about the human self." Like alternative healers of all stripes, New Thought figures "played out their passions upon living bodies, closely scrutinized for signs of self-control or dissolution and attuned to promises of beauty, longevity, corresponding suppression and fulfillment of desire."[64]

Various New Thought figures' eagerness by the turn of the twentieth century to broaden the rewards of right thinking and right speaking to include the acquisition of wealth and material prosperity served as a telltale indication that numerous participants were less than concerned with escaping the bonds of earth. Ralph Waldo Trine's book *In Tune with the Infinite*, published in 1897, illustrated this tendency well: "suggest prosperity to yourself. See yourself in a prosperous condition. Affirm that you will before long be in a prosperous condition. Affirm it calmly and quietly, but strongly and confidently. Believe it, believe it absolutely. Expect it,—keep it continually watered with expectation." Utilizing imagery that would eventually circulate freely throughout U.S. culture, Trine continued:

> you thus make yourself a magnet to attract the things that you desire. Don't be afraid to suggest, to affirm these things, for by so doing you put forth an ideal which will begin to clothe itself in material form. In this way you are utilizing agents among the most subtle and powerful in the universe. If you are particularly desirous for anything that you feel it is good and right for you to have, something that will broaden your life or that will increase your usefulness to others, simply hold the thought that at the right time, in the right way, and through the right instrumentality, there will come to you or there will open up for you the way whereby you can attain what you desire.[65]

In the end, the more popular expressions of New Thought and mind-cure that circulated throughout U.S. culture during the twentieth century—and influenced pentecostal culture in significant ways—were suffused with similar celebrations, not negations, of the distinctly this-worldly rewards available to those who rightly calibrated their minds.

As New Thought and mind-cure diffused throughout U.S. society beginning in the early twentieth century, they fed into another prominent development that also requires clarification: the emergence of a distinctive therapeutic culture. At the turn of the twentieth century, economic and technological changes spurred a profound reorientation in American life, as predominant producer-oriented values increasingly gave way to a consumer-oriented therapeutic sensibility fixated on the joys of conspicuous consumption, the pursuit of maximal health, and the rewards of self-realization. Early pentecostals' stress on divine healing created natural affinities with the burgeoning therapeutic ethos, and later adherents magnified these connections as they increasingly described pentecostal healing in terms that resonated with manifestations of the therapeutic in the broader culture.[66]

In stressing the merger of pentecostalism with mainstream therapeutic and consumer culture, I am not looking to rehash well-worn critiques of the self-absorption characteristic of much of modern U.S. society, nor am I arguing that the transformation of pentecostal healing should be read as a straightforward tale of accommodation wherein the faithful abdicated their religious heritage for a denuded substitute bereft of spiritual depth and substance.[67] Pentecostals did relinquish many of the holiness strictures bequeathed to them from their predecessors in favor of a more indulgent ethos over the course of the twentieth century, and overt supernaturalism lost ground to the Spirit's use of more mundane pathways of healing. Focusing solely on these trajectories, however, neglects the deeply embedded resistance to strictly naturalistic and materialistic outlooks that continued to shape pentecostals' and charismatics' view of the world, and overlooks adherents' steadfast refusal by the late twentieth and early twenty-first centuries to accept characterizations of more scientific, naturalistic modes of health and healing as somehow disconnected from divine activity. In mimicking metaphysical models, many of the faithful blurred the boundaries separating natural and supernatural healing in ways that freed them to draw confidently on the healing insights of modern science without relinquishing their vision of the world as drenched in the presence of the Spirit.

Several terms employed throughout this book also require extra attention. First introduced in 1926, the term "holism" has been employed in a variety of contexts, many of which have been only tangentially related to the restoration of sick bodies.[68] Even in the arena of physical healing, more historical models of holism intent on recovering humanity's connections to past ways of life differed from social models focused on situating the individual in her broader communal context, which in turn diverged from more organismic models stressing the importance of biographical details in structuring each individual's experience of disease.[69] Religion complicated the picture even further. On one end of the spectrum, holism involved explicitly religious conceptions of health treatments; on the other, it referred to *any* attempt to combat the depersonalizing effects of reductionistic medicine, whether by cultivating the patient-doctor relationship, highlighting the confluence of social and psychological factors in the etiology of disease, or implementing a host of other practical improvements in health care delivery. Doctors throughout the twentieth century who were uncomfortable with the direction of modern medicine, for example, offered their own internal critiques of the discipline, many of which had no connection to religious belief.[70] For my purposes, when I reference holistic healing trends, unless otherwise noted I typically have in mind efforts to reform health care by introducing a specifically religious element into the healing process.

Like holism, the terms "natural" and "nature" prove much more complicated to define than might appear at first glance. For one, conceptions of "natural healing"—especially in the hands of American individuals friendly to metaphysical forms of religion—quite frequently encompassed the operation of spiritual powers and forces working through more mundane physical substances and objects. Even where theoretical distinctions existed between nature and supernature, and between the earthly and the spiritual, in practice such boundaries often proved quite permeable and were difficult for adherents (including pentecostals) to maintain consistently.[71] Suffice it to say that though I differentiate "natural healing" from "divine healing" at several points in order to distinguish nonreligious forms of healing from spiritual alternatives that called for an avoidance of medicines and other "this-worldly" remedies, I also draw attention throughout this book to the potential slippage between these two categories and to pentecostals' and charismatics' increasing attraction to healing paradigms that straddled the nature/supernature divide.

Terminology aside, it is also important to note that this book is not meant to reflect an exhaustive catalogue of healing in the pentecostal movement throughout the twentieth and early twenty-first centuries. Rather, I specifically am interested in innovative healers' increasingly explicit spiritualization of natural means of healing. My goal is to chronicle the dramatic changes at work in the healing practices of numerous believers, focusing mostly on the writings of well-known pentecostal and charismatic leaders. While it would be a mistake simply to conflate the proclamations made by prominent figures with the actual practices of the average pentecostal or charismatic, the popularity of the figures and trends discussed in this book suggests a significant degree of overlap between the healing choices the faithful made in their day-to-day lives and the healing messages they encountered.

In addition, whenever possible I zero in on pentecostal figures whose ministries anticipated the late-twentieth-century changes in pentecostal and charismatic healing. Such figures include Oral Roberts, Franklin Hall, and healing evangelists influenced by the teachings of E. W. Kenyon. As these names suggest, most of the innovation in pentecostal healing over the course of the twentieth century occurred outside the formal control of traditional pentecostal denominations; as such, I focus on independent ministries much more than on the official denominational pronouncements regarding healing. In order to substantiate my argument regarding the connections between early pentecostal healing and its successors, when I discuss charismatic groups and individuals who operated outside of explicitly pentecostal contexts, I emphasize figures who managed to disseminate their views via communication outlets known to attract a high proportion of pentecostal readers and viewers (representative mediums include the magazine *Charisma*, founded in 1975 and published by the influential charismatic clearinghouse Charisma Media [formerly Strang Communications], as well as the Trinity Broadcast Network [TBN], which began in 1973).[72]

My argument regarding the evolving relationship between pentecostals and their metaphysically inclined rivals should not be read as another salvo in the battle between pentecostal and charismatic insiders and their critics regarding the orthodoxy of specific emphases. In the 1980s, Dave Hunt, T. A. McMahon, and D. R. McConnell, for instance, fought to expose what they believed to be the "heretical" metaphysical origins of beliefs and practices closely tied to the pentecostal-charismatic movement, several of which are covered in this book.[73] Both critics and defenders of metaphysical-style trends among pentecostals and charismatics doubtless will find in these pages additional ammunition to advance their disparate theological agendas. Be that as it may, I make no attempt to address the theological questions and issues at stake in the trends I describe, except where such theological debates explicitly shaped the history of healing in the pentecostal-charismatic tradition. My main purpose throughout is to call attention to the changing nature of pentecostal healing over the course of the twentieth and early twenty-first centuries, and to highlight the significance of this story for pentecostals' transformation into major players in the U.S. religious marketplace.

It is no accident that this book is subtitled "A History of Pentecostal Healing" as opposed to "A History of Pentecostal and Charismatic Healing." While I address various charismatic healers who reworked pentecostal emphases, I situate their contributions specifically in relation to the history of pentecostal healing. By arguing that the late-twentieth-century changes to pentecostal healing expanded in important respects on preexisting inclinations already present in the earliest expressions of pentecostalism, I do not mean to deny the fact that several charismatic healers drew on sources of influence well outside of traditional pentecostalism. I identify several of these lines of influence throughout this book. That said, the narrative thread throughout the book remains focused on the trajectory of pentecostal healing.

In a manner somewhat analogous to believers' attempts to straddle the natural/supernatural divide by the turn of the twenty-first century, I, too, ultimately attempt to straddle sharp differentiations separating the "pentecostal" from the "metaphysical." Though these categories are never fully interchangeable or free of important distinctions, a careful look at the history of pentecostal healing suggests that individuals representing them were never quite as far apart as it may have appeared. With the exception of studies of the Word of Faith and inner healing branches of the pentecostal-charismatic movement, histories of pentecostalism and other conservative forms of Christianity typically provide minimal commentary on the interconnections and resonances— as well as tensions—that existed between adherents and proponents of metaphysical brands of religion.[74] In this book, I attempt to fill this lacuna by highlighting pentecostals' and charismatics' ever-increasing willingness over the course of the twentieth and early twenty-first centuries to borrow and appropriate rival metaphysical practices, and by stressing aspects of early pentecostal culture that harmonized with metaphysical emphases and eased pentecostals' transition toward their previous rivals.

Once believers discovered new ways modern medicine and other natural means could coincide with their belief in supernatural agency, the long-standing affinities to metaphysical forms of spirituality in the pentecostal tradition increasingly moved from the background to the foreground. Pentecostal and charismatic healers did more than just appropriate and market key aspects of traditional medicine, alternative medicine, and psychological forms of healing. Whether they realized it or not, many of the faithful also reprioritized existing themes in the pentecostal heritage when they explicitly sought to Christianize rival healing practices by merging them with divine healing. Pentecostals and charismatics throughout the twentieth century discovered innovative ways to baptize the natural world in the Holy Spirit. Believers in the later decades of the twentieth century simply did so much more explicitly than their forebears, attracting an ever-growing audience in the process.

1

Pentecostal Healing in the Early Twentieth Century

In 1927 John Straton, a Baptist pastor in New York City who gained notoriety for his staunch fundamentalist views, found himself embroiled in a bitter dispute with several deacons in his church after he established a series of regular healing services. According to the dissident deacons, the healing services involved "'Holy Roller' and 'Pentecostal,' practices," accompanied by "rubbing people with oily hands," and "working up 'ecstasies.'" Straton vehemently denied the charges, promising a sermon entitled "Why I Am Against Pentecostalism." After reading the *New York Times* correspondent's definition of pentecostalism in his coverage of the events, few would question Straton's decision. According to the reporter, "[Pentecostalism] refers to a form of worship in which the members of the congregation permit themselves to enter a state of wild excitement bordering on hysteria, some times on frenzy. Shouting, leaping, groveling, violent muscular tremors and sometimes rigidity are among its manifestations."[1]

As the journalist's comments indicated, early pentecostals' healing practices contributed to a broader pattern of cultural isolation that placed the faithful well outside the bounds of mainstream respectability. The faithful frequently gave as good as they got, however, feeding off their sense of rejection and enthusiastically taking up the battle against any and all detractors. "The religious press is against us," exclaimed A. J. Tomlinson, general overseer of the pentecostal Church of God based in Cleveland, Tennessee. "The world's press is against us. The ministers of all denominations, of a hundred millions strong, are in opposition to this truth. The independent holiness press and ministry are all against us, but the conflict is on, and we dare not retreat and forsake our Captain, and leave Him to fight on the field alone."[2] Few early pentecostals could match the rhetorical bombast of Tomlinson, yet his remarks highlighted the degree to which many believers felt besieged, not just by the secular press but also by fellow Christians. Pentecostals often reserved their sharpest barbs, in fact, for fellow conservative evangelicals who failed to appreciate the saints' special relationship with God. "Men who formerly stood high in religious ranks as great evangelists . . . have gone down to utter ruin, and many times death, just because they failed to recognize God in this present day Latter Rain outpouring of the Holy Spirit, and tried to hinder the work of God," warned an eventual leader in the Assemblies of God, J. Roswell Flower, in 1910.[3] While Flower's comments accurately captured the deep antagonism characteristic of pentecostals' relationship with other religious groups, including evangelicals, such claims obscured adherents' profound indebtedness to previous generations in numerous arenas, including that of divine healing.

Early Pentecostal Healing

When pentecostals articulated their vision of healing, they perpetuated various emphases already prevalent in the nineteenth-century divine healing movement. Like several of their predecessors, pentecostals zealously promoted the idea that healing was "in the atonement" and purchased by Christ's death on the cross. In a "What We Believe" section of the *Pentecostal Holiness Advocate*, F. M. Britton, a former leader in the Fire-Baptized Holiness Church, which merged with the Pentecostal Holiness Church in 1911, put the matter succinctly: "Since the forgiveness of sins and cleansing from all sin is provided for in the atonement, we do not need any other remedy for our sins, or sin, and in the same way we do not need any other remedy for healing but faith in the atonement."[4] A contributor to the *Weekly Evangel*, an Assemblies of God periodical, implored his audience to resist "the enemy" in two key areas: "his attempting to put sickness on our bodies, and also his bringing up our sins against us." Quoting 1 Peter 2:24, the writer praised God for a "complete Atonement" that successfully beat back Satan's attack on both fronts. In case the reader had any doubt regarding the very this-worldly benefits purchased by Christ's death, the writer confirmed that these promises applied "here, even in this life."[5] Sufferers attending the myriad pentecostal services appearing across the United States quickly learned that their promised healing rested on the same secure foundation that procured their salvation from sin.

The saints' unshakable confidence in God's healing promises also mirrored late-nineteenth-century healers' single-minded focus on the centrality of faith in the healing process. As a writer explained in a 1926 issue of *Golden Grain*, a periodical published by the West Coast–based healing evangelist Charles Price, God commanded believers to pray for the sick; therefore, Christians had no reason to doubt that God wanted to heal. "The prayer of faith does not have an IF in it," and Christians needed to understand that "GOD WILL NEVER HEAR THE PRAYER OF DOUBT." If it was not God's will to heal, "HE WOULD NEVER HAVE COMMANDED IT," the author continued. In Scripture, God told the elders in the church to "pray and believe and I will heal." Therefore, it was

"THE ELDERS' BUSINESS TO PRAY AND BELIEVE AND LEAVE THE RESULTS WITH GOD." Period.[6] C. H. Mason, who helped found the predominantly black Church of God in Christ, taught the faithful in 1919 simply to pray: "My God, thou canst deliver, I'm trusting." "Have faith in God," he continued, "the Lord maketh . . . thy bodies whole."[7]

Lest any doubt the efficacy of faith, early pentecostal literature deluged believers with stories of God's miraculous intervention in response to their prayers. In one such example, an article in the *Apostolic Faith*, the flagship periodical of the early pentecostal movement, told of a "rough-looking man" who came to the Azusa Mission on crutches and in search of healing after being kicked by a horse. The man told his story to those assembled and quickly found himself surrounded by the saints, who "prayed the prayer of faith," laying hands on the man's head. A few moments later, the man "jumped to his feet, looked amazed, and said, 'It's done! It's done!'" He then proceeded to walk around the tent "walking as good as anybody."[8]

In addition to the saints' calls for a doubt-proof trust in God's healing guarantee, another sure sign of pentecostals' ties to late-nineteenth-century evangelicalism involved adherents' consistent focus on the importance of prayer and fasting for building up their faith as they sought divine intervention. Devotees joined three days of corporate fasting "for more power in the meetings" in the early months of the famed 1906 Azusa Street revival that helped kick-start the pentecostal movement, for instance, and members of the Church of God in Christ set aside three days for prayer and fasting prior to their annual convention in order to prepare themselves as worthy recipients of God's presence.[9] Believers targeted much more than illness with their intercession, yet healing proved one of the most prominent themes. Testimony after testimony recounted by numerous pentecostal sufferers suggested that their dedication to fasting and prolonged periods of prayer played an important role in establishing an unshakable confidence that they had done their part; having prayed and fasted, it was now only a matter of time before God would come through and intervene supernaturally to heal. In one story recorded in 1921 by Aimee Semple McPherson, the Los Angeles–based healing evangelist and pentecostal celebrity, she recalled her encounter with a man confined to a cot due to "tuberculosis of the spine." "Brother," she asked, when he was brought to her at healing revival, "have you faith that Jesus Christ will heal you now?" "Sister, I have," he responded. "I have been praying and fasting, and I know that He is able and willing!" During the same set of healing services, McPherson also met a paralyzed twenty-year-old woman. Again, despite the fact that she had never walked, McPherson reported that "her relatives and grandmother have been praying and fasting all day, and 'know' she will be healed. Sure enough, in a moment, she is up and walking to and fro across the platform, hands uplifted, face transformed."[10]

If early pentecostals carried forward a variety of themes associated with the late-nineteenth-century divine healing movement, they also modified the

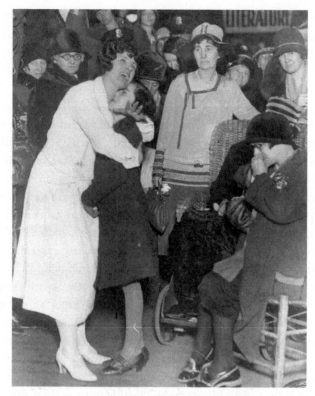

Figure 1.1 Aimee Semple McPherson praying over a sick girl at a healing meeting in Denver. Denver Public Library, Western History Collection, call no. Z-135; and Flower Pentecostal Heritage Center.

healing paradigms inherited from their predecessors in significant respects. Early pentecostals tended to embrace the more radical applications of faith-cure teachings, including a strong emphasis on spiritual warfare in the healing process, as well as absolute prohibitions against seeking out medical aid.[11] Nineteenth-century evangelicals who promoted divine healing highlighted sin as the true root of sickness and reflected a similar penchant for muscular expressions of God's healing power, but they usually did not share pentecostals' strong emphasis on deliverance from demonic powers. Here, pentecostals' connections to the separatist holiness groups of the 1880s and 1890s played a crucial role in establishing the close connection between spiritual warfare and divine healing in pentecostal thinking. Many of the earliest pentecostals hailed from "come-outer" Methodist groups who decried the stagnation they sensed in more mainstream Methodist churches. Benjamin Hardin Irwin, a forerunner of the pentecostal movement who identified the baptism in the Holy Spirit as a distinct third work of grace that followed sanctification, derided Methodist leaders' lack of moral backbone. The founder of the Fire-Baptized Holiness

Church called them "hog eating, nicotine professors of holiness, chewing, smoking, snuffing, and smelling like a hog on a dung hill, filthy, depraved and nasty." "Yet," he lamented, these depraved individuals remained "in good standing in the church."[12] Pentecostals imbibed the combative ethos evident in the ministries of individuals such as Irwin, which in turn helped shape their conception of healing as a pitched battle against hostile forces.[13]

The activities of radical healers John Alexander Dowie in Zion City, Illinois, and Frank W. Sandford in Durham, Maine, proved especially influential in nurturing adherents' attunement to the spiritual powers that opposed their search for healing. Numerous early pentecostals—including figures such as Charles Parham, who helped establish pentecostals' trademark teaching regarding the baptism in the Holy Spirit and speaking in tongues—associated in one way or another with Dowie and Sandford. These figures' insistent connections between Satan and illness, along with their flamboyant, aggressive style and staunch repudiation of physicians, prefigured later pentecostal themes.[14] In 1897, Dowie directed readers of his *Leaves of Healing* to Acts 10:38. "You will see," he explained, "that the Apostle Peter declares that He [Jesus] 'went about doing good, and healing all who were oppressed of the Devil.'" "Notice that all whom He healed, not some," Dowie continued, "were suffering from Satan's evil power."[15] An outside observer's comments regarding Shiloh, Sandford's community in Maine, captured the culture well: "At times when matters go especially wrong," the writer explained in 1905, "they decide that the devil has come upon the hill in person to make trouble." In such cases Sandford and his followers went to the "armory" on the property and armed themselves with real-life "bucklers and shields and weapons." Then "with Bible in hand," they "sally forth with cries of defiance to drive Old Nick off the hill top." "They don't see him go, of course," the author added, "but a sense of comfort and satisfaction comes to them after a time and they know he has fled."[16]

Like Sandford and Dowie, pentecostals engaged in spiritual hand-to-hand combat with Satan on the battlefield of their bodies, and the Prince of Darkness remained public enemy number one in the war for health. A commenter in the *Apostolic Faith* articulated in 1907 the assumptions supporting the saints' view of illness: "Every sickness is of the devil." In the Garden of Eden, humans were "pure and happy and knew no sickness." When the "unholy visitor [Satan] came in to the garden," though, Adam and Eve's "whole system was poisoned and it has been flowing in the blood of all the human family down the ages."[17] Frequently Satan employed demonic emissaries in his attacks on the bodies of the saints. "Demons are of a multiplied variety," wrote one pentecostal in 1910 for the *Pentecost*. Alongside the "unclean demons" and "witchcraft and fortune-telling demons" catalogued by this particular believer, it is striking how many of the demons related to the body and health. There were "deaf and dumb demons," demons of "insanity" and of "various forms of sickness" (not to mention "screeching and yelling demons"). "There are demons that act more particularly on the body," the writer continued, "or some organ, or appetite of the body."[18] In the words of F. J. Lee, the second general overseer of the Church of God in Cleveland, Tennessee, demons alternately wrecked havoc in believers' bodies, minds, and spirits: "When the spirits attack the body there is pain and sickness; when they attack the soul it is insanity; when they play on the spirit, actuate the spirit, it is sin."[19]

Considering the intimate connection pentecostals frequently saw between demonic powers and sickness, deliverance frequently played a key role in the healing process. When C. H. Mason described the healing of a woman on crutches in 1911, he indicated that after praying and laying hands on her, "Satan was rebuked at once." Following this prayer, she walked on her own unaided.[20] Elsewhere, Mason described how "hundreds have been healed by my laying on hands and praying to God to rebuke the enemy (the devil)."[21] The widely popular itinerant healing evangelist Maria Woodworth-Etter, known for the prevalence of trance-like phenomena in her meetings, recounted the story of a woman who had been tormented for nine years ever since a "restless, shaking spirit had taken hold her." Following prayer, "this nervous spirit went out and she slept for nine hours."[22] Another woman testified in 1907 how God gave her the "discernment of spirits," after which she suddenly could see the "epileptic demons, demons that had been tormenting me so long." Following four days of prayer and fasting along with a "hard fight with the devil," she finally obtained victory.[23] Though pentecostal ministers acknowledged the impact of factors other than demons in hindering healing, such as unconfessed sins and immoral habits, the frequent testimonies linking restored health with deliverance highlighted the supernatural framework that informed believers' basic assumptions regarding the nature of sickness and its cure.[24]

Early Pentecostals and the Medical Establishment

Given mainstream physicians' naturalistic understanding of disease, they repeatedly found themselves in pentecostals' crosshairs. Most late-nineteenth-century divine healing advocates insisted on the superiority of divine healing when compared to natural means such as medicines, which put pressure on their listeners to rely solely on God in the healing process, yet they usually proved less strident than pentecostals in their criticisms of doctors and medicine.[25] The well-known faith-cure proponent—and homeopathic physician—Charles Cullis, for example, included the following disclaimer in his 1879 book on divine healing: "I do not in any wise wish to detract from the valuable services of the medical profession, of which I am a member. I only desire to prove to the world that 'man's extremity is God's opportunity,' and that when the 'profession' pronounces a case hopeless, the promise of God remains as a testimony to the truth of His Word."[26] Right after he left no doubt regarding the incompatibility of the "law of faith" and recourse to means, A. B. Simpson nonetheless clarified: "We do not imply by this that the medical profession is sinful, or the use of means always wrong. There may be, there always will be, innumerable cases where faith cannot be exercised; and if natural 'means' have, as they do have, a limited value, there is ample room for their employment in these cases."[27]

Whereas some early pentecostals admitted that medical care could be beneficial for non-Christians, few could be characterized as friends of the medical profession at the turn of the twentieth century. In the "Questions Answered" section of a 1908 issue of *Apostolic Faith*, the editor responded to the direct question "Do you teach that it is wrong to take medicine?" The answer, most likely penned by the early Azusa Street revival leader William Seymour, was simple and to the point. "Yes," he wrote, "Medicine is for unbelievers." The acceptable "remedy for the saints of God" involved prayer and the anointing of the sick with oil, as detailed in James 5:14.[28] When the early pentecostal evangelist and chronicler of the pentecostal movement Frank Bartleman endured a series of illnesses, he confidently proclaimed, "I never feared disease and vermin in the work [among the poor in the slums]. And God kept me. I threw away my own medicine bottles of which I had several when I was first converted, and had never heard of Divine Healing. It seemed an easy matter to trust the Lord for my body when He had done so much for my soul."[29] A. J. Tomlinson reflected the same staunch repudiation of the medical profession. "Haven't you sworn to obey the commands of your Lord?" he asked his readers in 1913. "Doesn't He tell you what to do in case of sickness? And does He say if that fails to call for a physician?" Tomlinson continued: "Die rather than go contrary to the plain teaching in God's Word!"[30]

For some pentecostals at least, Tomlinson's words reflected more than just hyperbolic bluster. Tomlinson's own successor in the Church of God, F. J. Lee, died of cancer in his early fifties and steadfastly refused medical help right to the end.[31] "We know that many ordinary Pentecostals followed their leaders' advice to avoid medical treatment," the historian Grant Wacker explains. "Editors never liked to advertise the [pentecostal] movement's failures, but the evidence repeatedly hints that hundreds of members died or allowed their children to die rather than resort to worldly means."[32]

For many pentecostals, reliance on human aid seemed antithetical to their understanding of the spiritual nature of disease; sickness's origin in spiritual realities necessitated otherworldly solutions far removed from physicians' prescriptions. According to the Canadian-born Lilian Yeomans, a doctor turned divine healing advocate, "all human remedies . . . are not radical enough; they fail to reach the cause of the trouble."[33] Moreover, resorting to medical and other naturalistic healing methods denied the ready availability of God's power for all who called on him. As one commenter in the *Church of God Evangel* put it in

1918, the "Lord's People" were expected to trust God for both their health and that of their children. Those who "resort to remedies" dishonored God's name. "I do not see how people can be doing the will of the Father and take medicine," the writer continued, "when the Father has arranged for their healing by the power of God."[34] "If that once victorious saint now calls a physician of the world to come with his drugs," wrote another in 1920, "this has a tendency every time to mummify the subject until at last he stands as a spiritual mummy, not having any spiritual victory." Such a believer "can't testify to the thing that seems to stir the devil the most—divine healing."[35] Some of the saints allowed that the use of "medicine, drugs or remedies" may have been "all right for the children of the world," yet for the true saint, spiritual vitality required an unflinching confidence in the availability of divine assistance and no-holds-barred warfare against Satan's physical attacks on the body.[36]

Physicians' greatest sin, then, involved their embrace of naturalistic explanations of reality that downplayed a role for supernatural powers. One of the original architects of a distinctive pentecostal theology, Charles Parham, lambasted "scientists, infidels, and higher critics—a trinity of the same species," for their disbelief in the face of the "miraculous and supernatural, as though the unseen God, who governs all forces, were incapable of causing humanity to feel and realize His saving and healing power." "Medical science and her practicers," he continued, "are mentioned throughout the Old and New Testament in connection with those guilty of the vilest sins against God and humanity."[37] Dead, formalistic churches lacked the "old-time salvation attended by all its fullness and power," and "medical missionaries" were among those promulgating this powerless gospel. "The Lord is wearily waiting for the modern church," Parham added in 1911, "with its medical missionaries, to do something." Due to modern Christians' failure to draw on the supernatural resources that facilitated dramatic signs and wonders (such as divine healing), God "has chosen to again give His wisdom, grace, healing, miracles, and empowerment in speech through a restored Pentecost to carry this wonderful Gospel to all the world."[38]

Without hesitation, fellow pentecostals would have cheered Parham's diatribe against the naturalistic assumptions espoused by physicians and other unbelievers, yet less spiritual, more mundane forces also shaped adherents' antagonism toward the medical establishment. Scientific and technological advances fascinated early pentecostals just as much as they did other Americans, and pentecostals' attitudes toward medicine should not be read as an outright rejection of science and its benefits. Rather, the saints frequently castigated physicians for their faulty scientific claims, and for the way they peddled fraudulent medicines and practices that frequently did more harm than good. Such sentiments reinforced the deep-seated class warfare that separated pentecostals from the increasingly powerful professional class of doctors even as they reflected the state of the medical establishment at the turn of the twentieth century.

While physicians were busy climbing the U.S. social ladder, many pentecostals remained rooted in a "plainfolk" culture. "Plainfolk were not necessarily poor folk: the status was largely self-ascribed," writes the historian of pentecostalism R. G. Robins. "Most came from ranks of society low enough to have grounds for discontent with the status quo but high enough to aspire to reshape it and to have enough resources to form institutions capable of bearing those aspirations." More than economic standing, Robins argues, the key hallmark of plainfolk culture "was one's appropriation of the lore of the honest, hardworking ordinary American."[39] To a significant degree, early pentecostals' disavowal of medicine and physicians flowed out of the sharp class differences separating them from the growing professional class of physicians.

Indicative of the class warfare at work in early pentecostals' rejection of medicines, a frequent complaint levied by the saints against doctors centered on the way medical professionals preyed on the poor for their own gain. In the words of one early pentecostal, written in 1914, medicine was nothing more than a quintessential "humbug and fraud and largely a scheme invented by tricksters to make money."[40] "I do not need to point out to you the thousands of wealthy druggists and physicians," explained A. J. Tomlinson to his readers in 1913, "made so by the ill fate of the millions of unfortunates who have doped themselves with pills and patent medicine."[41] When a doctor happened to give good advice regarding practical prescriptions for health, asked another, why not obtain it directly from the Bible "without money and without price"?[42]

Class warfare aside, pentecostals' biting critiques of the medical establishment highlighted the faithful's marketing savvy as they learned to distinguish their healing brand in a crowded marketplace. The disparagement they frequently heaped on doctors also brought into sharp relief numerous pentecostals' marked lack of confidence in the accuracy of physicians' claims. A healing related by a woman in the Pentecostal Holiness Church in 1920 reflected a recurring motif in pentecostal discourse regarding healing. After turning her illness over to God, she finally discovered healing from "growths that doctors and remedies had never reached. I found more healing in the hem of Jesus's garment than in all the remedies I could get from doctors."[43] The typical testimony, as in this account, cast physicians in a distinctly negative light; having sought out medical advice, sick individuals turned to supernatural healing after they discovered the doctor's medicines and regimens powerless to heal. (Ironically, testimony after testimony culled from early pentecostal periodicals told of adherents who had visited a doctor.) While the presence of myriad statements referencing doctors' visits calls into question just how committed the average pentecostal was to the rigid antimedicine rhetoric spilling from pentecostal pulpits, the content of most of these reports also suggests that for a significant proportion of early pentecostals, their rejection of modern medicine stemmed not only from spiritual concerns but also from a very practical assessment of the efficacy of the drugs offered by physicians. "If medical science were God's chosen way of meeting our need in sickness," Yeomans insisted in 1926, "it would not be so uncertain, unreliable, fluctuating, and changing, nor so diverse in its teaching."[44] The title of a testimony published in the *Church of God Evangel* succinctly captured the same principle: "Healed When Doctor Was Dismissed."[45]

Early pentecostals were certainly not alone in their conclusions. Important advances were made in medical science during the late nineteenth and early twentieth centuries—the acceptance of germ theory in the second half of the 1800s, for instance, transformed scientists' conceptions of disease and its transmission—yet these advances had not yet produced much in the way of reliable medicines, for example the antibiotics that later appeared in the twentieth century. In fact, it was not until the late nineteenth century that a significant number of U.S. physicians shifted away from forms of therapeutic practice that stressed the local, context-dependent nature of illness in favor of methodologies rooted in the conclusions of experimental science and indiscriminately applied to different patients.[46] As Abraham Flexner's famous 1910 report on the condition of U.S. medical education attested, many individuals who attached "M.D." to their names received their degrees from institutions with few resources and even fewer reservations about awarding diplomas. In the words of one historian, the Flexner report demonstrated that "claims made by the weaker, mostly proprietary schools in their catalogues were patently false. Touted laboratories were nowhere to be found, or consisted of a few vagrant test tubes squirreled away in a cigar box; corpses reeked because of the failure to use dissecting rooms. Libraries had no books; alleged faculty members were busily occupied in private practice. Purported requirements for admission were waived for anyone who would pay the fees."[47]

Given the state of medical education, it is no wonder numerous pentecostals viewed doctors as professional con artists who touted their medical degrees to profit from medicines that were useless at best, downright dangerous at worst. In articulating their opposition to medical science, many early pentecostals drew on the types of condemnations of medicine they would have heard from the pulpits of protopentecostal healers such as John Alexander Dowie. Time and time again, Dowie pointed to the competing claims of allopathic, homeopathic, osteopathic, and hydropathic physicians, to name a few, to drive home his point that no scientific consensus existed regarding the nature of disease or its cure. "There is nothing, apart from scriptural considerations altogether," he wrote, "so purely speculative and so wholly unscientific as the practice of medicine." "Science is accurate knowledge," he wrote at the turn of the twentieth century; "where is there any accurate knowledge in medicine?"[48]

In similar fashion, when the early pentecostal W. A. Redding compiled a series of statements in a 1919 issue of the *Latter Rain Evangel* by a variety of scientists and medical doctors who questioned the efficacy of medicines, he accused physicians of doing more than going against the instructions in God's word regarding proper avenues of healing; he accused them of going against the very dictates of proper science. Redding quoted a French doctor who admitted that "medicine is a great humbug. It is nothing like science. Doctors are mere empirics when they are not charlatans. . . . I must repeat to you that there is no such thing as *medical science*." "I grant you, people are cured," the Frenchman continued, "but how? Nature does a great deal, but *doctors do devilish little*." Using the words of the president of the Philadelphia Medical Society, Redding went on to insist that physicians relied on the "spirit of speculation" and based their "pompous recommendations" on medical claims that "differ very widely from every other species of evidence." For Redding, the practice of medicine was nothing more than deceptive practices masquerading as empirical truth.[49] John G. Lake, a pentecostal pastor in Spokane, Washington, well known for his emphasis on healing, likewise quoted a U.S. surgeon who described surgery as a "confession of helplessness. Being unable to assist the diseased organ, we remove it." Lake found another expert who confirmed that there "is no such thing as the science of medicine. From the days of Hippocrates and Galen until now we have been stumbling in the dark, from diagnosis to diagnosis, from treatment to treatment."[50]

As these statements suggest, many early pentecostals did not reject science in general so much as they rejected medical science in particular; they frequently praised other modern advancements in science and technology. "In our own country—a young giant among nations—do we find some of the greatest strides," boasted a contributor to the *Church of God Evangel* in 1918. "Six great transcontinental trunk lines connect the Atlantic and Pacific shores. The 'iron horses' hurry over the plains . . . and slide down the other side with their long trains of freight and human souls behind them."[51] The writer read these developments as a sign that the end of time was near; nevertheless, the article pulsed with a palpable excitement regarding the amazing capabilities afforded by modern technological advances. G. F. Taylor, the Pentecostal Holiness Church leader and editor of the *Pentecostal Holiness Advocate*, spoke for many fellow pentecostals when he suggested in 1920 that premillennialists like himself who looked for the imminent Second Coming of Jesus to restore justice and peace on the earth nevertheless "appreciate the telegraph, the telephone, the automobile, the airship, and all other modern inventions for good" (though he quickly added that premillennialists "do not see that these things are bringing the world to Christ").[52] In his attempt to spur believers on to new spiritual heights, Tomlinson likewise wrote admiringly of the scientific spirit of discovery. He praised astronomers who constantly produced "new and more powerful glasses for the purpose of discovering, if possible, new worlds." He spoke of "diving bells and torpedo-boats" that assisted exploration of the "depths of the sea." "Balloons and airships are carrying [humans] above in the air, all in search of the unseen and unknown. The physical world is full of excitement, wild prophesies and projects," he observed.[53]

The saints' enthusiasm for modern advancements disappeared, though, when discussing the "false" science of medicine. More than just ineffective, many pentecostals thought medicines patently dangerous. One believer simply could not understand why Christians would ever surrender to the "doctor's care for him to dope with strong medicine that the human body was never created to receive or endure" instead of placing their families' well-being "in the hands of God."[54] Parham singled out medical science as the "octopus-god Molloch, in whose arms [individuals] have confidently laid so many of their loved ones and seen them perish." He acknowledged the benefits of "sanitary and quarantine laws" but mocked medical science's lack of success. "Medical science stands with fettered hands," he proclaimed, "in the presence of consumption, catarrh, cancers, fevers and many other diseases." Given the fact that physicians now had over "4000 years practice," Parham hardly could understand why individuals still allowed themselves to be "doped, blistered, bled and dissected" when the field of medical science had gained "little more" insight since biblical times.[55] For her part, the midwestern healing evangelist Maria Woodworth-Etter cited a Dr. Bell who wondered "how much more divine power" would be required to "overcome both the disease and the ill effect of the drug" as opposed to simply curing the disease itself.[56] Redding quoted one M.D. who admitted that "all medicines are poisonous" and another who acknowledged that physicians had "*destroyed more lives than war, pestilence and famine combined.*" In short, the "world . . . would be happier if drugs were unknown."[57]

Believers' attempts to isolate the failures of the medical profession from other forms of knowledge—including, at times, valid forms of medical knowledge—created a niche for more moderate voices and made it possible for some of the saints to blur the distinction between naturalistic explanations of disease and their own more spiritual views. A few early pentecostals, for example, sought to explain the germ theory of disease by claiming a close connection between germs and spirits. "Diseases are produced in the human system by animalcules, microbes and bacteria and these germinate into disease," one Church of God (Cleveland, Tennessee) adherent acknowledged. "I agree with Brother Lee that these germs are demons and they cause all diseases."[58] (Years later, Gordon Lindsay, a prominent promoter of the post–World War II healing evangelists, claimed much the same. He admitted that "a boil is caused by a germ" but quickly added, "we see that Satan is the agent by which germ diseases are made to afflict humanity.")[59]

A different type of moderation was modeled by E. N. Bell of the Assemblies of God, who took pains to differentiate between a rejection of medical science associated with the efficacy of medicines—which he did not view as a science at all—and other valuable tasks physicians performed, such as surgery and nursing those who were ill. He specifically approved of optometrists, who based their practices on "optics, or the laws of light as applied to vision," which reflected "a real science and not largely guesswork as is the administration of medicines." "Dentistry," he added, "is a much more accurate science than materia medica." In the end, Bell insisted that his goal was "not to run down the doctor" and that he believed that any doctor, "if he is an honest one," would agree with his claims, "for I got these facts from physicians themselves."[60]

The type of moderation expressed by Bell began to appear with greater frequency by the late 1910s and 1920s, due in part to the impact of the influenza epidemic in 1918 that killed tens of millions worldwide and affected approximately 25 percent of the U.S. population. A willingness to back away from the most uncompromising positions regarding the use of natural remedies was apparent especially among certain individuals associated with the Assemblies of God. While this trend likely reflected the average constituent's relative wealth and social standing compared to adherents in other denominations, the debates over divine healing that broke out in the Pentecostal Holiness Church and the Church of God (Cleveland, Tennessee) in the late 1910s indicated that other pentecostals as well were willing to challenge the most radical teachings regarding divine healing.[61]

In a few exceptional cases, a handful of early pentecostals openly expressed their approval of believers who consulted physicians. Hugh Bowling and Watson Sorrow, Georgia Pentecostal Holiness pastors, created a stir when they defended the use of remedies. "I have never stated that healing by medical aid was divine healing," Bowling averred in 1920, "but do state I see no Bible [*sic*] to condemn any one for receiving medical aid, and I see nothing to teach that such aid will hinder God working in a supernatural way." Comments such as these triggered alarm among denominational leaders who sought a trial of Bowling and Sorrow for deviating from the teachings of the church, and the pair eventually formed their own denomination.[62] It is instructive, though, that the editor of the *Pentecostal Holiness Advocate*, G. F. Taylor, initially adopted a position quite similar to that of Bowling and Sorrow. The original leaders of the Pentecostal Holiness Church, he wrote, taught that "there is healing in Jesus Christ absolutely independent of all material aid." That said, he went on to note that the church had "never objected to any one having a physician or taking remedies." Those actions simply should not be confused with divine healing. Taylor overstated the support in the denomination for the use of "means" and eventually sided with purists during the high-pitched debate over the use of various remedies in the denomination in the early 1920s. The very fact that he could claim otherwise, though, highlighted the fact that not all early pentecostals toed the party line when it came to the use of natural forms of healing.[63]

Exceptions notwithstanding, the typical perspective voiced by pentecostal leaders in the earliest decades of the pentecostal movement suggested that they felt they had good hard data to prove that divine healing, not mainstream medicine, was just as reliable as true scientific and technological knowledge. More often than not, the testimonies believers heard week in and week out from fellow pentecostals confirmed the ineptitude of physicians even as they validated—at least for those in the pentecostal fold—their own approach to healing. As Yeomans pointed out, various prescriptions (including her grandmother's "spring medicine," consisting of sulphur, chamomile, sassafras, herbs, and molasses) may have proved to be "one huge blunder, or big mistake . . . but there is no mistake about God's remedies. They are unfailing, and we surely need them."[64] While immunity from disease was the "unrealized ideal of medical science," she wrote in 1926, it was "realizable by any simple child of God who will take his stand on the promises of God and not stagger at them through unbelief."[65] The saints were convinced that the evidence backed up their claims regarding the superiority of their brand of healing when compared to any and every other rival healing product hawked in the healing marketplace of the early twentieth century.

Early Pentecostals and Alternative Medicine

For all the vitriol early pentecostals directed at physicians, they still had plenty of ammunition in reserve for unorthodox healers in the United States at the turn of the twentieth century. Alternative practitioners frequently represented just one more stop in adherents' futile search for health before they embraced the truth of divine healing. A testimony recorded in 1928 and published by Aimee Semple McPherson, who founded the International Church of the Foursquare Gospel, described the plight of a family seeking treatment for their epileptic son. The family initially turned to a doctor who "did nothing for the child except to put him in warm water, and massage him." After their son showed no improvement, they then tried chloroform treatments, to no avail. Then they took him to a chiropractor. "Every day except Sundays we took him there for seven months," the father reported. Desperate, they finally found the help they needed at one of McPherson's healing services, when she introduced them to the "Great Physician."[66] In similar fashion, a pentecostal missionary in 1929 recounted his early interactions with alternative practitioners while seeking healing from a fever contracted in Africa. He first went to "the Clifton Springs Sanitarium at Clifton Springs, N.Y., but got very little help. I then tried allopath, homeopath, and osteopath treatments, and about every other path I heard about." Relief only came when he "tried God's path, and was prayed for in a Pentecostal meeting in Toronto, Canada."[67]

As these accounts demonstrate, in their rhetoric many of the saints simply lumped unorthodox physicians together with the reviled allopaths. In doing so, here again they followed in the footsteps of John Alexander Dowie. "Is the science of medicine homeopathy, allopathy, hydropathy or psychopathy?" he thundered in 1899. "Which of the 'paths' that lead to the grave is it?" Highlighting the competing theories of healing represented by the various practitioners of natural healing, Dowie continued, "let those who say that medicine is a science just agree on which school is scientific. Certainly the *similia similibus* men who say that like cures like are not in agreement with the *contraria contraribus* men who say that the contrary cures the contrary."[68] Like Dowie, several early pentecostals considered the sheer number of conflicting approaches to healing a confirmation that healing could not be found by relying on human wisdom; only God provided a reliable cure.[69]

The relationship between physical healing and pentecostal conceptions of salvation highlights another key distinction that separated pentecostals from alternative practitioners. Though healing functioned as a crucial plank in pentecostals' message to the world, they were also very concerned about the hereafter and not simply about their quality of life on earth. The salvific dimension of their program—centering on the basic Christian narrative regarding bondage to sin and the atoning work of Jesus's death and resurrection—set pentecostals apart from those alternative practitioners who, despite the moral overtones in their teachings, tended to maintain a more thoroughly pragmatic focus on the restoration of physical health. The practical consequences stemming from these differences were significant: due to their explicitly religious status, pentecostals usually did not have to deal with the same licensing battles that plagued other alternative healers, nor did they receive formal payments as health-care practitioners (though this began to change by the end of the century as certain healers sold nutritional products). All of that said, pentecostals, like other alternative healers, never doubted that God was very concerned with alleviating their physical suffering in the here and now.

Ultimately, the common denominator uniting adherents' criticisms of alternative healing practices came down to a basic prioritization of the spiritual world over and above anything associated with human power and the natural world. "It is not in the region of psychology (the science of the soul), nor in the region of physiology (the science of animal and vegetable life) that we must look for help," Dowie taught. Rather, "it is in the region of pneumatology (the science of the spiritual nature of man) that we must look."[70] True divine healing was a thoroughly spiritual affair predicated on an individual's openness to God's direct intervention, and only God's direct intervention. Any other explanation bypassed the centrality of God in the healing process.

Pentecostals' single-eyed focus on a nonhuman, nonnatural otherworldly power in divine healing helps explain why the faithful often reserved their most direct criticism for mental healers who operated under the banner of Christian Science, New Thought, and Theosophy in the early twentieth century.

In stressing the power inherent in intangible thoughts and the ethereal mind, proponents of mind-cure came closer than any other group in approximating pentecostals' commitment to a thoroughly spiritual form of healing, and many pentecostals assumed that mind-cure advocates derived their power from evil supernatural forces. A commenter in the *Pentecostal Holiness Advocate* did not mince words when asserting that "'spiritism,' 'Christian Science,' 'Theosophy,' 'New Thought' . . . all belong to the false prophet class of the last days, classified by the Scriptures as the teachings of 'seducing spirits and doctrines of demons,' that is doctrines taught directly or indirectly by demons."[71] A writer for the *Pentecostal Evangel* warned that "such isms as Christian Science, Psychology, Unity, Spiritualism, New Thought, Theosophy, and many others. . . . are not God." They all use "a few scriptural truths misapplied and deny practically the fall of man, making their particular ism the thing for man to follow and making men believe that the Bible endorses them." Not only were these mind-cure advocates "not God," this writer added, but the "devil himself heals people through these isms."[72] Ernest Williams, general superintendent of the Assemblies of God, allowed in 1935 that "perhaps most of the healing reported by those who do not believe in the atonement of Christ result from psychology or mental suggestion." Less than comfortable with such a conclusion, he quickly cast doubt on all purported non-Christian healings, claiming that it was entirely possible that they came directly from Satan, who "could easily withdraw his power thus letting nature rebuild what he had destroyed."[73]

Even those believers who confidently concluded that mind-cure was just another variation on natural healing, such as the Pentecostal Holiness leader G. F. Taylor, nevertheless discerned a manipulative intent animating its practitioners. "As a system of healing, Christian Science is a fraud," he wrote in 1918. "It is a well known fact that despondent and melancholy feelings will have their effect in the physical system," Taylor clarified, "and so will pleasant and cheerful feelings, and Christian Science seeks to take advantage of these in order to pose as a system of healing."[74] Pentecostals' competitors could find solace in the fact that at least a few believers recognized a degree of efficacy in their rivals' practices, yet it is clear that early pentecostals had no intention of building a bridge of cooperation.

Beneath Pentecostals' Official Rhetoric Regarding Healing

For all the venom early pentecostals directed at physicians, orthodox and unorthodox alike, a careful look at the sources reveals a much more complicated picture regarding pentecostals' relationships with fellow unorthodox healers and spiritualized forms of natural healing. The party line regarding healing endorsed by the first generation of pentecostals should not obscure the very significant areas of overlap that frequently linked pentecostals to their rivals in the metaphysical tradition.

In some instances, pentecostals appeared simply to veer off-message as they utilized their competitors' rhetoric to describe the healing process. Charles Parham sounded very much like a New Thought practitioner in 1911 when he described the thoughts of God as "waves of wisdom that have been let loose by the minds of the church of the past ages, until the wisdom of the ages, floating ever upon the waves of ether, are at your command to draw from." Just as some New Thought practitioners easily adopted the emerging ideas regarding the sub-conscious at the turn of the twentieth century, Parham saw the subconscious as a point of contact between the divine and the human. "Let us know," he wrote, "that it is possible for God to speak through the subconscious mind by His Holy Spirit's power, until . . . it is tuned to catch the deeper thoughts of God and of the ages."[75]

If Parham's use of New Thought terminology and the language of the subcon-scious was an exceptional case, the frequency of early pentecostals' condemna-tions of healers with ties to metaphysical healing traditions serves as another clear tip-off regarding the saints' familiarity with competing healing methodolo-gies. At least a few demonstrated a thorough grasp of their competitors' theo-ries. Lilian Yeomans devoted an entire chapter of her 1926 book *Healing from Heaven* to the subject of Christian Science, recounting her dogged pursuit of healing from an addiction to morphine and chloral hydrate by any means neces-sary before finding relief in John Alexander Dowie's Zion City. She recalled plunging "up to the neck" in Mary Baker Eddy's *Science and Health*, "reading it every waking moment, or nearly so." As she refuted Eddy's claims, comparing them to various biblical passages, she referred the reader to specific pages and even specific paragraphs in the 1917 edition of Eddy's *Science and Health with Key to the Scriptures*.[76] Along much the same lines, William D. Gentry, who even-tually became an Assemblies of God pastor in Chicago, demonstrated a thorough knowledge of various alternative healing methodologies in *The Problem of Life, or the Royal Road to Health*, published in 1916. (The former homeopathic physician spent no less than twenty-seven pages refuting various aspects of Christian Sci-ence alone.) Lest readers doubt Gentry's competence to compare the efficacy of divine healing with the other healing options available in the early 1900s, he inserted a detailed testimony into the book that recounted his careful interroga-tion of "mind healing, healing by prayer, spiritualistic, mediumistic healing, Christian Alliance healing, Christian Science healing, [and] hypnotism," among others, prior to joining the divine healing camp. The title page also called atten-tion to the homeopathic textbook and concordance he had authored before he came to the conclusion that God was the "ONE and the only ONE to whom we can go when sick, suffering and tormented, to secure speedy and perfect healing."[77]

Ultimately, pentecostal believers' connections to their competitors' healing methodologies involved much more than rogue pentecostals reading from the wrong script. For one, even individuals who radically opposed all natural forms of intervention could nevertheless heartily "Amen" unorthodox physicians' sermonizing on the evils of medicines and drugs.[78] Like their pentecostal counterparts, the majority of unconventional doctors were convinced that medicines caused more harm than good and bypassed the gentler remedies afforded through attunement with the natural world. Though Parham vigorously disagreed with alternative doctors' methods, he at least understood why many found unconventional healing practices appealing. Considering the dangers associated with medicines, he asked: Why should it be surprising that many individuals were turning instead "to osteopathy, Christian Science, hypnotic and magnetic healing"?[79] Along the same lines, Dowie proclaimed a "sneaking fondness for the Homeopath." Referring to homeopaths' practice of infinitesimal doses, he confided: "The thing about the Homeopath that one likes is that one may take a whole bottleful of his medicine without resultant harm." Though hardly an endorsement for a homeopath to be proud of—Dowie added that "you might just as well put a few spoonfuls of your medicine into Lake Michigan, and then administer lake water by the bucketful"—his comments indicated a degree of appreciation for homeopaths' (relative) avoidance of medicine when compared with the level of medicines contained in prescriptions doled out by "regular" M.D.s.[80]

In addition to their shared antagonism toward the medical mainstream, for both pentecostals and unorthodox practitioners alike, healing required a holistic approach; by definition it engaged the spiritual aspects of a person's being and involved the restoration of harmony between the physical body and intangible powers that permeated human bodies and the entire cosmos. An anonymous contributor to the *Apostolic Faith* pointed to the full-person healing received during early pentecostal revival meetings in 1907. Jesus's "blood cleanses from all sin, and brings health, joy, salvation, and eternal life."[81] What more did a person need? Pentecostals' focus on the correlation between personal sin and sickness as well as their insistence that healing and not just salvation flowed from Christ's atoning death on the cross likewise encouraged believers to connect spiritual and physical transformation in their thinking. "One great proof that healing is in the Atonement," the healing evangelist Charles Price wrote in 1930, "is that salvation for the soul and healing for the body have always gone hand in hand."[82] For pentecostals, physical healing was only part of the multifaceted salvation purchased through Christ's death. Christ transformed the entire person: body, mind, and spirit.

Pentecostals and other unorthodox practitioners were also united in their opposition to traditional physicians' prioritization of theoretical knowledge over the practical insights gained through experience and intuition. If a therapy worked, both groups argued, who needed a theoretical explanation to justify putting it into practice? According to the medical establishment's detractors, doctors lost sight of common sense in their pursuit of a scientific ideal, fighting healing practices that alleviated suffering due to scruples over whether or not these practices made sense in light of current scientific knowledge.[83] As one 1917 advertisement for chiropractors in Duluth put it, "You cannot get around fact no matter how skeptical you are. . . . 'Results' are the great arguments that will win. If you would know what Chiropractic can do, ask the person who has given us a fair trial."[84] "Osteopathy increased in popularity," wrote a defender of the discipline for the *El Paso Herald* in 1912, "for the simple reason that it gave people relief without risk—also, without undue expense. Those who were sick usually got well, and if any of their friends suffered, they, too, were inclined to take up Osteopathy."[85] The lack of doubt these comments show epitomizes the type of "know-so" confidence that buoyed alternative physicians of all stripes in their interactions with critics.

Early pentecostals inherited a similar rock-solid confidence in intuition and in the knowledge gained through experience from nineteenth-century evangelicals who were convinced that their immediate perceptions of the world around them confirmed their deepest religious convictions. In what the historian Mark Noll has termed "methodological Common Sense," evangelicals asserted that "truths about consciousness, the world, or religion must be built by a strict induction from irreducible facts of experience."[86] Whereas many evangelical theologians tended to locate proof of Christianity in the miracles described in scripture or in observation of nature, participants in the pentecostal movement (along with other radical evangelicals) discovered the same assurance in daily events and in their own physical experiences of the supernatural.[87] For pentecostals, no doctor's theory could sway a believer's confidence in the reality of his or her experience of divine healing; divine healing worked, and that was all pentecostals needed to know. Reporting on her own healing revivals in 1921, Aimee Semple McPherson insisted: "If 'Seeing is believing' one could not be a doubter long. Blind eyes were opened, deaf ears unstopped and the lame in several instances left their crutches behind, leaping and jumping with joy as they went away." McPherson was convinced that these healing services "preach a louder and more convincing sermon than the most eloquent words ever could do."[88] According to both pentecostals and alternative practitioners, their methods produced results more reliable than so-called medical "science." Doctors could keep their theories; pentecostals knew where to go when they needed a sure answer to their suffering.

Significant points of similarity even united pentecostals with mental healers in the tradition of New Thought and Christian Science, though the saints would have balked at the comparison. On the most basic level, as with New Thought practitioners who emphasized the power of positive thoughts, an irrepressible optimism emerged time and time again among the early saints. Scholars, in fact, have suggested that early pentecostal teachings "sometimes verged on realized eschatology" wherein their end-times theology associated the last days with a promised "Latter Rain" that brought with it brighter and sweeter experiences "by the day."[89] Life in the Spirit was nothing less than "heaven below."[90]

More specifically, early pentecostals' insistence that believers confidently expect physical healings despite the presence of countervailing symptoms closely resembled mind-cure adherents' emphasis on the transformative energy inherent in positive thinking and affirmative prayers. Just as Christian Scientists and New Thought adherents accentuated positive possibilities in the face of negative circumstances, pentecostals—like nineteenth-century practitioners of the "faith-cure" who came before them—frequently taught believers to go about their daily lives as if they were not ill. Believers did not go as far as Christian Scientists in denying the reality of sickness or of evil, but they often directed sufferers to signify their faith by disavowing apparent realities.[91] As the influential healer and editor Carrie Judd Montgomery wrote in *The Prayer of Faith* prior to joining the pentecostal movement, "the great point to remember just here is that God's word is true and we must believe it in spite of every apparent contradiction. These contradictions, if they occur, can be only *seeming* ones, for God is always faithful; but the devil, who is the father of lies, often deceives us into believing feelings and circumstances instead of God's word."[92] Other pentecostals picked up on the same emphases. As one believer explained, though sick, God's instructions were to work, and "I obeyed although all the symptoms of disease remained." "The work I had planned that day was a washing," the writer continued, which was "not an encouraging prospect for one who could scarcely walk through the house." True to his word, God rewarded obedience, and the symptoms disappeared when the work was completed. The author's conclusion? "Attempting the seeming impossible opens the channel through which the supernatural current flows, and healing is the result."[93] Another pentecostal woman drew on similar themes in her description of faith in the periodical published by the healing evangelist Aimee Semple McPherson: "Faith questions not; takes no account of circumstances or of symptoms. Faith is *positive, decisive*—claims healing on the promises of God and presses on until the manifestation comes in the body, 'calling things which be not as though they were.'"[94]

Natural Healing in Early Pentecostalism

Perhaps the most obvious connection linking early pentecostals specifically with their more nature-minded counterparts in the U.S. healing marketplace involved the various concessions some pentecostals made acknowledging the potential impact of natural forces and behavioral choices on the healing process.

The most typical pentecostal overtures to natural forms of healing involved those pentecostals who followed in the footsteps of earlier evangelicals and admitted the value of preventative habits that aided the body's natural ability to ward off disease. In 1920, one reader of the *Pentecostal Holiness Advocate* asked why the editor claimed that it was "'our duty' to keep our teeth picked of particles of food, and our bodies washed with soap in order to keep off disease—would it not be just as much our duty to take something to purge our system from malaria in order to keep off fever and other diseases?" In his response, G. F. Taylor carefully differentiated between habits and practices that maintained health and those that repaired health. "Jesus did not die to pick our teeth nor to wash our hands, but He did die to heal our bodies of disease," the editor reasoned. As such, if an individual's "system has malaria in it, you are already diseased, and Jesus died to heal you. Jesus did not die to put clothes on my body to keep me warm; but if through some means I take cold, He died to heal me." In addition, every individual had the responsibility to avoid exposure to diseases. Those who act carelessly in this regard "do so contrary to the will of God." "I do say it is our duty to pick our teeth and wash our hands," he concluded, "but that these things are not parallel with the taking of drugs."[95] God would have pentecostals "observe the laws that govern the body," added a contributor to the *Pentecostal Evangel* in 1921. "Good food, air, sunshine, exercise, are consistent with the will and provision of God for our bodies. Be natural. Don't overeat. Don't starve. 'Let your moderation be known to all men.' Don't worry. Don't hurry. . . . A morning walk is a splendid adjunct to the morning watch."[96]

Judging from comments scattered throughout various pentecostal periodicals, numerous saints would have viewed a good number of the "natural" prescriptions doled out by alternative healers as nothing more than good common sense. In 1930 Alice Luce, a British-born missionary in the Assemblies of God, condemned alternative practitioners' search for "drugless" medicines, arguing that just because "man has made drugs from herbs does not prove that God ever intended them to be put to such a use." Luce nonetheless would have agreed with alterative healers who stressed the importance of a natural diet for the maintenance of health. "Does not common sense itself tell us that it is better to take the iron needed by our bodies in the form of spinach, lettuce, or other foods made by God Himself rather than in drugs which are made by man?" she asked. "Who else understands the composition of the human body or its needs so well as He who made it?"[97] The pentecostal healer Lilian Yeomans acknowledged in 1923 that some physicians offered valuable advice regarding "foods, exercise, bathing, etc., which we require to keep us in first-class condition." Significantly, she suggested that these insights were available not only in scripture but also in nature itself: "While the Scriptures are all-sufficient on every point, there is no doubt that it is profitable to study God's Word as we find it written in Nature, where we find 'sermons in stones and songs in running brooks,' and especially in the fearful and wonderful structure of our own bodies."[98]

As the foregoing comments indicate, many saints were especially open to dietary science and the assumption that good eating habits helped lay the foundation of physical health. "The regulation of the proper amount of the proper food and drink is temperance," wrote the editor of the *Pentecostal Holiness Advocate*. Intemperance involved taking "food or drink in violation of the laws of health." Such choices marked a "violation of nature's laws, and a depreciation of her gifts."[99] William Piper, pastor of the pentecostal Stone Church in Chicago, warned his listeners: "Violate the laws of health and you will suffer in your body. You can not be a glutton and not eventually suffer some way in some part of your physical system. . . . Violate a moral or violate a spiritual law and you will suffer the consequences of that violation."[100] As the subtitle to his book indicated, the former homeopathic physician William Gentry offered readers chapters full of "Instructions and Advice HOW TO LIVE. WHAT TO EAT. WHAT NOT TO EAT AND WHY."[101] Likewise, the founder of the Church of God in Christ, C. H. Mason, stressed the importance of eating foods such as fruits, vegetables, and nuts. He even went so far as to hire a staff dietician during the 1930s, and the denomination's magazine, the *Whole Truth*, published a column beginning in 1934 providing "short articles on the matter of body, food and true health" written by an expert "regarding the six great principles of the science of dietetics."[102] (Individuals less attuned to dietary science nonetheless could reach similar conclusions, for example the early pentecostal who thanked God for deliverance from a "morbid and gluttonous demon.")[103]

Figure 1.2 C. H. Mason, founder of the Church of God in Christ. Flower Pentecostal Heritage Center.

Beyond admissions regarding the benefits of proper diet, exercise, and hygiene, at times pentecostals offered qualified approval of alternative practices while attempting to maintain a sharp distinction between the healing power of nature and truly miraculous divine healing. In 1923, one pentecostal teacher tried to answer the question how a man who had been "a broken man physically, financially, and spiritually" nevertheless had "improved in health" and become a "strong, prosperous, happy man" after consulting a Christian Scientist. Instead of denying the healing, the teacher relegated the benefits of Christian Science to the "*natural* powers God has given" to all humans. Pentecostal healing, conversely, proved a *genuine* miracle effected by divine intervention.[104] Similar logic spurred the first general superintendent of the Assemblies of God, E. N. Bell, when asked in 1916 if natural means of healing should be employed when children were involved—a subject of considerable interest to pentecostals, considering governmental actions against religious groups that refused medical care to minors. Bell clarified that he did not speak for the General Council of the Assemblies of God as a whole but nevertheless indicated that he for one would not object if an adherent consulted a doctor in such a situation, though he recommended that they "call a physician who will not give poisonous drugs, such as Physio-Medicos, Osteopaths or Homeopaths."[105] If a doctor's efforts help at all, he later added, it was because "he will work with nature, and help thus, if he knows how. He will give you proper directions about nursing, and such like, which is often more important than the medicine he gives."[106] In at least one instance, a pentecostal woman went so far as to claim that God himself commanded a mother to take her child to a homeopath physician for healing of epileptic fits. As Fannie Reif recounted in the *Latter Rain Evangel*, "after months of prayer and persuasion" the child initially received relief simply through the mother's prayers. When the epileptic fits returned in a year, however, the "Lord spoke to the woman . . . that she should get a doctor for her child." Initially resistant to the idea, the woman eventually relented and went "to a homeopathic doctor, who gave her some little pills." The results would have shocked the sensibilities of many pentecostals who read Reif's account: "After the child took one dose of the pills she never had another fit, and was healed from that time on." Though Reif explained God's deviation from his stated healing plan as an attempt to deal with the mother's pride "because she was so critical and harsh of His children who did not believe as she did," it is nevertheless significant that when God directed the woman to a doctor, he pointed her to an alternative physician.[107]

Not surprisingly, other pentecostals condemned their fellow believers' willingness to countenance anything other than "pure" divine healing. An author in the periodical *Golden Grains* lamented the fact that the "use of lemonade, ginger tea for a cold, a plaster for an ache, alcohol for outward application is urged by some, but they fail to recognize that the use of the natural will interfere with and retard the workings of the Supernatural. We are apt to trust in what we are doing rather than in the Lord."[108] Of course, condemnations of this sort regarding the use of natural remedies would have been unnecessary if believers had shown no inclination to resort to "means."

In the end, pentecostals' clear prioritization of direct divine intervention did not always equal a denial of unorthodox healers' effectiveness, and despite their differences, pentecostals stood much closer to alternative healers than they did to orthodox physicians. Believers shied away from unorthodox healers' explicit metaphysical language conflating divine power with the healing power inherent in nature, yet more than a few early pentecostals defied sticklers in their movement and distinguished between the unnatural prescriptions provided by physicians and common-sense natural remedies and habits that maintained health and aided the body's God-given ability to self-heal.

Metaphysical Themes in Early Pentecostalism

If early pentecostals stopped well short of openly affirming metaphysical assumptions regarding the nature of the supernatural, other more subtle similarities that often extended beyond pentecostals' discourse regarding healing nevertheless linked the faithful to the worldview of their metaphysically inclined rivals. Most important, pentecostals' conceptions of the Holy Spirit frequently looked a lot like unorthodox physicians' descriptions of impersonal powers that flowed throughout the human body yet operated outside a Newtonian universe governed strictly by the laws of chemistry and physics.

On the one hand, pentecostals never intentionally promoted impersonal notions of God. A major critique pentecostals levied against metaphysical groups, and especially Christian Scientists, in fact, involved their depersonalization of God. "As to its Christianity," wrote the editor of the *Pentecostal Holiness Advocate*, "Christian Science is void of every spark thereof." Included in a long laundry list of Mary Baker Eddy's mistaken assertions, the author included Christian Scientists' denial of "the personality of God, the personality of Satan." Such issues lay at the "very foundation of Christianity." Therefore, "Christian Science is not Christian at all."[109] Concurring with the assessment of Christian Science made by a man she had read about who compared the Bible with Eddy's *Science and Health with Key to the Scriptures*, Lilian Yeomans concluded: "So you are taught to think of God as a Principle merely. Well, it seems to me that there isn't much left of the Book after the lady that found the 'key' gets through with it."[110]

Despite pentecostals' attacks against Christian Scientists and others due to their conceptions of an impersonal God, quite frequently the faithful depicted the third member of the Trinity as a substance-like force strikingly similar to chiropractics' concept of the "Innate," the otherworldly power that osteopaths associated with electricity, not to mention Christian Scientists' description of the "Divine Mind." Here, pentecostals' utilization of natural terms to describe the Holy Spirit built on biblical passages that compared the Spirit to forces of nature. Jesus, for example, likened the activity of the Holy Spirit to wind. Just as the "wind bloweth where it listeth, and thou hearest the sound therof, but canst not tell whence it cometh, and whither it goeth: so is every one that is born of the Spirit."[111] Similarly, the arrival of the Holy Spirit on earth following Christ's ascension coincided with "a sound from heaven as of a rushing mighty wind, and it filled all the house where they were sitting. And there appeared unto them cloven tongues like as of fire, and it sat upon each of them."[112] Another common image utilized by pentecostals involved references to the "Shekina glory." An extrabiblical term, it generally referred to palpable manifestations of God's presence when the saints gathered in worship. "The great Shekina glory rests upon us day and night, and we are filled and thrilled with the power of the Holy Spirit," one believer wrote. "Today the Shekina glory rests day and night upon those who are baptized with the Holy Ghost, while He abides in their souls," William Seymour said. "For His presence is with us. Glory to His name."[113]

In a less theological vein, pentecostals also likened the Spirit to everything from electricity to liquids, fire, and modern forms of energy production. Early pentecostals' choice of imagery here reflected the way technological advances were dramatically changing everyday life for most citizens in the late nineteenth and early twentieth centuries. The "electrification" of the United States during the period serves as a case in point. Electrical lines first appeared in cities during the 1880s, quickly transforming the U.S. landscape. Used initially for public street lighting, electricity soon facilitated public transport, provided power to factories, and eventually entered the average home. Telephone, telegraph, lighting, and other power lines crisscrossed downtown areas—so much so that laws were quickly passed requiring underground wires due to concerns over safety and aesthetics. Describing the period, one historian suggests that mechanization "took command"—not only of the means of production but also of the public's imagination, as technological advance permeated the consciousness of Americans.[114]

Religious believers were hardly immune to these changes. Specifically regarding the saints' depictions of the Holy Spirit, the writings of Martin Wells Knapp, an important radical holiness figure who directly influenced early pentecostal leaders such as William Seymour, foreshadowed later pentecostal themes. Describing his baptism in the Holy Spirit, Knapp recounted in 1887 how "in an instant I was made just as conscious of the Divine Presence as ever man was of the company of an earthly friend." Quickly transitioning to a much more impersonal description of the spirit, Knapp continued, "I felt the presence of a gentle, unseen power upon my head. Then a wave of divine power and love, causing a sensation something like an electric shock, only inexpressibly pleasurable, rolled over my entire being."[115] Elsewhere, Knapp again employed markedly physical language to characterize the presence of God in a meeting. Once all of the necessary requirements for a revival were met, he wrote, then "surely will the spiritual temperature rise, the air become heavy with spiritual moisture and charged with electricity from above, and soon the Church become the center of a cyclone that shall be awfully destructive to all spiritual buildings that are not founded on the Rock of Ages."[116]

Knapp's inclination to describe the Spirit as a palpable force and source of energy quashed dualistic conceptions of the relationship between spiritual and natural realms, and pentecostals picked up where he left off. "It is one of the most difficult things in all the world for people who are not familiar with the ministry of healing to comprehend that the Spirit of God is tangible, actual, a living quantity, just as real as electricity," wrote the healing evangelist John G. Lake. The Holy Spirit is "just as real as any other native force."[117] A smattering of testimonies culled from the periodical *Apostolic Faith*, associated with the initial Azusa Street revival in Los Angeles, illustrated similar trends. Celia Freeman recounted that on "March 13th, 1907, the electrical shock of the Holy Ghost from heaven fell on me. I died seemingly and I became helpless as a babe."[118] Brother George E. Berg claimed that the Holy Spirit felt like "balls of fire . . . [that] went through me from the crown of my head to the soles of my feet." He literally felt his heart enlarged. Far from a mere metaphor, Berg recounted real fear that that the "vessel might not hold the glory and power that seemed to rush into me like water."[119] A Brother Hezmalhalch told how the Holy Spirit manifested through a young girl. "As I went toward her," he reported, "I shall never forget the power I felt when about two feet from the child, I felt as if batteries of mighty power had seized my body and the whole was one great reservoir of electric forces."[120] Such portrayals of the Holy Spirit would continue to appear in testimony after testimony throughout the twentieth century.

Pentecostals' impersonal descriptions of the Spirit as a substance-like force reinforced their belief that healing power could be transmitted via humans or other physical objects, just as electricity could pass from one point to the next via power lines. Believers frequently administered healing by laying hands on the sick and anointing them with oil, or by placing Bibles, pentecostal periodicals, or handkerchiefs that had been prayed over on the sufferer's body.[121] In stressing the ability of natural objects to convey God's healing presence, the saints tapped into a long-standing tradition in Christianity. The practices of laying hands on the sick and anointing with oil and the use of handkerchiefs were all mentioned in the New Testament, while throughout history numerous Christians also made use of holy relics believed to carry healing power or icons believed to convey the divine presence.[122]

Specifically in a U.S. context, adherents' assumptions regarding God's use of material objects and human bodies to convey his power built on significant precedents in the evangelical tradition that closely paralleled the metaphysical principles espoused by other groups. Commentators on European Pietism, a precursor to U.S. evangelicalism, note a persistent anti-Aristotelianism, a penchant for mysticism, and an attraction to Paracelsus's "vitalist understandings of nature" rooted in "concepts of macrocosm and microcosm, the unity of the universe and its reflection in the small world, man."[123]

The mechanical philosophy that became dominant by the eighteenth century challenged the metaphysical-like intellectual framework embraced by some early evangelical groups, though the close association of physical and spiritual realms by no means entirely disappeared. John Wesley, for instance, insisted throughout his writings that the human frame could be a direct conduit of the Holy Spirit. (Not coincidentally, Wesley's contact with the Moravians provided a direct link to earlier expressions of evangelicalism in the Pietist tradition.) By advocating such positions, Wesley countered individuals working out of the Reformed tradition, such as the eighteenth-century theologian Jonathan Edwards. Edwards by no means disavowed the importance of personal encounters with the Holy Spirit—quite the contrary, he stood as one of the most important defenders of this experiential form of Christianity that he inherited from his Puritan forbears—but he did seek to maintain a sharp distinction between the pure activity of the Spirit and humans' tainted thoughts and actions.[124] Following in the footsteps of the Protestant reformer John Calvin, Edwards highlighted the disastrous consequences of sin on human nature. Due to these assumptions, Edwards distinguished phenomena such as fits, trances, and the like from "true religion." To do so, Edwards employed naturalistic explanations that separated those phenomena from the world of direct supernatural activity. At most, they could be seen as symptoms of supernatural activity, but not as supernatural in and of themselves. Wesley, however, embraced bodily manifestations as the direct activity of the Holy Spirit.[125]

Some nineteenth-century evangelical healers employed Edwardsean distinctions in an effort to distinguish their own use of oils and the laying on of hands from "magical" Catholic practices and from the metaphysical assumptions undergirding mesmerism and the approaches of other mind-cure healers who frequently utilized similar "magnetic passes" of the hands to induce health. In defending their healing rituals, these evangelical healers insisted that the use of oil and human touch simply aided faith by symbolizing the imperceptible work of the Spirit. On occasion, early pentecostals voiced similar explanations regarding the use of physical objects such as oil.[126] Fine-grained theological distinctions regarding the precise inner workings of the laying on of hands and of anointed handkerchiefs likely mattered little to those late-nineteenth-century parishioners who were seeking relief from painful illnesses; such certainly seemed to be the case for numerous early pentecostals as they appropriated the same practices. Commenting on revival services held in London, E. N. Bell stated approvingly, "To [the revival leaders] the age of miracles is not past; the laying on of hands no figure of speech, but a material fact which drives pain and disease from their bodies. The blind see, the deaf hear, and cripples walk."[127] When one pentecostal mother in Superior, Colorado, sought healing for her daughter's earache, she simply "laid her on the [Pentecostal] Evangel paper and prayed for her, and she was healed."[128] Similarly, a woman who suffered from "ulcerated nerves" testified to the relief she found after she "went out on the front porch, began reading, and pleading the blood; and believing, and aplied [sic] the handkerchief. Oh glory! The power of God fell on top of my head and ran to the end of my toes like electricity. . . . Oh glory! I don't feel like the same woman."[129] One healing evangelist was confident enough to guarantee the longevity of the power made accessible through the use of a blessed handkerchief: "As long as the cloth lasts, the power of God will operate, if faith is exercised."[130] In short, by focusing on physical objects and human bodies as transmitters of divine power, and by accentuating their Wesleyan heritage, early pentecostals mimicked the metaphysical inclination to blur rigid differentiations between natural and supernatural realms.

In another telltale indication of the similarities between early pentecostals with their metaphysical counterparts, time and time again believers highlighted the predictability of the Holy Spirit's actions. The healing power delivered by the Holy Spirit represented a divine right purchased by Christ's death—as much the right of the believer as salvation; pentecostal healers typically viewed healing as a straightforward transaction wherein faith-filled prayers reliably procured healing. Many described faith as a gift from God, to be sure, yet the responsibility for accepting and acting on that gift lay squarely with the believer. According to Lilian Yeomans, faith "is a gift and must be appropriated."[131]

It was in large part due to assumptions such as these that early pentecostals often found fault with the sufferer and his or her lack of faith when healing failed to materialize. When illness persisted, the healing evangelist Maria Woodworth-Etter explained, "there is a lack on the part of the individual somewhere; for God's part is complete, *and when ours is, the work must be done*."[132] Along similar lines, the Assemblies of God pastor William Gentry of Chicago wrote: "The [healing] work commences just as soon as the case is laid upon Him [Christ], according to the Scriptures. Therefore any person may be delivered and healed who will meet the conditions prescribed in the New Testament, and do and have done for them what the Lord has provided."[133] Pentecostals would have vehemently denied the resemblance, yet alternative healers such as homeopaths, chiropractors, and practitioners of New Thought and Christian Science were hardly the only religious groups on the U.S. scene at the turn of the twentieth century highlighting the tangible benefits that automatically accompanied a formulaic engagement with unseen powers.

At least a few believers went so far as to describe divine healing as patently scientific. "If we could make the world understand the pregnant vitality of the

Spirit of God," wrote the pentecostal healer John G. Lake, "men would discover that healing is not only a matter of faith, and a matter of the Grace of God, but a perfectly scientific application of God's Spirit to man's needs."[134] Lake's mentor, Dowie, also insisted on the scientific nature of his view on divine healing. Describing a service in which he spoke on divine healing, he recounted how the message "fell with great spiritual power and impressiveness into the hearts of the many strangers present. . . . It was Scriptural, logical, scientific and convincing."[135] The healing evangelist F. F. Bosworth, who has been described as the "most respected healing evangelist of the 1910s and 1920s," insisted that it was the opponents of divine healing who abandoned true science. "Being governed by natural sight is unscientific because it does not take into account all the facts," he wrote. In particular, "healing by natural means only is unscientific because it overlooks important facts—the supernatural agency in disease as well as the privilege of the supernatural in its recovery."[136]

Many outsiders of course would disagree with Dowie, Lake, and Bosworth's definitions of "science" and the "scientific." Their comments nevertheless help explain why pentecostals' treatment of the Holy Spirit so often mimicked alternative, metaphysical healing systems premised on the existence of an invisible realm that functioned as predictably and reliably as the visible, natural world. While pentecostals would point to the Bible as the ultimate source of their confidence that God would in fact heal, their tendency to depict the Holy Spirit as a substance-like force—as predictable and reliable as any natural law— buttressed their "know-so" assurance that healing was readily available to all that believed. As their descriptions of the Holy Spirit suggested, at times early pentecostals resembled their competitors more than they would have liked to admit.

Despite the overlap between metaphysical assumptions and early pentecostalism, these similarities did not translate into a widespread acceptance of unorthodox methodologies as valid avenues of healing. For most pentecostals, the various forms of alternative healing available to Americans in the early twentieth century remained unholy alternatives to the pentecostal churches' teachings regarding divine healing. Even in the few cases when pentecostals admitted the efficacy of competitors' practices, they usually contrasted these outcomes with the superior results offered via divine healing. Early believers never would have admitted the metaphysical leanings in the pentecostal movement or consciously approved of the drift away from more traditional notions of God as a personal being.

At the heart of pentecostals' critiques of unorthodox healers stood pentecostals' conviction that these alternative healing methodologies lessened the believer's absolute reliance on God's power; alternately, the prayer of faith bypassed any "natural" intermediaries in the healing process. Though real, the resemblance between pentecostal healing and healing in explicitly metaphysical traditions remained largely in the background. It remained for later generations of pentecostals and charismatics increasingly to depict natural substances and the mind as necessary mediators that facilitated the flow of God's power into the human body and emotions. In the process, the door opened for dialogue between pentecostals and some of their most bitter rivals.

2

Midcentury Transitions

In 1953, a pentecostal layman wrote in the *Church of God Evangel* of the strong ambivalence he felt when consulting a physician. "I purchased the medicine," he explained, "and I can truthfully say I lived up to the prescription which [the doctor] gave me." He "felt so condemned" about using medicine, though, that it hurt him "almost more to do what I was doing than the actual suffering I went through." Even so, he implored the reader, "please do not think I am knocking doctors and medicine, because I know that doctors are helping so many people."[1] The tortured comments of this believer highlighted the dramatic transformation, well under way by midcentury, in pentecostals' attitudes toward rival healers, and in particular toward medical professionals.

As early as 1932, a regional superintendent in the Assemblies of God could list doctors alongside lawyers, ministers, scientists, and aviators as "men who succeed . . . men who have prepared for life's battles in their particular line and are qualified to meet the obstacles which come before them."[2] Doubtless some old-timers did a double take in 1940 when one pentecostal compared the reliability of scripture to the prescriptions doled out by well-trained physicians: "A good doctor prescribes the right regime, so does God's Word."[3] Other believers claimed that doctors were particularly valuable converts, since "few have more opportunities to reach souls than the Christian doctor."[4]

The dramatic changes in pentecostals' attitudes toward the medical establishment represented just one of many practical concessions made by the pentecostal faithful as they established themselves as a permanent presence in the United States. Already in the early decades of the pentecostal movement, some adherents began to deviate from the strict logic of their premillennial beliefs wherein expectation of Christ's imminent Second Coming nullified the value of political activity, and a number of saints joined with their fellow Americans in a show of patriotic fervor to actively support the U.S. government in World War I. Around the same time, a similar reconsideration of pentecostals' reticence toward investing time and energy in long-term endeavors led many believers to shed their antiinstitutional bias and develop denominations and licensing requirements for ministers in an attempt to regulate the pentecostal movement and ensure its longevity.[5] As a direct result of changes such as these, pentecostal churches slowly began to look more and more like their fellow evangelicals' congregations, paving the way for the inclusion of pentecostal denominations in the nascent National Association of Evangelicals beginning in the 1940s.[6] Specifically in the realm of healing, over time individuals with a penchant for antimedical diatribes increasingly found themselves at odds with more moderate factions pushing for mainstream respectability.

Whether they realized it or not, pentecostal leaders who stressed the complementary nature of divine healing and orthodox medicine mimicked a characteristic feature of postwar evangelicalism as a whole. Midcentury evangelicals of all stripes still sought to transform their fellow Americans into God-fearing, Bible-toting believers, yet many viewed the scorched-earth policy of Fundamentalist firebrands as counterproductive, eschewing an antagonistic stance toward the broader culture. Opting instead for what one sociologist has referred to as "engaged orthodoxy," evangelicals constantly looked for ways to translate their message into idioms as palatable as possible to the broader culture without abandoning their core convictions.[7] Pentecostals who downplayed the more radical antimedical positions on healing associated with the pentecostal movement reflected a very similar sensibility, which in turn facilitated believers' continued assimilation into the broader evangelical world, not to mention the broader U.S. culture as a whole.

Besides the evangelicalization of pentecostalism, another development spurring the saints' new-found appreciation of medicine involved the average pentecostal's improved social standing—especially following World War II—which deflated the class-based antagonism toward doctors characteristic of the early pentecostal movement. Organizations such as the Full Gospel Business Men's Fellowship International (FGBMFI) catered to a wide variety of pentecostal and charismatic professionals, including doctors, and signaled their growing presence among the faithful. Founded by the pentecostal businessman Demos Shakarian in 1951, this interdenominational group offered a venue for fellowship and evangelism. In stark contrast to popular conceptions of pentecostals as uneducated, poor Christians operating out of tents and rural churches, the FGBMFI often met in hotel ballrooms and the like. In the realm of education, in 1955 individuals in the Assemblies of God established the first pentecostal liberal arts college, Evangel College, which was followed a decade later by the dedication of Oral Roberts University. In sum, beginning in the 1940s and 1950s, believers gradually grew accustomed to the presence of pentecostals in their midst who had M.D.s, Ph.D.s, and J.D.s after their names.[8]

More important than all of these influences, the medical establishment's growing prestige—and success—made it much more difficult for pentecostals to shrug off physicians' claims regarding the power of medicine. The first signs of orthodox physicians' eventual monopolization of the U.S. healing scene emerged toward the end of the 1800s. In the later decades of the nineteenth century, the application of germ theory paved the way for the widespread use of antiseptic surgery and for improvements in public health, such as efforts to purify public water and milk supplies. These advances not only contributed to a sharp decline in instances of water and food-borne diseases but also bolstered the U.S. public's appreciation of medical science. Though "wonder drugs" such as antibiotics had yet to appear, physicians' improving diagnostic abilities further abetted their increasing authority by the turn of the twentieth century.[9]

Medical science's accomplishments by the early 1900s only hinted at the success and power orthodox medical practitioners would enjoy as the century progressed: medical scientists introduced the use of sulfa drugs and subsequent antibiotics such as penicillin during the 1930s and 1940s. They developed several new antiviral vaccines during the 1940s and 1950s. Rapid progress in immunology, pharmacology, and surgical technology eventually opened the door to death-defying surgeries, including the first successful heart surgery in 1952, a successful kidney transplant in 1954, and the first human heart transplant in 1967.[10]

Doctors in turn converted medical science's growing technical mastery into social authority. Medical professionals successfully lobbied for strict licensing and educational guidelines during the first half of the twentieth century, emerging "as the strongest and most influential profession in America."[11] According to one historian, the twenties in particular saw the consolidation of professional power in the medical profession, as doctors' "prestige, aided by the successes of medical science, became securely established in American culture. The twenties were a decade when legislators, district attorneys, AMA [American Medical Association] publicists, and public health officials took up the war against 'quackery' as a great cause of enlightened government and exposed and prosecuted 'cultists' and operators of diploma mills."[12] Comments made by James Angell, a psychologist and president of Yale University, at a 1931 meeting of the American College of Surgeons epitomized physicians' aggressive promotion of their guild. "Conscious of our own rectitude, engrossed in the joy of scientific investigation, proud of our guild accomplishments," Angell told his audience, "we stand astounded that our worth, sincerity and scientific attainments are not universally acknowledged; that the faith healer, cultist and quack share with us even in small part, in the confidence of the public. With outraged feelings we threaten to expose and fight them." The key to this battle, he argued, and the "only effective measure to combat these evils," involved the "education of the public as to the principles of scientific medicine and its victories over disease."[13]

The correspondence between the timing of the medical establishment's consolidation of its power and pentecostals' acceptance of physicians reinforces the notion that a pragmatic evaluation of medicine's effectiveness likely played an important role in many early believers' initial rejection and ultimate embrace of physicians. As orthodox physicians increasingly flexed their muscles and garnered more and more proof to support the efficacy of their methods, pentecostals who had previously dismissed physicians as frauds would have felt mounting pressure to reconsider their relationship to modern medicine. Coupled with the changing socioeconomic status of the average pentecostal by midcentury, the medical profession's expanding monopoly on healing set the stage for believers' dramatic about-face in their attitudes toward physicians. As the twentieth century progressed, more and more evidence confirmed a new default approach to divine healing among pentecostals: increasingly it was seen as a complement to, not a substitute for, medical care. Many learned to accept their doctor's assessment regarding the nature of their illnesses while simultaneously situating their diagnoses to fit with a "more encompassing religious weltanschauung" emphasizing God's control over events, or the role of demonic powers operating behind the scenes.[14]

Countervailing Trends

The ascendancy of the medical establishment did not provoke a uniform reaction on the part of all pentecostals. Whereas the majority of them simply learned to accept doctors as valid healers without abandoning their belief in specifically supernatural forms of healing, others responded to the juggernaut of medical orthodoxy by reasserting the superiority of divine healing over any and every rival method. For these individuals, many of whom drew the ire of the formal pentecostal denominations, the growing body of evidence pointing to physicians' success only upped the ante as it elevated the temptation believers faced to trust in natural pathways to healing.[15]

In many respects, the time was ripe by the end of World War II for no-nonsense demands that the pentecostal movement return to its roots. The steady gentrification of the movement concerned those who had known the fervor of the early days, and believers must have longed for an antidote to the existential angst associated with living in the newly inaugurated nuclear age. The fear that the Communist government of the USSR sought to destroy the United States, along with the formation of the state of Israel in 1948—which believers read as a harbinger of the end-times, given their interpretation of specific biblical prophecies—only confirmed the saints' long-standing conviction that they were in fact living in the last days.[16]

In the midst of all of this postwar uncertainty and expectation, the rise of the New Order of the Latter Rain in 1947, which first appeared across the Canadian border in North Battleford, Saskatchewan, provided powerful answers to some of the deepest concerns held by North American pentecostals. Convinced that other pentecostals had lost the power of the Holy Spirit, Percy Hunt and George and Ernest Hawtin, among other leaders, condemned denominationalism and stressed the role of present-day apostles and prophets in restoring the super-natural power of the New Testament church. In addition to accentuating the imminent return of Christ, New Order ministers reaffirmed the link between physical healing and deliverance from demonic powers. Many in the established pentecostal denominations saw the New Order as divisive and dangerous due to its emphasis on contemporary prophets who criticized the status quo, yet the emphases of the New Order quickly spread and were especially influential in in-dependent pentecostal churches. Myrtle D. Beall of Detroit and Thomas Wyatt of Portland, Oregon, in particular helped spread New Order teachings beyond Canada and into the United States. (Years later, several figures with New Order ties continued to wield influence in the burgeoning charismatic renewal during the 1960s and 1970s.)[17]

The appeal of the New Order in pentecostal circles coincided with a devel-opment that had even greater implications for healing in the pentecostal movement: the emergence of a postwar healing revival. Led by larger-than-life personalities who promised the faithful dramatic demonstrations of the power of God, the pentecostal healing revivals of the 1940s and 1950s seemed to signal a pentecostal retreat from accepting medical professionals before the new attitude toward doctors would have a chance to take firm hold. Ministers who often operated independently of the established pentecostal denomina-tions, such as William Branham, Oral Roberts, Jack Coe, and A. A. Allen, drew crowds who gathered in the thousands under revival tents, hungry to see su-pernatural manifestations and spectacular healings.[18]

As with their New Order counterparts, apocalyptic prophecies related to the Cold War frequently appeared in the periodicals of the midcentury healing re-vivalists. At the same time that religious Americans, more broadly, were seeking to shore up their faith and safeguard it against the threat they felt from "god-less Communism," figures such as Allen, who eventually established his head-quarters in southeastern Arizona after surrendering his credentials with the Assemblies of God, saw the healing campaigns and supernatural testimonies as a bulwark against antireligious forces. "So, keep your eyes on these people who claim that nobody is getting healed!" Allen instructed. "Either they are Com-munists, or (perhaps without even knowing it!) they are assisting the Commu-nists in their plan to destroy the Church in America!"[19]

Midcentury healing evangelists also joined their New Order counterparts in their stress on deliverance from demons. The chief coordinator and organiza-tional guru linking the various healing evangelists, Gordon Lindsay, affirmed that in a "very real sense, Satan is responsible for all sickness." Nothing had changed since the days of Christ: a "great number of sick people who come for-ward to be prayed for are oppressed, obsessed, or possessed by demon spirits."[20] The view of cancer espoused by the Oneness pentecostal healing evangelist Wil-liam Branham, a towering figure in the healing revivals, typified many healers'

Figure 2.1 A crowd of people underneath a tent at one of William Branham's healing campaigns in Kansas City, Kansas, in 1950. Gordon Lindsay is standing at the pulpit. Flower Pentecostal Heritage Center.

instinct to link all manner of illnesses with the demonic. According to Branham, cancer usually started with a bruise, which damaged a cell, which in turn opened the door for a demon to enter the body. The demon then "starts growing, he begins to multiply cells. . . . Cell on top of cell, cell on top of cell, cell, any way, any where, just they have no form of nothing like a human being after its nature."[21] To truly deal with the root of the problem, then, required deliverance.

Other healing evangelists echoed Lindsay and Branham's sentiments. According to T. L. Osborn, an independent evangelist who attracted a large following both in and outside North America, when he first heard Branham's explication of the nature of disease, "the whole matter began to clear up for me." He and his wife concluded that "sickness is of the devil, and we have power over the devil in Jesus's Name. . . . We'll rebuke the devil that has bound and possessed their bodies with disease; we'll cast out the evil 'spirits of infirmity'; the diseases will then die, and the sick will recover."[22] The Tulsa-based healing evangelist Oral Roberts claimed a special ability to sense God's healing power in his right hand

and also to detect the presence of demons. (Branham described a very similar experience when he prayed for the sick, though he felt the vibrations in his left hand, and also discussed the presence of a special angel who facilitated his ministry.)[23] Though Roberts eventually moderated—but by no means relinquished—his emphasis on evil supernatural powers, during his early ministry in particular, demons loomed large as a source of illness.[24]

Not all ministers emphasized the demonic to the same degree, to be sure. Numerous testimonies appeared without any mention of demonic interference, zeroing in instead on the centrality of faith, while in other instances healers recognized other factors that fed into illness. Lindsay acknowledged in 1948 that "worry, anxiety, all of which indicates a lack of submission to God and His will may bring on symptoms of serious ailments"[25] Along similar lines, at one point the popular Texas-based healing evangelist Jack Coe attempted to draw a contrast between the emphasis on demons in other ministries and his own approach to healing. Coe warned that "there is a definite difference between demon possession and sickness!" "I have seen many men praying for the sick," he added, "and almost without exception, they would say, 'You demon of headache, gall-stones, etc., loose this person!' Everything was a 'demon,' whether it was fallen arches or arthritis. I DON'T BELIEVE THAT! You will seldom hear me call a sickness 'A Devil.'"[26] While Coe's comments underscored the very real diversity separating the various deliverance evangelists, his characterization of fellow healers simultaneously confirmed the widespread stress on deliverance that permeated much of the healing revival, especially before its decline in the late 1950s.

Midcentury Healers and the Medical Establishment

Not surprisingly, considering the stark distinction between physicians' understanding of sickness and the spiritualized framework espoused by the deliverance evangelists, strong antimedical rhetoric persisted among many of the midcentury healing ministries. O. L. Jaggers, who experienced great success early on yet eventually fell out of favor with large segments of the pentecostal movement due to exaggerated claims and controversial teachings, lamented in 1949 believers' growing comfort with the medical establishment, and their inclination to turn to medicine before the Great Physician. Such a "modern, half-hearted, apologetic view on Divine healing by some Pentecostal ministers has caused many hospitals to be visited all too frequently by Pentecostal people," many of whom allowed "the temple of God, our physical body," to be "mutilated and butchered on! What a declaration of unbelief!"[27] Coe, who once attended one of Roberts's healing crusades so that he could measure the tent and order a slightly larger one for himself, went so far as to warn his listeners that anyone who sought medical aid would be forced to accept the "mark of the beast" and be identified with Satanic forces during the last days of human history before Christ's return.[28] In addition to more moderate statements suggesting that God provided physicians to assist nonbelievers, in 1959 Osborn pointed the faithful to verses in 2 Chronicles and Isaiah long used by pentecostals to warn against the use of doctors: "Asa died in his sickness because he sought 'not to the Lord, but to the physicians,'" whereas in Isaiah 38 "Hezekiah lived, because he sought not to the physicians, but to the Lord."[29] "Do you believe God turned His work over to the church, His anointed, Holy Ghost filled believers as was in evidence on the day of Pentecost," A. A. Allen said, "or did He turn His work over to manufacturing plants, drug companies, and medical centers? Can you find one place in the Bible where Jesus ever said He turned his job over to medicine, drugs, surgery, or doctors? . . . If that group of doctors is being used of God to heal the sick, and if God is healing through those doctors, why is it that they are fighting me and what I preach from the Word of God?"[30]

The basic issue at stake for these healers, much as it had been for earlier pentecostals, could be encapsulated in a simple question: Should the sick person trust God or rely on natural means of healing and human aid? Every illness proved a litmus test of the individual's level of faith and standing before God. The success of the medical establishment only heightened the stakes in these pentecostals' search for God's best path to health and healing.

For all their claims regarding the superiority of divine healing when compared to any other "means," it is interesting to note the way many of the midcentury pentecostal healers insisted that they had no intention of disparaging the medical community or the usefulness of their work; most of the prominent deliverance evangelists avoided early pentecostals' denunciations of the medical establishment as inherently unreliable and useless.

Oral Roberts stood out in the midcentury pentecostal healing scene due to his very clear support of the medical profession, a theme that appeared early on in his ministry. In 1949, Roberts admitted that there were instances when "nature has not been weakened beyond its power to resist disease," in which case the body "responds to medical treatment since the doctor can assist nature."[31] "The herbs from which our most curative medicines are extracted were made by God," he later reminded his followers, "and the skill in their most effective use is a gift of the Almighty God."[32] "I believe God gives us good doctors," he added in 1957. "I believe he gives us good doctors because he wants man to be well." On the basis of these assumptions, Roberts insisted that God expected humans to make use of natural healing methods. Of course, doctors had limitations, and certain things were beyond their control. When humans reached those points of limitation, God's power was then available. "I am expected to do for myself the things which I can do," Roberts explained. "But the things beyond my power and beyond the power of any other mortal man are in God's power, and I come to God boldly, believing in him that he can raise me up as the Bible promises."[33]

If Roberts's unflinching approval of modern medicine separated him from many of his fellow healing evangelists, others also found ways to qualify their antimedical rhetoric. As might be expected, in at least a few instances the healing evangelists' tenacious resolve to rely on divine healing and only divine healing faltered when God seemed to withhold his healing touch. Branham, for example, always insisted on the primacy of divine healing, yet his beliefs were put to the test when his wife developed a tumor. Despite their prayers, the tumor continued to grow. Severely discouraged, Branham and his wife relented and went ahead with the surgery, concluding that their "faith is not sufficient."[34]

Perhaps on the basis of experiences such as these, several of the revivalists were willing to concede that physicians and medicines could maintain and preserve health, even if they could not heal. Many of the healing evangelists would have agreed with the response given in a "Questions and Answers" section of the main periodical of the midcentury healing revivals, the *Voice of Healing*.

Reprising a theme that appeared among some of the more moderate early pen-tecostals, the author admitted that physicians could "assist nature" and aid in-dividuals recuperating from illness, though "God alone can heal." That said, "medicines and drugs are not necessary for those whose faith is in Christ, the Great Physician."[35] "I'm merely telling you that doctors cannot heal," another revivalist explained. "They can keep you alive and I thank God for them. I wouldn't want to live in a city without them. I believe in them. But I don't be-lieve they can heal."[36] Such sentiments help to clarify the seemingly contradic-tory claims made at times by the healing evangelists. A 1953 sermon delivered by Branham in Indiana serves as case in point. Just before assuring his audi-ence that "there's not one speck of medicine ever did cure any sickness," he told his listeners, "I salute every doctor. Yes, sir. Every medical science, God bless them for the help that they've done for people." Branham's biographer suggests that statements such as these pointed to the evangelist's belief that "medicine merely kept the body clean while God performed healing."[37]

Another option available to healing evangelists as they navigated their rela-tionship with the medical establishment was simply to differentiate between the healing pathways open to believers and unbelievers. In the same book in which he defined illness as demonic in origin and quoted Bible verses regarding the dangers of seeking medical aid, Osborn articulated themes reminiscent of com-ments made by F. F. Bosworth: "Since sickness is of Satan, every manner of re-lieving the suffering must be ordained of God." "Every means of relief must be a blessing," he continued, "whether it be the 'prayer of faith,' or the 'gift of heal-ing,' for those who serve God faithfully and who believe and trust His divine promises, or 'medical science' for those who do not serve God, and who do not have faith in God's divine promises to heal."[38] In a similar vein, immediately after stressing the sharp disconnect between divine healing and the medical es-tablishment in a 1961 article, Allen quickly clarified: "I am not writing to con-demn, belittle, or discourage the use of medicines or drugs by people that have no faith or trust in God."[39] For both Allen and Osborn the problem with believ-ers' utilization of natural approaches to healing was that they stole glory away from the almighty God.

Midcentury healing evangelists were not the first pentecostals to carve out a valid role for doctors while simultaneously giving primacy to divine healing. Considering the midcentury healers' resurrection of dramatic healing exor-cisms, however, this type of disclaimer revealed the progress the medical estab-lishment had made during the twentieth century in convincing even the most skeptical observers of the usefulness of their services. Given the close associa-tion between illness and demon possession on the part of the healing evange-lists, and considering the fact that natural healing nearly always took a backseat to the possibility of extraordinary supernatural intervention, most of the high-profile independent pentecostal healers throughout the midcentury decades did more to reinstate the antimedical implications of pentecostals' traditional antagonism toward the medical profession than they did to challenge these attitudes. Still, even here amid individuals intent on reviving the connections between divine healing and spiritual warfare, an (often grudging) respect for advances in medical science emerged.

Pentecostals and Naturopathic Medicine at Midcentury

Whereas most of the midcentury deliverance evangelists could not stomach an open acceptance of medicine as a pathway to health that was as valid as divine healing, a few discovered other ways to modify their healing methods and elevate the importance of mundane activities and choices alongside faith. In the process, these figures directly appropriated unorthodox healing paradigms to articulate visions of healing that in practical details differed little from certain forms of alternative healing in their attempt to bring the power of natural substances and the power of the mind into unity with divine power.

The connections between diet and divine healing proved especially attractive to some, given the long-standing emphasis on dietary discipline in the pentecostal movement. From the start, numerous early pentecostals placed overeating alongside a host of "worldly pleasures" threatening to extinguish the spiritual life of the believer, such as "movies, theaters, cards, the dance, Secret societies, unholy alliances, gluttony, tobacco, extravagant dress, newspaper filth, Lord's day desecration."[40] As the Canadian pentecostal A. G. Ward warned readers of the *Latter Rain Evangel* in 1928, "some folk feast so much that when it comes to a fight with the power of darkness they are of no more value than a wood-chuck. If you feast and overload your stomach, you had better count yourself out when it comes to a conflict with the powers of darkness."[41]

Pentecostals' explanations regarding the benefits of fasting paralleled in important respects the therapeutic paradigm espoused by naturopathic physicians. First promoted in the United States by Benedict Lust in the first decade of the twentieth century, "naturopathy," which literally meant "nature disease," generally referred to alternative approaches to healing that zeroed in on the importance of cleansing the body of inner impurities capable of inhibiting a cosmic energy or "life force" that most naturopaths believed flowed through the human body. Key to naturopathic philosophy was the idea that the true source of sickness was unnatural habits and choices, as opposed to factors outside of the body. Though practitioners did not deny the existence of bacteria and viruses, they saw harmful germs as symptoms of bad choices and not as the source of illness. If restoring self-control proved insufficient to combat the sickness, then more active, nature-friendly methods were brought into play. The emphasis on the individual's responsibility for disease added a moral dimension to naturopathic physicians' healing program and proved an important point of continuity with more traditional religious interpretations of illness.[42]

In stressing the spiritual purification and spiritual power attained through fasting, early pentecostals accentuated holiness themes that sounded strikingly similar to naturopathic teachings, though pentecostals were much more concerned than naturopaths with spiritual toxins such as pride, lust, and selfishness that distracted the saints from their desire for God. According to E. B. Noel, a pentecostal from West Virginia writing in 1928 for the *Church of God Evangel*, in order to receive healing from God, the faithful should first "strip [themselves] of every earthly or worldly lust, or lustly extravagance, of all selfishness and self-will, call a fast and get down to business before God."[43]

Despite the very different notions of toxicity that frequently separated the two groups, as well as pentecostals' belief in a very personal God, in other respects pentecostal discourse fit neatly with naturopathic themes. Smoking, alcohol, and a variety of other substances and practices deemed to pollute the human body, for example, were strictly off-limits. "Can a man or woman be in full fellowship with the Assemblies of God and use coffee?" one early pentecostal asked E. N. Bell. The believer may have been relieved to learn that the Assemblies of God had "never made an issue of hell or heaven over coffee," yet the very fact that such a question could be asked highlighted adherents' seriousness regarding such matters. In a manner very similar to naturopathic teachings, total abstinence from unholy substances coupled with fasting purified the body in preparation for the presence of the Holy Spirit.[44]

The similarities between pentecostal fasting and naturopathy set the stage for midcentury pentecostals such as Franklin Hall, who openly endorsed naturopathic conceptions of physical healing starting in the late 1940s. An eccentric figure in the pentecostal movement, Hall consistently stressed the role of fasting in releasing God's healing power within the body. As the title of one of his more popular books proclaimed in 1946, believers could experience *Atomic Power with God through Prayer and Fasting*.

Whereas Hall was well known in pentecostal circles around midcentury—leaders of the New Order of the Latter Rain credited his teachings with helping launch their movement—he was not always well received. His more radical teachings regarding "bodyfelt salvation" (a teaching that stressed the possibility of a continuous, dynamic physical experience of the "Holy Ghost fire" that brought health and healing) alienated him from many of his fellow evangelists, and he became increasingly isolated. Despite these challenges, one insider familiar with the pentecostal healing evangelists of the period claimed that "every one of these men down through the years followed Franklin Hall's method of fasting."[45]

Like other pentecostals, Hall frequently highlighted fasting's distinctly spiritual benefits. He labeled true fasting an inherently "anti-pleasure measure."

Thus, "if one is fasting mainly for greater success in business, or for selfish material welfare, or for healing only, or some other personal object—this is an unacceptable fast to God." The real aim of any true fast rather was the pursuit of "spiritual pleasure."[46] Along similar lines, fasting served as "perhaps the best way to kill the old man of pride. Pride lives on the appetites, and fasting masters the appetites, therefore pride may be eliminated by a person who will fast occasionally for at least a week or more."[47] Hall, in short, envisioned fasting as *the* crucial discipline connecting the believer to God. "Fasting is the most potent power of the universe placed at the disposal of all believers," he concluded. Comparing the power obtained through fasting to the power of the atom bomb, Hall sought "to show to the Christian an even greater power for his spiritual progress that can definitely be obtained through 'fasting and prayer.'"[48]

Hall's focus on the spiritual benefits of fasting and his tendency to link the practice with health and healing all mimicked the priorities of earlier believers. Hall went well beyond his predecessors, however, by employing heavy doses of explicitly naturopathic philosophy in his promotion of bodily discipline. Here Hall mixed his own intuitions regarding the functions of fasting with information gleaned from various research studies related to nutrition. He was convinced that evil spirits were attracted to filth and that accumulated toxins in the body invited demonic activity.[49] Fasting purged the body of these toxins, since fasting lived "on the very poisons one wishes to abolish." When combined with a healthy diet, food abstention helped prevent everything from the common cold to cancer. On this last point, Hall highlighted studies conducted on rats where the "irritating matter coming from canned foods, preservatives, spices, and drugs" caused cancer. Sounding very much like a twentieth-century version of the health reformer Sylvester Graham in his denunciations of overstimulation, Hall asked: "If animals get cancer by eating our spiced up, overseasoned, depleted food, then why should we expect to overcome the consequence of such eating?" On the basis of such findings, Hall grouped foods into different categories that represented the full spectrum of "stimulation." These ranged from water (nonstimulating) to coffee, spices, and alcohol (very stimulating). He said that physicians in San Francisco and Chicago with whom he was "personally acquainted" put "cancer patients on a twelve to fifteen day fast followed by raw vegetable and fruit juices, and many are cured." For Hall, results such as these confirmed fasting's potential as a natural solution to a wide variety of "disorders or growths which any physician knows are caused by auto-intoxication brought on by overeating." Articulating a theme that would recur with regularity among later figures in the pentecostal-charismatic movement, he concluded that scripture was "far ahead of health authorities and medical science."[50]

Hall was quick to characterize the physical benefits of food abstinence as "secondary blessings of fasting," yet he clearly saw fasting as the cornerstone of physical well-being.[51] If he had his way, all individuals would incorporate the practice as a regular part of their lives. "Regardless of the great spiritual results of a week or two of fasting now and then," he wrote, "our earthly tabernacle so greatly needs this fast for cleansing that everyone owes it to himself to take a fast of this kind three or four times a year at the very least." He went on to specify specific times of year when fasting would prove most beneficial. In the spring it made sense to fast, since at that time "our bodies are heavily laden with toxic poisons, more than at any other time," due to the typical "heavy winter diet." He also recommended fasting at the end of summer "as a safety first measure against the wintry colds and for fortitude," and at midwinter to "insure good circulation to the system when exercise is at the minimum."[52]

Judging from testimonials published in Hall's ministry magazine and books, his emphasis on the practical benefits of fasting and diet struck a responsive chord among readers. Glenn Espich, a barber in Fort Wayne, Indiana, detailed numerous healings that occurred as he prayed for others during his twenty-eight-day fast. "My eyesight is fifty percent better," he beamed; "arthritis has left my body and there are no more aches in my arms." A Brother Albert Fredrick Rowe reported after fasting for twenty-three days: "I feel much better in every way, both in body and spirit. I feel young again and in shaving my beard it cuts as easily as it did when I was twenty or thirty." Wayne Moufrey of Decatur, Illinois, believed that "cancer is passing from my system and I also have a bad case of sinus that is being cleansed."[53]

Despite the influence of Hall's teachings, most of the other healing evangelists did not emphasize fasting to anywhere near the extent Hall did. While Hall did more than any other pentecostal at midcentury to disseminate naturopathic assumptions regarding the importance of a natural diet and of cleansing the body of impurities, more than a few pentecostals worried that his single-minded focus on the importance of asceticism and diet denied the importance of God's supernatural assistance.[54]

Hall was very aware of these criticisms. He simply did not agree with fellow believers' inclination to maintain such a strong distinction between natural and supernatural activities. "I have had people say my articles on FASTING contained too much about the natural," he acknowledged. Nonetheless, he insisted that an individual "never comes to God except he first comes in the natural, and then in the spiritual." Here Hall drew a parallel linking his description of healing to his unique understanding of the salvation process: "A sinner first makes a natural step toward God before he gets saved. First, he kneels in the natural after he is convicted, then he opens his lips naturally to start a prayer to God. The breath that he breathes to God is natural, his voice is natural, in that he cries out to God in confession as he surrenders his all to God for acceptance; he yields all of his natural powers to God before the spiritual new birth takes place. . . . No one can come to God, saved or unsaved, for any need, large or small, without coming first to God in the natural." Applying the same logic to fasting, Hall concluded: "When a fast is undertaken it starts in the natural and ends in the spiritual. Natural things in their proper places do play a great part when consecrated to God in drawing us into the spiritual." In truth, Hall claimed, Jesus Christ "spoke more about wealth and that which pertains to food and eating than about anything else in His ministry."[55]

Hall was not the first pentecostal to depict fasting as a gateway to healing and supernatural power. As such, some of the changes represented in his teachings are best classified as changes in degree, not kind. Hall's clear appropriation of naturopathic justifications for fasting and dietary discipline nevertheless downplayed the centrality of faith in the healing process and pushed believers much closer to explicit metaphysical assumptions premised on the healing power of nature. Several of Hall's teachings placed him well outside the pentecostal mainstream at midcentury, yet as the twentieth century progressed, more and more pentecostals and charismatics joined him in blurring the distinction between supernatural healing and natural healing, and between God's direct intervention and the healing power associated with natural processes and substances.

Pentecostals and Mental Healing at Midcentury

Around the same time that Hall taught pentecostals to purge their bodies of toxic waste, a very different—yet equally influential—tributary in pentecostal healing also took shape. Unlike Hall's purgative program for healing, this branch of pentecostal healing drew on the powers inherent in thought as opposed to the power of fasting, and on psychotherapists and mental healers' fascination with the mind as opposed to the naturopathic instincts of other alternative healers. Considering the fact that psychology and psychoanalysis appeared as archenemies of religion during the early twentieth century—due in large part to the legacy of Sigmund Freud—linking divine healing and mental healing in the minds of pentecostals proved no small feat.

The earliest generation of pentecostals, in fact, usually condemned psychologists and psychotherapists right alongside other rival healers. Donald Gee, a British pentecostal and editor of the journal *Pentecost*, whose writings reached many North American pentecostals, confirmed the saints' deeply entrenched opposition to any and all forms of psychological discourse. "Psychology is an unnecessary bogey to many Pentecostal people," Gee wrote in 1936, "if psychic or 'soulish' manifestations are regarded as almost on a par with the positively demonic." From his perspective, he found many teaching "the rubbish that every activity of the soul is 'fleshly' and 'carnal' in a wrongful sense, and therefore to be utterly condemned and swept away from among those who long for pure movings of the Holy Spirit in their midst."[56] Twenty years after he made these comments, Gee found himself fighting the same battles in the pentecostal movement. "Truth constantly suffers from extremists," he wrote, "and unfortunately there have been preachers who have publicly blamed almost all ailments and abnormal conditions of body or soul upon demon-powers. . . . It panders to love of the dramatic. . . . We do well to recognise that mental illness is quite often illness; in the usual sense of the word. Disease has attacked the brain. There need be nothing supernatural about it."[57] According to Gee, many pentecostals saw psychology as impotent to describe, much less address, humanity's deepest needs.

More than just incompetence, early pentecostals discerned sinister forces at work among mental healers, frequently branding psychologists and psychoanalysts as degenerate atheists determined to bypass reliance on God's power or any recognition of his laws. Early pentecostal criticisms of psychology in this regard reflected concerns shared by conservative evangelicals and fundamentalists of the period regarding psychology's promotion of moral relativism.[58] Writing for the *Pentecostal Evangel* in 1928, one believer admitted that other times and places throughout history had witnessed rampant immorality, yet he worried that "in our day these things are being boldly lifted out of the class of the immoral and questionable and being raised to the place men once gave to honored and sacred things." In particular he singled out the theories associated with "evolution, psychology, and sociology,—teaching that, in the name of science, boldly challenges every accepted standard of morality that the world has held to for ages."[59] During the mid-1940s, G. H. Montgomery of the Pentecostal Holiness Church, who eventually edited Oral Roberts's publications, likewise lamented the "systematic campaign at work to promote and encourage disobedience to parents" that had been at work in U.S. society for "years." "Much of the so-called child psychology," he wrote, "contributes directly to the practice of juvenile disobedience and delinquency. The ban on punishing children for their misconduct has in many cases put the child on the throne and the parents at his feet." In turn, "disobedience to parents is lawlessness in infancy."[60]

The early pentecostal Jonathan Perkins's 1924 account of his past interactions with a psychology professor reflected the intensity of many pentecostals' resistance to psychology. Perkins recounted his trip years before to a "university city" where he had visited both the insane asylum and the state university in town. He first went to the insane asylum, where he encountered a woman who believed herself to be Queen Victoria. Afterward, he attended a class on religious psychology, where he was "amazed and then amused to see the close physical resemblance between the professor and the inmate of the insane asylum." To his dismay, he watched as the professor "deeply entangled [the students] in his web of unbelief, as a spider does a fly." Though Perkins never feared that the professor "would harm the Bible . . . I did know that he was destroying faith. I could not shake off the feeling that there was more similarity than contrast between the college professor and the insane woman." If truth be told, the professor's "moral insanity was worse than hers, for it was of a poisoned stream flowing down into the minds of the young, withering the tender flowers of faith." Perkins concluded his account "grateful that it took more than a bloodless and effeminate professor . . . to do away with my mother's Bible."[61]

Not surprisingly, similar skepticism surrounded early pentecostals' denunciations of any form of healing associated with psychotherapy. In her discussion of the biblical story of Jesus healing a lame man, Lilian Yeomans, a former physician, asked, "Did the multitude glorify Jesus Christ?" "Never," she answered. "They had their own idols to whom they hastened to ascribe the praise for what had been accomplished." According to Yeomans, not much had changed in nearly 2,000 years. In biblical times, the idols were "Jupiter and Mercurius. Today they have different names, suggestion, mass-psychology, the sub-conscious self, (what wonders has that marvelous being not accomplished)."[62] In 1929, Charles Price warned his listeners regarding the futility of psychology and psychoanalysis: "There is no philosophy. There is no psychology. There is no ism, there is no psycho-analysis, there is no mental concentration, there is nothing in the realm of mental physics, there is nothing in all the world can deliver a man's soul from the guilt of sin BUT FAITH IN THE ATONING BLOOD OF JESUS CHRIST."[63] He admitted that "mental attitude will sometimes make the outlook on life brighter," but he nevertheless categorized psychology and psychoanalysis as "twentieth century 'bunk'" because "it will never save a man's soul and it will never work a miracle in a man's body."[64]

Despite the withering criticism directed at psychologists and psychotherapists, the early days of the pentecostal movement saw a few signs of pentecostal openness to the field of psychology, especially among moderate figures who focused more on it as a science explaining the habits of the human mind rather than on psychoanalysis as a healing system. For these individuals, psychological insights could benefit believers, provided that they always tested the conclusions of psychology against scriptural principles. While the Assemblies of God leader E. N. Bell labeled courses on "hypnotism, clairvoyance and spiritism" taught in the name of psychology "positively evil," he concluded that there was "no harm in the Psychology taught in the schools and colleges if it is taught by a Christian in harmony with the Bible."[65] The editor of the *Pentecostal Holiness Advocate*, writing in the late 1920s, recognized that although "many preachers sanctified and filled with the Spirit" were standing ready to serve God in any capacity, they "do not get the results that should be expected under such circumstances." Pentecostals who wanted their ministers to speak the words of the Spirit and only the words of the Spirit would have recoiled at his conclusion: "What is the idea in all this?" he asked. "Any successful preacher has to use a good deal of psychology, whether he has any scientific knowledge of it or not. . . . In order to win men there must be made to them the proper appeals in the proper way."[66] Clearly at least a few early adherents believed psychology offered valuable insights for ministers and educators seeking to advance the pentecostal message.

In time, a growing number of pentecostals accepted more moderate stances regarding the benefits of psychological theories, though when it came to pentecostals' views of healing, movement toward psychologists and psychiatrists' distinct understanding of the curative process did not appear until midcentury, when pentecostal healers began to acknowledge the fact that many ailments originated in anxiety and mental illness. While references to demonic powers by no means disappeared, prominent leaders increasingly allowed for a much greater role for the mind in both sickness and its cure, thereby naturalizing their understanding of healing to a significant degree.

A constellation of forces contributed to the new-found openness to psychotherapy among some pentecostal healers. Changes in the fields of psychology and psychiatry played a role. The flood of mental health issues stemming from the experience of U.S. soldiers in World War II in particular spurred psychotherapists' willingness to look to outside resources such as religion to help them address the needs of their patients; in turn, the growing number of psychotherapists who saw religion as an ally in their battle against mental illness likely contributed to conservative U.S. Christians' willingness to make use of psychological findings.[67] A historian writing of midcentury evangelicals' attitudes toward psychology indicates that believers "took comfort in the growing prominence of ideas drawn from psychologists and psychiatrists—Adler, Fromm, Horney, Erikson, Jung, Rogers—who seemed to possess a solicitous attitude toward religion, or who at least did not wear their lack of piety on their sleeve."[68]

Innovative religious leaders also initiated a dialogue with psychology and psychotherapy that attracted more and more interest as the century progressed. In 1906—the same year as the famed Azusa Street Revival—the Emmanuel Movement started by Elwood Worcester represented an early attempt to merge religion and clinical psychology. Worcester, a minister at the Emmanuel Episcopal Church in Boston, and his assistant Samuel McComb worked to provide an "orthodox alternative" that countered the widespread success of rival healing movements such as New Thought and Christian Science. The valid core at the heart of many of the new healing movements, Worcester contended, was the "wonderful healing power that has been discovered within the mind." Focusing on the naturalistic assumptions espoused in the burgeoning fields of psychology and psychiatry, as opposed to the metaphysical mind promoted by Mary Baker Eddy and others, Worcester went so far as to insist that the biblical miracles described in scripture, rightly interpreted, fit with the conclusions promoted by twentieth-century psychology.[69] The Emmanuel

Movement, as his following came to be known, lost momentum in the 1910s after garnering national attention during its early years, yet others picked up the slack. Richard C. Cabot, a Harvard physician who had worked with Worcester, the Presbyterian minister Anton Boisen, and others, eventually helped form in 1930 the Council for Clinical Training of Theological Students, which focused on providing clinical training for ministers to help prepare them for the numerous types of suffering they would encounter. By 1946 *Peace of Mind*, by the Reform rabbi Joshua Liebman, which incorporated heavy doses of Freud alongside religious claims, sat atop the *New York Times* bestseller list for over a year. A few years later, in 1952, Norman Vincent Peale, the famed advocate for Christian forms of positive thinking, garnered similar levels of attention with his *Power of Positive Thinking*. Heavily influenced by the New Thought tradition, Peale spearheaded efforts to create the American Foundation of Religion and Psychiatry.[70]

All of these developments paved the way for pentecostals' (and more generally conservative Christians') eventual participation in a U.S. self-help culture saturated with references to popular forms of psychology. The most immediate impact of these developments during the 1950s could be seen in midcentury healing evangelists' references to mental health studies highlighting the prevalence of mental forms of illness. As in other areas, Oral Roberts was one of the first to appreciate the rising interest in mental health in U.S. society. "While I was studying Psychiatry in Phillips University," he wrote in 1948, "my professor pointed out that about one-tenth of the population was either insane now or would be before their death. A great physician has prophesied that there will be 12 million mental and nervous cases resulting from World War II and the peak would come in 1956."[71] When "worry and fear grip your spirit and your mind is tormented with doubt," he added in 1949, "then nature is unable to function and there is no doctor nor medicine that can bring recovery to your body from sickness and disease."[72] Of course, Roberts offered a very different solution for mental illness than did psychotherapists. What psychologists labeled "dementia praecox or schizophrenia, or a 'split personality,'" Roberts branded demon possession. Roberts nevertheless confirmed his appreciation of "the earnest effort of these men to help suffering humanity" at the same time that he maintained the importance of a deliverance ministry.[73] In the mid-1960s, Roberts went further in his praise of psychiatry, even as he sharpened his distinction between what psychiatry and Christianity had to offer suffering individuals. "Psychiatry likes to go inside the mind and find the festering sore and let the matter run out," he taught. "It helps a person talk himself out, empty himself and face up to his negatives. It assists the person in emphasizing the corresponding positive so that he can look on life with a real positive strength in his mind." Christianity went "further than psychiatry. It is actually an injection of life."[74]

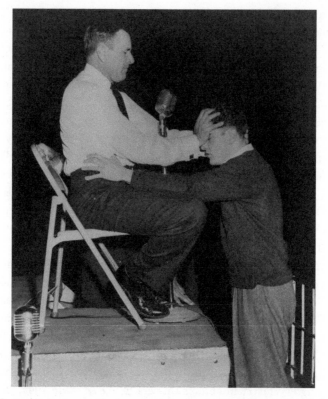

Figure 2.2 Oral Roberts praying for a man's healing in Hempstead, New York, in 1958. Flower Pentecostal Heritage Center.

In the late 1950s and early 1960s, several other leading figures in the pente-costal movement likewise expressed their conviction that mental illness was on the rise and flooding society with an overwhelming number of individuals in need of relief. "Men's bodies are being assaulted by the powers of hell," the popu-lar Indiana-based pastor and broadcaster Lester Sumrall warned in 1965. "The same is true of the minds of men. There has never been as many mental phobias and problems as there are right now." "It is the minds of men for which Satan is battling the hardest today," he continued. "But remember, *God can heal the mind just as easily as He can heal a little finger.*"[75]

At times, pentecostal figures also reflected the budding public interest since midcentury in the psychosomatic nature of various physical maladies.[76] In 1964, Sumrall instructed readers that "a broken spirit will actually have a physical effect, a truth that medical science is now beginning to learn." He cited a survey conducted in New Orleans of "gastro and intestinal diseases" wherein "74 per cent of the patients were suffering from these illnesses that were caused by fear and emotions." In addition, "authorities at New York University say emotional stress and strain cause 76 per cent of all the ills of the patients received in the

Out-Patient Hospital." Sumrall's conclusion? Physical disease frequently "begins with the soul and the spirit."[77] Along similar lines, Gordon Lindsay, the organizational genius who helped spur the resurgent healing movement among pentecostals around midcentury, observed in 1964 that "almost half of the people in the prayer line are suffering not from organic diseases, but from nervous conditions, neuroses, oppression, depression, fears, complexes, etc." Lindsay associated these problems with the "work of oppressing spirits which are sorely affecting and depressing the people of God," yet his comments indicated his appreciation of the role of the mind in bodily sickness.[78]

Healing evangelists were by no means the only believers tracking medical professionals' growing attentiveness to the connection between mind and body. In 1960, the Assemblies of God's *Pentecostal Evangel* reprinted an article written for the American Tract Society by an M.D. who referenced the psychosomatic origin of numerous illnesses in order to highlight the spiritual solution provided by God: "every day I have patients come to me for help who, I find, have no organic disease but merely a functional ailment caused by worry, anxiety, fear, and the like."[79] Writing in the Church of God's denominational periodical in 1961, the editor-in-chief, Charles Conn, drew on similar assumptions in articulating a distinction between faith healing and divine healing. According to Conn, unscriptural faith healing "presupposes that the disease is in the mind or the emotions rather than some organic disorder." In turn, this mental change then "routs the imaginary ill." Though Conn's schema delegitimized mental forms of healing in relation to "true healing," he acknowledged the limited "therapeutic value" of ordinary forms of faith.[80]

Not surprisingly, considering his long-standing critique of pentecostals' knee-jerk rejection of psychology, Donald Gee went even further than most other pentecostals at midcentury in terms of his approval of mind-based healing methods. In the early 1960s, he instructed North American readers of *Pentecost* that "purely psychic" healing should not be condemned or despised, though "it should be kept in the hands of those who know its dangers as well as its possibilities." Like the vast majority of his fellow believers, however, Gee was also convinced of the superiority of supernatural deliverance. "Probably the most acid test of the genuinely supernatural in healing comes through the passage of time," he added. "A purely psychic, and therefore natural, healing experienced in a crowd will pass off when the suitable psychological conditions have ceased, or when the potency of auto-suggestion has run its course." Gee clearly prioritized supernatural healing over and above mental forms of healing, yet his comments stand out in that he so easily affirms the validity of psychological methods for addressing individuals' needs.[81]

As a testament to just how widespread interest in the mind's role in illness became, even the flamboyant pentecostal healer A. A. Allen at times indicated a nuanced appreciation of the connections between mind and body. While Allen was quick to associate psychiatry with atheists and Communists, a 1959 article contended that "America's number one sickness today; America's number one disease is MADNESS—which is none other than the nervous disorders, the insanity, and the mental trouble from which millions of people today are suffering."[82] Though Allen usually attributed insanity and mental illness to demonic activity, at times he appeared open to more naturalistic explanations as well; he especially was interested in psychosomatic theories of illness.[83] Referencing *Live at Peace with Your Nerves* ("the greatest thing I have ever read," Allen exulted), by the psychiatrist Walter Alvarez, Allen wrote: "The majority of people who are seeking aid of medical science and surgery actually do not need surgery nor medicine! They are not sick! Their affliction is the result of nervous tension; it is caused by worry, anxiety, disappointment!" He then went on to describe for his readers the nature of the placebo effect. He recounted a discussion he had with a physician who offered patients different-colored pills that contained the same ingredient so that they could benefit from the psychological impact of taking many pills, concluding that "many times [the pills] have no medicinal value, they only have a psychological affect on you, because you believe they are going to help you!" Excited by these findings, Allen exclaimed, "God's children shouldn't be disappointed, shouldn't worry!" "Some of these physicians and psychiatrists know something," he admitted. Allen's new-found knowledge regarding the psychosomatic origins of illness changed more than just his conceptualization of illness. When individuals asked him to pray for high blood pressure, he increasingly began to tell them: "I am not going to do it. I am going to rebuke that foul thing that has caused your nervous tension. When that nervous tension is gone, your blood pressure is going to be normal; or, likewise, your indigestion will be gone."[84]

Pentecostals and New Thought at Midcentury

If most pentecostal healers remained tentative in their overtures to modern psychotherapy at midcentury, that hesitancy evaporated when the topic turned to a more general discussion of the power of right thinking and right thought to positively affect the healing process. Here pentecostal healing increasingly converged with a powerful current in U.S. religion rooted in the late-nineteenth-century New Thought tradition and popularized earlier in the century by Ralph Waldo Trine and others. Much like their New Thought counterparts, more than a few believers were thrilled to learn that they could speak positive realities into existence, provided that their desires matched the desires of God.

Telling individuals they could have what their hearts longed for was a surefire recipe for success, and by the middle of the twentieth century, New Thought assumptions had made significant inroads into mainstream Protestant discourse. No one figure represented the mainstream of New Thought better than Norman

Vincent Peale. Initially a Methodist minister, Peale eventually accepted a pastorate at the Reformed Marble Collegiate Church in New York City. While in New York Peale rocketed into the national spotlight due in large part to his books, including the wildly popular *Power of Positive Thinking*. As Peale admitted, his works reflected New Thought teachings, and in effect he mediated New Thought principles to a largely Protestant audience—the majority of whom would not have recognized the source of Peale's inspiration. In a transparent reference to Trine, for example, Peale indicated in 1952 that "every great personality I have ever known . . . has been a person in tune with the Infinite. Every such person seems in harmony with nature and in contact with the Divine energy." In a line that could have easily been lifted right out of the pages of a New Thought treatise, he added: "By learning how to cast [obstacles] from the mind, by refusing to become mentally subservient to them, and by channeling spiritual power through your thoughts you can rise above obstacles which ordinarily might defeat you."[85] Throughout, Peale demonstrated a "metaphysical preference for affirmative prayer" as well an inclination to describe God in more impersonal metaphysical terms as energy and force.[86]

The willingness of pentecostal healing evangelists to publish articles by Peale in their ministry magazines serves as a sure sign that the message of positive thinking was reaching pentecostal circles. As early as 1949, Oral Roberts published Peale's article "Christ's Healing Power" in his ministry magazine *Healing Waters*. Though the article was not specifically about positive thinking, it nevertheless described healing in classic New Thought terminology. In the article, Peale drew on New Thought practitioners' vision of the world as permeated with divine energy to describe Jesus's healing ministry. "Here was a man through whom the tides of the Infinite were flowing," Peale wrote, "and the people were conscious of that power." In 1961, Gordon Lindsay's *Voice of Healing* similarly published "How Faith Shapes Events," an article by Peale that stressed the creative possibilities that emerged when someone acted on faith in God's provision and goodness instead of dwelling on negative circumstances.[87] Only a handful of Peale's articles made their way into pentecostal periodicals, to be sure, yet their presence highlights New Thought adherents' success in making their movement's message palatable to a broad range of individuals.

The midcentury evangelists' incorporation of Peale's article also spoke to the growing convergence of pentecostal healing with New Thought practitioners' distinctive stress on the power of words to shape reality. The late-nineteenth-century mind-cure proponent Warren Felt Evans's works in particular played a pivotal role in shaping New Thought adherents' understanding of the power inherent in thought and speech. According to Evans, words served as "one of the principal mediums through which mind acts upon mind."[88] Evans's conception of the power of words fit neatly with his understanding of the metaphysical manner in which the spiritual and material worlds interpenetrated one another.

As one historian writes, just as Evans conceived of a "spiritual body" as an intermediary that "bridged the world of pure spirit and the material realm of the body," he also "saw a bridge between principles and facts, between causes of illness and their unpleasant effects. The bridge, as a chapter title announced, was the 'sanative power of words.'" Such a high valuation of speech in turn led New Thought practitioners to emphasize the importance of affirming prayers that focused on positive possibilities while ignoring negative circumstances and appearances, such as manifestations of illness.[89]

Among pentecostals, the influence of the evangelist and author E. W. Kenyon provided a direct link to New Thought–style teachings. Steeped in the Higher Life teachings circulating among radical evangelicals during the late nineteenth century, Kenyon added to this mix a healthy dose of New Thought–inflected metaphysics predicated on the power of the mind and speech to shape an individual's world.

Kenyon sharply distinguished his teaching on the power of "positive confession" from other metaphysical healers. True spiritual healing, he argued, "is not mental as Christian Science and Unity and other metaphysical teachers claim. Neither is it physical as the medical world teaches. When God heals, He heals through the spirit." Kenyon also advocated a robust conception of belief as distinct from mental assent. "Mental Assent is standing outside the baker and coveting the cake in the window," he explained. "Faith," however, "is always now. Believing is acting on the Word."[90]

Despite Kenyon's attempts to distance his teaching from that of mental healers in the New Thought tradition, the practical guidelines for healing that he and his successors outlined for believers directly paralleled New Thought's focus on the power of affirming words and of positive thoughts. Throughout his works, Kenyon instructed adherents to repeat faith-inspired statements that countered negative and painful situations in their lives. Christ's death and resurrection purchased healing and power for every believer, he insisted, yet it remained up to believers to actualize these resources by aligning their thoughts and their speech with God's will. "In the mind of the Father, you are healed," Kenyon wrote. "Jesus knows that He bore your diseases. How it must hurt Him to hear you talk about bearing them yourself." Instead, believers should confidently proclaim their healing even before any physical changes manifested in the body of the sick person. "A positive confession dominates circumstances," Kenyon instructed, "while a vacillating confession permits circumstances to govern one. Your confession is what God says about your disease. A negative confession will make the disease stronger." Believers could demonstrate rock-solid confidence that their positive words and thoughts would materialize precisely because Christ's sacrifice established a new order of reality, already bought and paid for, that could only be nullified if the faithful failed to take advantage of the blessings and healings placed at their disposal.[91]

Kenyon did not explicitly credit New Thought as a source of influence on some his teachings, but the considerable overlap between his theology and New Thought positions, coupled with his exposure to New Thought ideas early in life while in Boston, and specifically during his time at Emerson College, suggest otherwise. While at Emerson, Kenyon would have been exposed to the teachings of individuals steeped in the New Thought tradition, for example the school's president, Charles Wesley Emerson, and Ralph Waldo Trine.[92]

It can be argued—and has been argued—that in emphasizing the power of positive thinking and positive confession, Kenyon brought to the fore themes that already were stressed to varying degrees among advocates of divine healing. In a manner very similar to New Thought believers, late-nineteenth-century evangelicals frequently taught the faithful to ignore symptoms as they laid hold of God's healing promises, and there is evidence that "verbal affirmations of scriptural 'promises'" often were encouraged in the divine healing movement of the nineteenth century. The degree to which Kenyon highlighted the role of confession in his teachings nevertheless suggests more than just an incidental resemblance to metaphysical mind-cure movements. It may be true, as Dale Simmons contends, that New Thought was not "*the* major contributing factor in the initial development of Kenyon's thought," yet this should not elide Kenyon's role as a conduit of New Thought–style teachings to his followers. As Simmons acknowledges, though the "pattern of publicly testifying as to one's attainment of spiritual blessings is apparent in the holiness movement, Kenyon's overwhelming emphasis on the absolute necessity of making positive confession and avoiding any hint of a negative confession is more akin to the practice of New Thought," and he stressed such teachings "to a point which is only comparable to that of New Thought."[93]

Among pentecostals, Kenyon's name remained relatively unknown, and he never formally identified with the pentecostal movement. His teachings, on the other hand, left an indelible imprint on the ministries of various early pentecostal figures, including the Chicago pastor William Durham and the healing evangelist F. F. Bosworth. Bosworth, whose ministry spanned the first half of the twentieth century, included in his widely influential *Christ the Healer* a chapter, entitled "Our Confession," that he directly attributed to the influence of Kenyon. "Healing is always in response to faith's testimony," Bosworth wrote. "Disease, like sin, is defeated by our confession of the Word. Make your lips do their duty; fill them with the Word. Make them say what God says about your sickness. Don't allow them to say anything to the contrary."[94] Bosworth's appropriation of Kenyon's teachings proved all the more significant given Bosworth's strong influence on the healing evangelists of the 1940s and 1950s, and *Christ the Healer* continued to be published by pentecostal and charismatic presses throughout the twentieth century.

In 1949, O. L. Jaggers confirmed the growing preoccupation with the power of words evident among some of the midcentury healers. If believers "expect

God to heal us," he explained, it was "tremendously important" that we "be controlled by the Holy Spirit constantly working in us in WORD."[95] In a more direct indication of Kenyon's influence, T. L. Osborn often read whole chapters of Kenyon's books as part of his sermons, and he received permission from Kenyon's daughter to reproduce in his own books her father's writings.[96] In a passage that was vintage Kenyon, Osborn wrote in 1959: "When we CONFESS HIS WORDS, then our High Priest, Jesus Christ, acts on our behalf, according to our CONFESSION OF HIS WORD, and intercedes to our Father for the benefits of the promises which we are confessing. He is the High Priest OF **our confession**." Christ's death served as the believer's Emancipation Proclamation; believers should "ACT accordingly. You should SPEAK accordingly. CONFESS your FREEDOM instead of your bondage!"[97]

The popularity of the New Thought–inflected emphases that were derived from Kenyon and were apparent in the writings of several midcentury healing evangelists would only expand in the later decades of the twentieth century, with the appearance of the Word of Faith movement and the rising popularity of Kenneth Hagin beginning in the mid-1960s. Like Osborn, Hagin did not hesitate to quote Kenyon's writings verbatim. (Unlike Osborn, Hagin never acknowledged his debt to the protopentecostal leader.)[98]

The future of pentecostal healing, it turns out, belonged to individuals who, in the tradition of Kenyon and Franklin Hall, harnessed insights closely tied to alternative healing traditions such as New Thought and naturopathy, not to mention mainstream medicine, and merged them with more traditional pentecostal practices. Both figures foreshadowed the innovative pentecostal healing paradigms that burst on the scene with increasing regularity in the later decades of the twentieth century. As A. A. Allen commented regarding his old-school methods shortly before his death in 1970, "There are no evangelists left that offer us any competition. We've got the field. Back in the late '40's and '50's, Jack Coe, Oral Roberts, O. L. Jaggers and 200 others, you know, there were 200 evangelists all praying for the sick, having healing revivals. Now they're nonexistent."[99]

Allen's eulogy of traditional faith healing may have been premature, yet his comments accurately captured the dramatic changes afoot in the pentecostal movement. In time, more and more believers embraced holistic models of health and healing premised on the inexorable connection between mind, body, and spirit. Many new faces helped spur the diminished role for the midcentury deliverance model of healing, as individuals built on the legacy of Hall and Kenyon by stressing the interconnections linking divine healing with dietary choices and the mind. It was a long-standing member of the old guard, Oral Roberts, though, who spearheaded the widespread popularization of holistic healing models, as he sought no less than to join divine healing with the insights of mainstream medicine.

3

Making Medicine Spiritual

For all of their star power in the early to mid-1950s, the independent healing revivalists experienced a rapid decline in the late 1950s and early 1960s, due in part to the fact that several of them decided to exercise their democratic right to undermine their own ministries. Part of the problem lay in over-the-top claims and promises—even by the revivalists' lofty standards—that began to be made in various ministries. "The first time in 1900 years," O. L. Jaggers exulted in 1959, "an exact formula has been given as to how to attain physical immortality in this World!!!! The fountain of perpetual youth, longevity, and eternal life in a physical body, has now been discovered in this world."[1] Jaggers's increasingly extreme positions isolated him from other deliverance evangelists, but he was not alone in testing the outer limits of credulity. Reports of healing made in A. A. Allen's ministry magazine mimicked the types of sensationalist claims made in the *National Enquirer*. At one point he told readers of the miraculous transformation of a man who literally had been born with alligator skin, and another woman testified that "God's reducing plan" had helped her shed 200 pounds instantly at a service.[2] The wife of a hermaphrodite confirmed an even greater transformation effected at one of Allen's meetings: all of her husband's "female organs, which had been quite prominent have shriveled up and disappeared." "Surely if anyone should be sure about this," she confirmed, "it would be his own wife, who has lived with him closely these three years. I know what I am talking about. God has changed him and HE IS ALL MAN!"[3] For a brief time, Allen even promoted a "raise the dead" initiative, though the program ran into trouble when some followers declined to bury their deceased relatives in hope of a miraculous turn of events.[4]

Even more damaging than the extreme claims made by the healing evangelists, scandals shook followers' confidence in the integrity of their spiritual heroes. Allen's well-known struggles with alcohol tarnished his image, for instance. Granville H. Montgomery published a series of articles in the early 1960s cataloguing widespread excesses associated with the revivals. A former editor in the Pentecostal Holiness Church, Montgomery eventually worked closely with Oral Roberts prior to a messy parting of ways that brought the relationship to an end. Shortly thereafter, Montgomery published his biting critique, exposing the evangelists' dirty laundry. Without naming names, Montgomery chronicled fraudulent healing claims, the lavish lifestyles enjoyed by many of the healers, and the misappropriation of funds that had been donated for specific causes and purposes. Indicative of the healers' penchant for gross exaggeration, Montgomery noted that over a two-year span various evangelists claimed roughly 3 million converts in Jamaica as a result of their meetings. The tally was quite impressive, especially considering the fact that the island's total population stood at 1.6 million.[5]

Even apart from some of the healing evangelists' scandalous behavior, with the arrival of the 1960s a new decade ushered in new concerns and a very different cultural frame of mind, as Americans turned their attention to Vietnam, feminism, civil rights, and the closely related counterculture movement. In addition, internal realignments related to demographic changes and the appearance of charismatic renewal fostered new expressions of the "spirit-filled life," even as they rendered the flamboyant revivalism of the deliverance evangelists less and less effective.[6] Pentecostal healers attentive to the rapidly changing landscape quickly realized that their survival depended on a willingness to adapt and evolve with the times.

Though overblown at times by historians and sociologists, social and cultural differences separated more traditional pentecostals from their charismatic kin, and charismatics' influence on the pentecostal healing tradition reflected these differences. Charismatics' greater openness to higher education and science proved of particular importance as their growing numbers during the 1960s and 1970s provided a font of new energy and ideas from individuals who lacked the antimedicine, antipsychology baggage carried by those with deep roots in the pentecostal tradition.

Indicative of many charismatics' unalloyed support of the medical establishment, Agnes Sanford, an Episcopalian healer in the United States who influenced numerous individuals associated with the charismatic renewal, unequivocally affirmed medical professionals in her extensive writings on healing. "We are not too proud to go to God's servants, the clergy, for our spiritual help," she explained in her book *The Healing Light*, originally published in 1947. "Why should we be too proud to go to God's servants, the doctors, for our physical help?" Sanford similarly approved of medicines. "All things are of God," she wrote. "The antibiotics, for instance, are a source of power implanted in nature for man's use, just as electricity is a source of power implanted in nature for man's use."[7] Significantly, by the 1960s several of Sanford's works were published by charismatic presses and increasingly reached a pentecostal audience.

Through his writings and especially through his friendship with Oral Roberts, William Standish Reed functioned as another harbinger of charismatics' impact on pentecostal healing. An Episcopalian physician, Reed circulated in various healing networks, for example the Order of St. Luke the Physician and Glenn Clark's Camps Farthest Out, that were comprised largely of individuals in the historic churches and that functioned as forerunners of charismatic renewal.[8] In 1962, he also founded the Christian Medical Foundation International with the intent of connecting physicians open to divine healing. Time and time again, Reed fought against the sharp segregation of medicine from faith. "I believe implicitly in the Healing Ministry of the Church of Jesus Christ," he explained in 1969. "However, I believe that this ministry should be used in conjunction with the best medical and surgical methods—not as a substitute for scientific methods."[9]

Kathryn Kuhlman's ministry stood closer to traditional pentecostalism than those of Sanford or Reed; hers, too, however, serves as one more example of charismatics' greater willingness to align themselves with physicians. Beginning in the 1930s, Kuhlman tasted significant success as she established the 2,000-seat Denver Revival Tabernacle, and early on in her ministry she encountered pentecostal healing stalwarts such as Charles Price. Healing did not become a focal point of Kuhlman's meetings until the late 1940s, though, and her relationship with pentecostals was strained due to her status as a divorcee and the fact that she did not emphasize speaking in tongues in her services. Despite the tense relationship at times between Kuhlman and pentecostals, and despite the fact that Kuhlman distanced herself from pentecostals' reputation for disorderly services and attention-hungry revivalists, she nevertheless recognized her indebtedness to the pentecostal movement. "I'm as Pentecostal as anybody who stands behind the pulpit," she declared in one radio broadcast. "I've taken my stand before the whole world. I've taken my stand before millions. I've declared my position. I'm as Pentecostal as the Word of God. But I want nothing to do with fanaticism. I want nothing to do with the demonstrations of the flesh."[10]

In 1950, an article in *Redbook* thrust Kuhlman into the national spotlight, and during the 1960s and 1970s she was a major force in the charismatic movement. In her focus on divine healing, Kuhlman criticized doctors for their tendency to discount the miraculous, yet she had no qualms about the validity of modern medicine.[11] "I have nothing against doctors, and hope they have nothing against me," she clarified. "I don't cure people—the Holy Spirit cures through me. Doctors cure people, too. I think doctors are wonderful."[12] The feelings were not always mutual; Kuhlman accrued her fair share of detractors in the medical profession over the years, most notably William Nolen. In his 1976 book *Healing: A Doctor in Search of a Miracle*, Nolen concluded that Kuhlman's healing claims were simply false, despite her evident sincerity.[13] Numerous other physicians who participated in Kuhlman's services, however, begged to differ. According to Kuhlmans' biographer, "through the years several doctors were willing—even eager—to appear at her meetings to assist in the healing ministry or speak a word of commendation."[14]

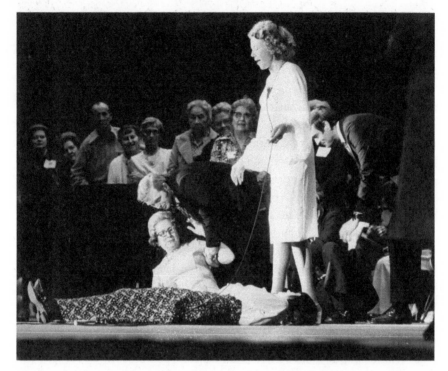

Figure 3.1 Ushers help congregants who have fallen to the floor during a 1973 healing service conducted by Kathryn Kuhlman. AP Photo/Tampa Tribune.

The ability of figures such as Sanford, Reed, and Kuhlman to influence the trajectory of pentecostal healing symbolized the growing significance of what have been called "zones of convergence" that appeared outside the formal pentecostal denominations in the second half of the twentieth century, as pentecostals interacted with believers tied to more established forms of Christianity in the United States.[15] The knack the midcentury healing evangelists had for attracting individuals from well beyond the pentecostal fold to their massive tents served as an early instance of this trend, as did the efforts of the South Africa–born pentecostal David du Plessis, who broke ranks with many of his fellow pentecostals in the early 1950s by cheering for ecumenism and working to establish a dialogue with believers in the historic churches. (In a move that stunned his fellow pentecostals, Oral Roberts went so far as to leave the Pentecostal Holiness Church and officially join the United Methodist Church in 1968.) Associations such as the Full Gospel Business Men's Fellowship International also helped bridge the pentecostal-charismatic divide. In the ensuing years similar sites for interaction and exchange between pentecostals and charismatics surfaced, including Oral Roberts University; Aglow International (formerly Women's Aglow Fellowship), an organization for evangelical women that started

as a counterpart to the FGBMFI; the "Jesus People Movement," a loosely organized youth movement that initially formed as a Christian alternative to the
1960s counterculture; and, in time, the Association of Vineyard Churches and
the Full Gospel Baptist Church Fellowship. The Christian Medical Foundation,
which Reed established with the help of the Assemblies of God physician Jere
Melilli, among others, can also be included in this list.

If the convergence of pentecostalism and charismatic renewal spoke to the
growing influence of charismatics on the saints, it also revealed the internal momentum already propelling increasingly upwardly mobile pentecostals toward the
evangelical mainstream. Specifically in the realm of healing, charismatics' comfortable relationship with medical orthodoxy added fuel to a fire that was already
at work transforming the pentecostal subculture. Numerous pentecostals—
especially those in the established denominations—had made peace with the
medical profession well before charismatic renewal emerged as a major force in
the 1960s. By 1961, for example, the executive director of the Division of Foreign
Missions of the Assemblies of God (now the Assemblies of God World Missions),
J. Philip Hogan, could commission Jere Melilli to assess the viability of a medical
program for Africa.[16]

Despite the clear openness to the potential of medical missions, such efforts
never gained traction, as detractors argued that denominational funds were
better spent on more direct evangelistic efforts aimed strictly at conversion. Melilli himself indicated that if he "were going to be a full-time missionary today,
I would not go to Africa as a medical missionary, but rather as an evangelist."[17]
Nonetheless, the simple fact that such missionary efforts garnered serious attention confirmed the fundamental shift in adherents' attitudes toward physicians. In 1964, Hogan clarified the denomination's position: medical missions
were not cost-effective, considering the denomination's priorities. "We never
have appointed a medical doctor," he explained, "and it is unlikely that we will do
so in the foreseeable future." That said, the denomination was "not critical of
missions that emphasize medical and educational programs, nor are we un-
mindful of the physical and material needs of people in countries where we
serve."[18]

Holistic Healing Paradigms

At the same time that more and more pentecostals were joining charismatics in
the suburbs and mirroring the behavior of their newly acquired neighbors, developments external to the pentecostal-charismatic movement provided another impetus for change, as a perfect storm took shape that fueled the surging
popularity of holistic healing paradigms in the broader U.S. culture. For one,

during the middle decades of the twentieth century more and more cracks began to appear in the armor of the medical establishment. Awareness of the limitations and negative implications associated with widespread use of the supposed "wonder drugs"—antibiotics—steadily grew beginning in the 1950s, for example, as evidenced by a 1957 article in *Time* castigating the uncleanliness of America's hospitals. Quoting a Dr. Carl Waldemar Walter, the piece suggested that "90% of the nation's hospitals are a menace to health." Due to lax standards, hospitals assured "maximal multiplication of pathogenic monsters [i.e., germs]." "Doctors rely too much on antibiotics," the article concluded, "ignoring the fact that bacteria which defy the antibiotics stay around hospitals."[19] In another very public failure, physicians frequently prescribed thalidomide to pregnant women in order to counteract the effects of morning sickness, which in turn caused thousands of unnecessary birth defects worldwide during the 1950s and 1960s.[20] To physicians' dismay, their profession's shortcomings contributed to diminished trust and respect from the American public, even if their position as the primary source of health care for the vast majority of Americans was never seriously threatened. The rapid rise in medical costs accompanying the increased reliance on medical technology only compounded the medical establishment's growing image problem.[21]

Internal critiques cultivated by members of the medical establishment contributed to the rise of holistic perspectives as well, further challenging reductive explanations of the healing process that treated the patient as little more than a collection of cellular processes. Already in the first half of the twentieth century, physicians such as George Canby Robinson and Alan Gregg mounted holistic-style criticisms, stressing the social components of medicine and the interconnections of psychiatry with standard medical care. Related efforts continued in the form of the midcentury psychosomatic movement.[22]

Beyond physicians' self-inflected wounds and in-house deliberations, the growing prevalence of holistic critiques specifically grounded in religious sensibilities added a distinctly spiritual dimension to debates regarding the efficacy of medical orthodoxy. The widely publicized efforts of figures such as Joshua Liebman and Norman Vincent Peale to harmonize religion with psychology and psychiatry during the postwar years set an important precedent legitimating religion's presence in such discussions, and in the sixties a new set of circumstances amplified the overtly spiritual criticisms of the medical establishment that appeared with increasing regularity. Congress loosened restrictions on the immigration of non-Europeans in 1965, for instance, opening the door for an influx of healing practices tied to Eastern religious traditions and well outside the pale of Western medicine. At the same time, the antiauthoritarian ethos exemplified by the civil rights movement and Vietnam protests, along with a growing disillusionment with the perceived artificiality of life in modern societies, abetted

Americans' willingness to experiment with natural, metaphysical paradigms that challenged orthodox physicians' privileged position and power. Taken together, each of these trends chipped away at the hegemony of the medical establishment and laid the groundwork for the reinvigorated presence of holistic health-care options stressing the religious dimensions of healing.[23]

Already steeped in their own "whole person" perspective on health and illness, those pentecostal and charismatic healers who were conversant with the emerging critiques of mainstream medicine from a holistic perspective readily incorporated similar language into their own discourse on healing. Roberts's biographer notes that by the 1960s he consistently stressed "wholeness," as opposed to mere physical healing, and as early as 1949 quoted a doctor who explained "that there is little medical hope for people whose souls are wrong with God, whose spiritual channels are blocked, whose minds are beset by fears and frustrations." Given the ultimate unity of the body, mind, and spirit, Roberts concluded that the "miracle of healing starts from within."[24] In 1960, Kuhlman likewise chided physicians for their lack of holistic focus: "Many of our fine medical men will agree that religion is good for mental healing, the healing of the mind. And they all agree that religion is healing for the soul. And yet few admit that the power of God for the healing of the body is reasonable." Approaches to healing premised on a sharp distinction between body, mind, and spirit made no sense to Kuhlman, "when after all the three are all interlocked."[25]

One of the most insistent charismatic voices spurring the emerging holistic sensibilities belonged to William Standish Reed, who drew on the inspiration of the Swiss physician Paul Tournier as he forcefully argued for nothing less than a reformation of modern medicine based on the principles of divine healing. A 1964 speech delivered to an audience at Oral Roberts University prior to its official opening outlined his concept of "logo-psychosomatic healing": "The logos is the spirit of man," he declared to his audience, "the psychi is the mind of man, and the somatic is the body of man. . . . We need someone who has the synthetic mind, who can take all of these various aspects of man and put us back together again." In a crucial move, Reed's vision required Christian—and more specifically pentecostal and charismatic—doctors. "The only kind of doctors that can fill this particular bill," he insisted, "are those who are baptized with the Holy Ghost because they do not know otherwise what the spirit is."[26] Whereas Reed sought to implement his vision by encouraging and organizing doctors who were open to the Spirit's healing work, his influence in the pentecostal-charismatic movement expanded exponentially due to his personal friendship with Roberts. Only someone with Roberts's clout could marshal the resources necessary to build institutions dedicated to training spirit-empowered physicians; in time, Roberts planned to do just that.

The "Holistic Health Explosion" of the 1970s

Roberts's vision for a spirit-centered medical school and hospital would not materialize until the late 1970s and early 1980s. In the meantime, the effects of skyrocketing medical costs, antibiotic-resistant strains of disease, and exposure to Eastern forms of medical care continued to spread throughout U.S. culture and challenge the medical establishment's authority. In the process came a "holistic health explosion," characterized by a growing chorus of voices stressing the inexorable ties between the spiritual and natural dimensions of health and wholeness.[27] One list of the hodgepodge of methodologies promoted at various holistic health conferences during the 1970s included "acupuncture, astrology, graphology, numerology, clairvoyance, biofeedback, homeopathy, naturopathy, nutrition, iridology, pyramidology, psychic surgery, yoga, faith healing, vitamin therapy, apricot kernel therapy, touch encounters, chiropractic, self-massage, negative ionization, and psychocalisthenics, among others."[28] "I didn't intend to let the 'discovery' of acupuncture turn me into a gullible person," an M.D. offered, "but I did resolve that I would no longer have a closed mind."[29]

Among pentecostals and charismatics, the proliferation of holistic healing models in U.S. society, coupled with the growing disaffection with doctors, helped to ensure the continued appeal of the divine healing message, though by this point most prominent healers readily affirmed physicians' abilities and usefulness while simultaneously highlighting modern medicine's limitations when divorced from knowledge regarding the spiritual component of human existence. In this respect, pentecostals and charismatics reflected the general trajectory of alternative healing in the late-twentieth-century United States: most Americans who experimented with unorthodox methodologies—and many did—nevertheless did so while still consulting their doctors.[30] Some pentecostal and charismatic leaders in fact seemed more concerned with tamping down overzealous promotions of the supernatural and clarifying their support of the medical profession than with proving the reality of supernatural healing. A Baptist M.D. from North Carolina writing for the charismatic journal *Logos* in 1975 lambasted those who mocked doctors or embellished facts so as to undermine the authority of physicians, cringing when pentecostal and charismatic testimonies "use sarcasm, and treat with cynicism [physicians] from whom we have sought help in the past—and from whom we will probably seek help in the future." In an effort to stress Jesus as the "Great Physician," the author believed some pentecostals and charismatics forgot the fact that Dr. Luke ministered alongside the Apostle Paul and was there "to tend the wounds" while also praying for healing.[31] The Assemblies of God also made its support of physicians crystal clear in a 1974 position paper on divine healing: "It is true that the Lord is the Great Physician," the authors noted, though it was also true that "the physician had an honorable place in Israel. . . . and Jesus also presented the medicinal use of oil and wine by the Good Samaritan in a favorable light."[32] Enthusiastic defenders of God's healing power continued to allow antimedical tropes to creep into their rhetoric, and some believers still saw reliance on doctors as a sign of weak faith, but widespread disavowals of medical care were a thing of the past.

Beyond the basic holistic assumptions implied by believers' inclination to jump into the healing prayer line after receiving instructions from their physicians, more voices—especially charismatic voices—offered explicit affirmations of holistic thought during the 1970s. The popular Catholic charismatic healer Francis MacNutt, for instance, stressed in 1974 that sickness could originate either in the spirit, the emotions, the body, or the demonic. Regardless of the differing roots of disease, MacNutt made it clear that the four categories easily bled into one another. Sickness of the spirit often contributed to emotional and bodily sickness, sickness of the emotions often contributed to spiritual and bodily sickness, and so forth. Complete healing, by extension, required an approach that addressed all four areas.[33] Barbara Pursey, a contributor writing for *Logos* in the late 1970s, likewise described the complex interplay between body, mind, and spirit in disease and its healing: "A disease in one area can spread and infect other areas where open doors of weakness exist," she wrote. "Conversely, healing can spread from the first point of contact—whether body, soul (mind, emotions, memory), or spirit—into other areas in time, when there is openness to healing love."[34]

The charismatic healers Charles and Frances Hunter illustrated a more popular articulation of similar holistic themes. Dubbed the "Happy Hunters" for their gregarious style, the healing duo crisscrossed the country conducting healing crusades that attracted thousands. From the start, the Hunters stressed their confidence in physicians, especially spirit-empowered physicians. "We believe in doctors, and praise God for their calling," Charles Hunter wrote in 1978. The problem arose when individuals relied solely on physicians "who are not baptized with the Holy Spirit" and therefore had limited resources at their disposal. According to Hunter, intractable diseases in particular such as cancer, diabetes, multiple sclerosis, and blindness were "mostly caused by spirits." Thus, unbelieving doctors simply "do not have the power nor understand how to deal with these 'persons without bodies.'" Significantly, Hunter's stress on the activity of spirits did not preclude natural and mental sources of illness, even in diseases where Hunter usually discerned spiritual activity. One woman who came to the Hunters for healing from pain in her side described the failed interventions of doctors, psychologists, and even other preachers. "With all those facts, I reasoned that it must be a spirit," Hunter explained. Embedded in Hunter's response was a baseline assumption that standard care could and would alleviate physical ailments rooted in nonspiritual causes, and Hunter expressed no reservations about the usefulness of professional health-care providers when purely natural forces were at work (though it is interesting to note that the physician who frequently traveled with the Hunters from early on in their ministry, Roy LeRoy, was a chiropractic doctor, not a traditional physician).[35]

Oral Roberts and the "City of Faith"

Of all the voices calling for more nuanced understandings of the interplay between supernatural and natural healing, in the end no one did more to mainstream holistic understanding of health and healing among adherents than Oral Roberts. What set Roberts apart from others who shared his criticisms of the limitations of conventional medicine involved his attempt to explicitly merge medical and spiritual models of healing by training "spirit-filled" doctors. According to his biographer, Roberts had contemplated opening a school of medicine at least since the early 1960s. Impressed by the medical missions employed by the Seventh-Day Adventists, he answered a query in 1963 as to whether or not the university would "turn out medical doctors as the Seven Day Adventist people are turning out." "God has a magnificent program in the future for this university," Roberts responded, "and He happened to tap on the shoulder some men who aren't scared of anything."[36] The first step in this direction occurred during the 1960s when Roberts put together plans for Oral Roberts University (ORU). Established in 1965, ORU eventually expanded beyond its focus on undergraduate education and included graduate schools, not the least of which included the school of medicine that opened in 1978.[37]

Getting the medical school accredited, it turned out, was not for the faint of heart. Roberts faced stiff opposition—especially from local doctors at other hospitals in Tulsa—in part due to concerns that he intended to build a hospital in the region (which in fact he did). In addition to the medical school, he also opened schools of dentistry and of nursing.[38] With each of these graduate programs, Roberts's vision entailed educating dentists, doctors, and nurses who would then utilize their training to bring healing to suffering individuals around the globe, and salvation as well. In 1976, he spoke of "physicians and dentists that I can envision going out from ORU's medical and dental schools into the far corners of the earth where God's light is dim and His voice is heard small, taking his love and healing power."[39]

Roberts sought to do much more than simply train medical professionals for missions. Apart from the sheer magnitude of his efforts, the key innovation represented by his creation of a medical school and his support of medical missionaries stemmed from his desire to transform the practice of both medicine and supernatural healing by merging the two. For Roberts, the explicit combination and commingling of medicine with spiritual forms of healing was nothing less than a "new concept in medical science."[40] The physicians trained at ORU would possess a revolutionary ability to heal based on their willingness to fuse supernatural and natural forms of healing. "There is a coming together for the first time, at least in my lifetime of the great healing systems of God," he wrote. "I believe that all healing is from God. I believe that He only has different 'delivery systems.'"[41]

Unlike most of his nonpentecostal counterparts in the holistic movement, Roberts saw in scripture a blueprint of God's plan to merge medical science and prayer. Jesus himself had affirmed "the need to merge all of God's healing systems," Roberts claimed, pointing to Jesus's statement in Matthew 9:12 that "it is not the healthy who need a doctor, but the sick." Due to the "scarcity of physicians . . . at the time," Jesus was unable to make the ideal a reality. Despite the lack of physicians during biblical times, Roberts concluded, the divine plan for combining the skills of doctors and spiritual healers began to take shape during the ministry of the Apostle Paul. Paul relied on divine intervention, as "miracles of healing were wrought by God through his hands." Alongside Paul's ministry, "suddenly there arose a physician" as well, "a skilled doctor by the name of Luke, and he joined Paul's powerful evangelistic team." Unlike the first generation of pentecostals, who often claimed that Luke stopped providing medicines after becoming a disciple of Christ, questioning whether he ever had at all, Roberts celebrated Luke's chosen profession. According to Roberts, once this healing tandem was formed, *the two streams of God's healing power started to merge.* Despite this hopeful beginning, the healing model provided by Luke and Paul, Roberts said, was not heeded by subsequent generations. Roberts observed that by the late twentieth century, the conditions present during Jesus's and Paul's lifetime had been reversed. Now there were "hundreds of thousands of physicians, men and women who are dedicated to healing people through medical skill," but far too few spiritual healers.[42]

By the mid-1970s, Roberts was convinced that the time was right to fulfill God's vision for merging these "two streams." "We are seeing thousands of doctors who are practicing at the top level of their competence who also believe that the inner spirit of man has to be touched by a greater power," he wrote. "Also we are seeing people who believe in the power of prayer going to their doctor gratefully, carrying their faith and accepting the great God-given and hard-worked-for gift that the physician brings. The two 'delivery systems' are coming together more and more every day."[43] With everything in place, all God needed was someone to implement the new vision of healing, and Roberts believed himself up to the task; he sensed God directing him to stand "in the gap to help unify these delivery systems of our healing Lord."[44]

The culmination of Roberts's dream emerged in 1977, when he announced plans to build the City of Faith. The blueprint for the complex, which opened in 1981, called for three buildings, including a thirty-story hospital with 777 beds, a sixty-story clinic, and a twenty-story medical research center. Directly in front of the buildings stood a sixty-foot bronze sculpture of praying hands. According

Figure 3.2 This sixty-foot bronze sculpture of praying hands originally stood at the entrance of Oral Roberts's City of Faith in Tulsa, Oklahoma. The two hands represented the merger of divine healing through prayer with healing obtained through modern medicine and physicians. AP Photo/Brandi Simons.

to a ministry brochure, "one hand represents the hand of prayer raised to God, the source of health and healing, and the other the hand of the physician raised in commitment to place all of God's healing power in operation for every patient and against every disease."[45]

In one sense, Roberts's venture was just one more in a long line of religiously affiliated hospitals in the United States. By midcentury, over 25 percent of all individuals in hospitals, in fact, found themselves in religious hospitals. While such institutions often offered additional resources meant to cater to the spiritual and not just physical needs of patients, in practical terms the medical care provided differed little—if at all—from the care provided at nonreligious hospitals.[46] But Roberts had very different plans for the City of Faith.

He pictured there "some of the greatest medical scientists of the world seeking a breakthrough for cancer, and heart disease, and studying the problems of aging, and researching in other problem areas in an atmosphere that's filled with prayer and faith."[47] As these comments suggest, Roberts's vision of a spiritualized medicine went beyond joining prayer and medicine in the treatment of patients. He also envisioned new forms of medical research being conducted within a spiritualized context. Roberts's beliefs regarding cancer underscored his assurance regarding the superiority of spirit-guided inquiry. Confident that

"God intends for there to be a medical breakthrough in cancer research," Roberts concluded that cancer had a "spiritual origin" and was "different from all other diseases." As he prayed for individuals suffering from cancer throughout his years of ministry, he would "smell this terrible odor" and "be reminded of Beelzebub which is the name of the chief demon." Though careful to clarify that he did not see cancer as a sign of demon possession, he nevertheless taught that "cancer had a relationship to this chief of demons, Beelzebub."[48] On the basis of these assumptions, Roberts asserted that "only in an atmosphere where God is uplifted, where men can have insights from God coming though their minds and spirit, only then will we ever find a breakthrough for cancer." As a complex dedicated to research conducted in an atmosphere charged with prayer, Roberts was supremely confident that the City of Faith would produce "one of the major breakthroughs in our lifetime."[49] "There must be a unifying of [medical research] with the power of the Holy Spirit," he concluded.[50] Both the medical school and the City of Faith testified to Roberts's desire for institutions where "prayer, medical science, and hard work mix for many miracles."[51] Pentecostal healing had traveled far indeed.

If not all pentecostals or charismatics imitated Roberts's insistent calls for an explicit merger of divine healing with natural healing, his efforts augured well for continued—and increased—cooperation between physicians and believers. Much like Kuhlman utilizing physicians in her services, in the 1980s Charles and Frances Hunter incorporated doctors' panels as part of their Healing Explosion services, asking physicians to provide insights into the nature of various ailments. Apparently, the healing couple had little trouble attracting physicians who shared their worldview: they dedicated three pages of their 1987 primer on divine healing to thanking medical professionals, listing over eighty specific doctors and nurses for lending their expertise to facilitate the Hunters' ministry. Describing these panels, the Hunters wrote: "We never know who is coming, but He always brings new experts from many fields of medicine." Participants included "medical doctors, orthopedic surgeons, pediatricians, obstetricians, podiatrists, chiropractors, ophthalmologists, opticians, optometrists, dentists, orthodontists, nutritionists, gynecologists, osteopaths, pathologists, surgeons, and other fields of medicine." The "great medical knowledge" offered by these professionals, they explained, "combined with the spiritual knowledge God gives, has brought about many healings which might not have otherwise been accomplished."[52]

The Hunters' incorporation of doctors into their meetings centered on a simple premise: physicians' ability to identify the specific sources of diseases allowed believers to target their prayers more effectively. Along these very lines, the Hunters' *Handbook for Healing* listed various diseases with brief descriptions of their medical causes. The reader suffering from arteriosclerosis learned that it involved a hardening of the arteries, for which the authors recommended a prayer calling for a "divine 'roto-rooter' of God's power to completely clean out all the arteries of all cholesterol plaques." Regarding Addison's disease, a failure of the adrenal glands, the Hunters indicated that healing prayer should "command a creative miracle—a new pair of adrenal glands." While it is obvious that the prescriptions offered by the Hunters usually bypassed any normal medical recommendations for various illnesses, they nevertheless saw medical professionals and their knowledge of the body as crucial participants in the healing process.[53]

No longer content merely to affirm the validity of physicians and medicines, denominational pentecostals did not lag far behind their charismatic counterparts as they, too, were busy discovering new forms of collaboration with mainstream medicine. In 1984, the leadership of the Assemblies of God surmounted the remaining internal dissent over funding medical missionaries and formally approved a medical missions program. Founded by Paul Williams, a physician trained in neonatology at the Washington School of Medicine (St. Louis, Missouri), HealthCare Ministries organized doctors, dentists, ophthalmologists, and other medical professionals for short-term humanitarian trips around the globe. Working in close association with local pastors and missionaries, the typical outreach consisted of a temporary clinic setup in a poverty-stricken area. Those who arrived for care received a basic exam and medicines while also spending time in a counseling area staffed largely by local ministers.[54]

In focusing on one- to two-week trips financed by donations and by the physicians who contributed their time and services free of charge, HealthCare Ministries differed from Roberts's efforts in a very important respect: it never took on the financial burden of supporting a full-fledged medical institution. Shortly after the ministry began sending teams abroad, in fact, the financial strains Roberts faced in attracting funding gained national attention with his infamous appeal for financial support for the medical school in 1987. As Roberts recounted the story years after the fact, to his dismay, students who graduated with their M.D.s decided that they simply could not afford to immediately go into the mission field while owing tens of thousands of dollars for their medical education. He recalled reacting skeptically to students' claim that they had to work in the United States to pay off their debts. Roberts expected students to enter the mission field on faith. "I operate solely by faith. If I could start at ground zero on the medical school . . . by faith only, why couldn't they?" "I probably thought that since I obeyed whatever God said to me, at any cost," he continued, "every other believer working with me would do the same."[55] Frustrated over ORU's inability to fulfill its mission and produce medical missionaries, Roberts went public with his claim that God would allow him to die if he did not raise $8 million to fund medical scholarships. Immediately following the announcement, he became the butt of jokes nationwide. "'Your Money or my life' plea is latest for savvy fundraiser," wrote the *St. Petersburg Times*. The author compared Roberts's latest call for money to past petitions, including his "publicity spectacular" insisting that a

900-foot Jesus had commanded him to finish the City of Faith.[56] Another writer reported with regret: "Mr. Roberts raised this cash for his apparently extortionist God . . . and lives on to ask for more and more and more." At least a few observers were disappointed when Roberts met his goal and forestalled his date with destiny.[57]

Frequently lost in the din of controversy surrounding Roberts's fundraising methods was his concern over the medical school's slow production of medical missionaries. The episode revealed just how far pentecostalism had come. Whereas numerous early pentecostals had considered doctors money-hungry frauds, roughly eighty years later, one of the most prominent ministers in the United States with a pentecostal background could claim that God would demand his life if adherents did not donate millions of dollars to fund the training of doctors.

As it happens, both the medical school and the City of Faith closed in 1989 due to financial difficulties. Ever the optimist, Roberts recast these negative events as part of God's plan—he even went so far as to tout the closing of the City of Faith as "one of the greatest victories not only of my life but in Christendom." He compared the closing of the City of Faith to the death of Christ. He recalled hearing God speak to him while in prayer: "Do you know why I did not permit [Jesus] to live to be 40, or 50, or 60, or 80? Or even more years in His physical and bodily form? . . . I had My Son to have His public ministry for only three years so My larger purpose would not be localized only in His physical presence in time and space." God then indicated that in a similar fashion he had Roberts "build the City of Faith large enough to capture the imagination of the entire world about the merging of My healing streams of prayer and medicine. I did not want this revelation localized in Tulsa, however." Now that the job of merging prayer and medicine "is done," the time had come to make the message known "to all people and to go into all future generations."[58] Roberts's rationalization regarding the closing of the City of Faith did little to placate critics who saw the venture as a colossal waste of funds, yet efforts to merge divine healing and medicine would in fact survive among pentecostals and charismatics—even thrive—in spite of the setbacks experienced in Tulsa.

The holistic message voiced by Roberts and others like him reflected the trajectory of the pentecostal-charismatic movement as a whole. As pentecostals encountered the rising prestige and effectiveness of the medical establishment over the course of the twentieth century, they faced a choice. They could continue to advocate divine healing at the expense of modern medicine, or they could join fellow charismatics and adapt their methods to fit with the increasingly persuasive evidence regarding medical efficacy.

The vast majority chose to adapt.

Some adapted simply by creating room for medical healing as a valid complement to divine healing. By the end of the twentieth century, pentecostals and

Figure 3.3 Interior and exterior views of the "flying hospital," an L-1011 retrofitted in the mid-1990s by Pat Robertson's nonprofit humanitarian organization Operation Blessing. Reprinted with the permission of Paul R. Williams.

charismatics expressed few qualms about visiting their physicians, and efforts similar to HealthCare Ministries continued to appear, most notably the Virginia-based charismatic Pat Robertson's launch in 1994 of a Medical Services Program as part of his larger nonprofit humanitarian organization Operation Blessing. Robertson's ability to raise millions of dollars in 1996 to retrofit an L-1011 plane to serve as the "largest fully equipped, self-contained airborne hospital ever built" provided vivid evidence of the seemingly unqualified acceptance of physicians in the pentecostal-charismatic movement by the end of the twentieth century. The aircraft included a three-station surgical suite as well as a dental suite and flew on mission trips to countries such as El Salvador, Ecuador, the Ukraine, and India.[59] As the "flying hospital" graphically illustrated, numerous pentecostals and charismatics did not think twice about utilizing the benefits of modern technological and medical advances even as they prayed for divine intervention.

Others, however, wanted more. Just as Roberts's attempt to blur the boundaries separating natural and supernatural forms of healing expanded on metaphysical tendencies in the early pentecostal movement that described the Spirit's work in impersonal, highly predictable terms, another breed of pentecostal and charismatic healers built on the metaphysical inclinations embedded in pentecostalism as they experimented with novel permutations merging divine healing with various forms of mental healing and psychotherapy. Freud would not have been happy.

4

Minding the Spirit

In the fall of 1978, Phyllis Wells shared her testimony with fellow pentecostal and charismatic women who subscribed to the charismatic periodical *Aglow: For the Spirit Renewed Christian Woman*. The wife of a minister, Wells recounted her steady spiral into deep depression following a series of medical issues coupled with an ongoing battle with "fear, feelings of inferiority, jealousy, and self-pity." Desperate for a way out of her personal hell, Wells eventually overdosed on pain-killers in an attempt to end it all. After her suicide attempt failed and her despair only deepened, Wells shared with readers how God miraculously broke through the "torture of [her] mind," audibly speaking to her. "I heard clearly these words," she remembered: "I will be your psychiatrist." Tears immediately streamed down her face as she repeatedly thanked the Lord for intervening. While her recovery was not instantaneous, from that point on God revealed the sources of her trouble, focusing in particular on her "warped attitude toward marriage." "He showed me that for eighteen years I had lived as a rebellious wife," pouting when her husband "preached on women being in submission to their husband." "Bit by bit," she recalled, God walked her through the healing process.[1]

While Wells's divine encounter illuminated the powerful hold of gendered notions of submission in conservative Christian circles, it also graphically illustrated pentecostals' and charismatics' appropriation of psychological methodologies since the 1970s. In the midst of her ordeal, Wells indicated that no less than God himself embraced the role of divine psychiatrist. Not all believers felt comfortable with such claims, to put it mildly, yet around the same time Oral Roberts set about convincing the faithful that medical healing not only complemented but should be fused with divine healing, two very divergent groups—practitioners of inner healing and Word of Faith healers in the tradition of E. W. Kenyon—elevated the mind to a central place in the healing process and steadily eroded the suspicion that many believers harbored against mental forms of healing.

If some pentecostal healers tentatively engaged psychology around midcentury, the appearance of charismatic renewal during the 1960s and 1970s rapidly accelerated adherents' appropriation of psychological jargon, much as it stimulated interest in the potential collaboration between divine healers and medical professionals. Here, pentecostals and charismatics mirrored other conservative evangelicals who likewise overcame the traditional resistance to psychology and psychiatry in their circles as they sought to move away from Fundamentalists' take-no-prisoners approach to the broader U.S. culture. Indicative of these changes, evangelical writers such as Charles Allen and Clyde Narramore popularized psychological concepts beginning in the 1950s, publishing books with titles such as *God's Psychiatry* and *Psychology of Counseling*. By 1965, the evangelical Fuller Theological Seminary formed a graduate school of psychology. With the arrival of the "Me Decade" of the 1970s, evangelical psychologists, ranging from James Dobson to Frank Minirth and to Paul Meier gained a national reputation as authoritative voices culling biblically sound insights from the previously despised discipline.[2]

Indicative of similar trends among some pentecostals and charismatics, in 1971 Jamie Buckingham, a prolific charismatic author with Southern Baptist roots, described dreams utilizing classic psychological tropes: "As the conscious goes to sleep and relaxes, the subconscious—that great storehouse of suppressed, repressed material that involves the larger part of the mind—comes floating to the surface. Often it will actually break out into the open, mixing with the conscious mind in sleep, causing us to dream." Buckingham went so far as to redefine baptism in the Holy Spirit using psychological terminology. He claimed that baptism in the Spirit involved allowing God to clean out the subconscious, and he instructed readers to make God the "Lord of the subconscious."[3]

Observers of twentieth-century U.S. therapeutic culture note how the "tacit conviction that self-realization was the largest aim of human existence" served as a common denominator uniting various manifestations of the therapeutic impulse, and pentecostals' and charismatics' participation in these trends was no exception.[4] By the 1970s, numerous charismatics and a growing number of pentecostals borrowed heavily from popular forms of psychology as they zeroed in on a wide range of emotional deficits confronting believers. A 1979 article described how "spiritual surgery" allowed Jesus to "cut away the growths of inferiority, unworthiness, condemnation, and inadequacy so that we can become the Spirit-filled person God created us to be."[5] Earlier the same year, *Charisma* published an excerpt from *The Fragrance of Beauty*, by the evangelical author Joyce Landorf. Throughout the excerpt, Landorf demonstrated a ready familiarity with the psychological buzzwords pervading the ubiquitous literature of self-help. She wrote of individuals hindered in their relationships with others due to their "low self-estimate" and of her husband's healthy "self-image" and "self-worth" due to his surrender of "ego" to the Lord.[6] Bob Mumford, who was ordained with the Assemblies of God before gaining prominence as a popular (and controversial) speaker in charismatic circles, indicated that "most of us exhibit emotional instability because we are caught between two basic fears. The first is the 'fear of absorption'; that is, the fear of losing your identity. . . . The second fear is the 'fear of isolation,' the fear of being left all alone." Emotional and mental instability often derived from a tendency to "bounce from one of these extremes to the other." As part of his prescription for mental health, he counseled his readers to "be real" and avoid playing a "'super-spiritual' role."[7]

A sampling of article and book titles that circulated in pentecostal and charismatic circles during the 1970s and 1980s provided further confirmation of believers' widespread participation in the U.S. self-help culture. "You Can Stop Feeling Bad about Yourself," one author promised,[8] while another taught believers how to go "From Rejection to Acceptance."[9] David Seamands, a United Methodist minister who embraced charismatic emphases and was well respected in the broader evangelical world, published in 1981 *Healing for Damaged Emotions*, which included chapters titled "Healing Our Low Self-Esteem" and "Super You or Real You?"[10] The front cover of a book by the popular charismatic author Rita Bennett, whose husband attracted national attention in the early 1960s when he embraced charismatic spirituality while serving as an Episcopalian priest, summed up the genre well: "You Can Be . . . Emotionally Free."[11] As was the case among conservative evangelicals more generally, pervasive denunciations of "the world" were steadily giving way to the rhetoric of self-esteem and self-realization.

Inner Healing

While some of the references to popular psychology by pentecostals and charismatics represented superficial engagement with the genre, several individuals advocated "inner healing" and pushed for a more sustained dialogue with psychology. On the whole, those who sought to merge spiritual forms of healing with the basic insights afforded by the discipline tended to identify more closely with the charismatic movement, as opposed to the traditional pentecostal denominations. Few had as significant an impact on pentecostals and charismatics in this regard as the Episcopal laywoman Agnes Sanford. Although she was more indebted to New Thought than the more formal methodologies associated with psychology and psychiatry, Sanford inspired numerous others who created a niche for mental healing among charismatics and some pentecostals.[12] Sanford's interest in healing initially was spurred by the illness of her third child, John. The Episcopalian minister who prayed for her son was strongly influenced by New Thought writers, and her experience encouraged her to explore the works of mental healers such as Mary Baker Eddy—whom she strongly disagreed with— and the New Thought writer Emmet Fox.[13] By the time Sanford embarked on her own healing ministry and began writing on healing prayer, New Thought assumptions permeated her books. In *The Healing Light*, initially published in 1947, Sanford described God and humanity in classic New Thought fashion, using the terminology of light, energy, and vibration. Humans were "made not of solid and impenetrable matter, but of energy," she insisted. Likewise, the various chemicals that composed the human body "live by the breath of God, by the primal energy, the original force that we call God." The "closer connection with God" established through prayer, then, allowed for an infusion of "abundant life—an increased flow of energy. The creative force that sustains us is increased within our bodies. The vibration of God's light is so very real that even a child can feel it."[14]

As with New Thought writers shaped by figures such as Emanuel Sweden-borg, Sanford's imagery of energy and vibration challenged dualistic divisions between the spiritual and the natural world in classic metaphysical fashion. Unlike later pentecostals and charismatics who mimicked metaphysical themes, Sanford never shied away from recognizing her indebtedness to traditions such as New Thought. Following a description of her healing philosophy in her auto-biography, she observed: "At this point some people may be thinking, 'But isn't this metaphysics? Isn't this the power of positive thinking?'" Sanford did not equivocate in her answer. "Certainly!" she wrote. "And I might point out that Jesus called it faith."[15]

The most significant adaptation of New Thought teachings by Sanford in-volved her focus on the power of the mind to effect healing. In a very literal sense, Sanford saw the mind as a crucial battleground governing the influx of divine energy into each individual. A properly calibrated mind allowed God's healing power to flow uninhibited throughout the entire person, body and soul. The untrained mind proved unaware of the healing resources at hand and unable to access the vital life-giving energies that perfected the natural world. "We must re-educate the subconscious mind," she wrote, "replacing every thought of fear with a thought of faith, every thought of illness with a thought of health, every thought of death with a thought of life." Such reprogramming of the mind al-lowed for the restoration of an individual's physical and emotional well-being.[16]

In her practical instructions to readers, Sanford frequently turned to the New Thought practice of visualization as a basic tool for attuning the mind to divine power. At one point she recounted her instructions to a G.I. recovering from a leg wound that required a bone graft. When she initially approached the soldier suggesting that he pray for healing, he responded simply: "But I don't know any-thing about God." Undeterred, Sanford coaxed a vague admission from the sol-dier that he at least believed "there's *something* outside of yourself." That simple acknowledgment proved all the opening Sanford needed to set in motion the healing process. "Well, then, ask that Something to come into you," she contin-ued. "Just say 'Whoever you are or whatever you are, come into me now and help nature in my body to mend this bone, and do it quick. Thanks, I believe you're doing it.'" The final crucial step in the healing process then required actively imagining and visualizing the healing. For the G.I., this involved making a "pic-ture in your mind of the leg well. . . . See the bone all built in and the flesh strong and perfect around it." When the soldier questioned the need for visualization, asking "Why do I do that?" Sanford answered simply, "Because that's the way you make it happen. No matter what you want to make, you first have to see it in your mind."[17]

Significantly, Sanford extended her focus beyond physical healing to include emotional healing, underlining in particular the centrality of forgiveness in the maturation of the Christian soul. She instructed readers to set aside blocks of time in order to allow the Holy Spirit to bring to remembrance any "unforgiven sins (or any uncomfortable memories, as we would probably call them)." She compared these unhealed memories to "splinters in the hand. The thing may be invisible, but as long as it is there it festers a bit. So the splinters of uncomfortable memories (unforgiven sins) fester in the subconscious and throw out into the conscious mind various symptoms of fears, nervous tensions, etc., of whose cause we are completely unaware."[18] Simply identifying these unhealed memories proved insufficient. Instead, confessing unhealed memories and receiving forgiveness opened the door for Jesus's presence and power to enter the individual. Drawing once again on New Thought terminology, Sanford explained: "God's love was blacked out from man [prior to Christ's death and resurrection] by the negative thought-vibration of this sinful and suffering world." In order to transform this dire condition, Jesus in turn "lowered His thought-vibrations to the thought-vibrations of humanity and received unto Himself man's thoughts of sin and sickness, pain and death."[19] For Sanford, the heart of the Christian life revolved around the healing exchange of an individual's sinful thoughts for Christ's thoughts.

As with physical healing, for Sanford, visualization facilitated the inner healing of the emotions as well. "In order to fill ourselves with His whole being," she wrote, "let us think of Him, imagining His presence, seeing Him with the eyes of the mind, trying to love Him with the heart." Once individuals had learned to identify with Christ as an ever-present reality within themselves, they in turn could learn to pray that others would also undergo a similar healing experience. "Having constructed by thought and will a picture of the patient well, peaceful and happy," Sanford explained, "we then ask Jesus Himself to go through us and abide in the one for whom we pray, resurrecting him after that likeness of all beauty that is Himself. And believing that He is doing so, we learn to see within the patient, Christ."[20]

Ultimately, both physical and emotional healing for Sanford depended on individuals' willingness to take responsibility for their healing by attuning their minds to God's ever-available presence in the universe. More important, through her influence Sanford mediated New Thought assumptions to individuals from a wide spectrum of denominational backgrounds, and by the 1960s her teachings were popular especially among charismatics. A historian in the charismatic movement, in fact, has referred to Sanford as the first theologian of the charismatic renewal.[21]

Perhaps the best known charismatic proponent of inner healing influenced by Sanford's teaching was the Roman Catholic minister Francis MacNutt. Mac-Nutt first encountered Sanford's ministry while attending a spiritual retreat conducted by Glenn Clark.[22] An important bridge between New Thought and the pentecostal-charismatic movement in his own right, Clark initiated his "Camps Farthest Out" in the 1930s. Modeled on intensive football camps for training athletes, these summer gatherings provided a time of spiritual renewal through prayer, lecture, and Spirit-inspired creative activities associated with the arts, for example dancing and painting. Like Sanford, Clark's writings represented a blend of Christian and New Thought emphases and frequently addressed the issue of healing. By the time MacNutt encountered Clark and Sanford in the 1960s, the camps had become a vehicle for leaders in the charismatic renewal to spread their message (many of whom expressed strong reservations regarding the camps' New Thought connections). In addition to Sanford and MacNutt, high-profile figures associated with the camps included Derek Prince, Ruth Carter Stapleton, and Merlin Carothers.[23] MacNutt walked away from the meetings deeply impressed with Sanford's teachings. Her teachings made sense, he wrote, "not only because Christ came to free us from the evil that burdens us, but also because it was in accord with what psychologists have discovered about the nature of man: that we are deeply affected not only by what we do, but by what happens to us through the sins of others and the evil in the world."[24]

In a sign of the trajectory of Sanford's teachings as they developed in the inner healing movement, MacNutt's approach lacked the controversial New Thought verbiage used by Sanford. The role of the mind in the healing process certainly remained a crucial element of his appropriation of the ministry of inner healing, yet MacNutt tended to utilize the terminology of popular psychology and self-help literature more than New Thought emphases on energy, light, and vibration. Sounding themes that many Americans had grown accustomed to hearing from mainstream authors, he described humans' deepest need as the need for love, and "if we are denied love as infants or as children, or anywhere else along the line, it may affect our lives at a later date and rob us of our peace, of our ability to love, and of our ability to trust man—or God."[25]

Despite his reliance on popular psychological paradigms, MacNutt made it clear to the reader that he did not see psychology as sufficient in and of itself to fully heal the wounds of the past. Describing his own past efforts to minister to individuals prior to his exposure to the inner healing movement, MacNutt indicated that the "most I was ever able to do as a counselor was to help the person bring to the foreground of consciousness the things that were buried in the past, so that he could consciously cope with them in the present." With the ministry of inner healing, however, he discovered that "the Lord can heal these wounds—sometimes immediately—and can bring the counseling process to its completion in a deep healing."[26]

MacNutt's understanding of psychology as a useful but ultimately insufficient ally in the healing process reappeared frequently in the writings of other inner healing practitioners. As one *Charisma* author wrote in summarizing the inner healing movement, "psychiatrists spend years with patients bringing to the surface experiences of the past which have left them crippled and disturbed. . . . Those who practice inner healing believe that the Holy Spirit can perform the same work of revealing the hidden, unhealed areas of our lives, but with one important difference. If the Holy Spirit reveals a wounded area, He also brings it to Jesus that it may be healed."[27] Rita Bennett's writings expressed an analogous ambivalence regarding psychology. Whereas psychologists could give "good advice," the ministry of inner healing superseded psychology by bringing divine resources to bear on the situation.[28]

For her part, Ruth Carter Stapleton, the sister of President Jimmy Carter and a well-known advocate for inner healing among charismatics, called on Christians to accept the valuable insights provided by the discipline despite its limitations.[29] "Many sincere and intelligent Christians mistrust psychology," she wrote in 1977. "When secular psychology claims that there is no need for 'the spiritual,' that emotional integrity is everything, that emotional integration is man's goal, [Christians] rebel." Though Stapleton understood such reservations, she held out the possibility of another, more fruitful relationship between psychologists and Christians. She noted that "growing numbers of sincere seekers have found emotional healing through the discipline of psychology." More important, "these people have also learned that Jesus Christ can enter the life and instill a sense of peace, love and power they have never known before which is obviously not a product of psychological therapy." Given the fact that "both of these positions have great truth," she envisioned an integration of the two insights under the banner of inner healing that would "bring authentic principles of psychology under the guidance and inspiration of the Holy Spirit. When this happens, people are healed, new ministers of inner healing are raised up, and the entire redemptive movement increases in quantum measure."[30]

The shift toward a more professional, scientific-sounding conception of the Spirit's work evident in Stapleton's and other charismatics' writings resonated in important respects with religion-friendly conceptions of psychology that circulated throughout U.S. culture in the twentieth century. Armed with the newly minted theory of the subconscious self, for example, at the turn of the twentieth century William James had attempted to mediate between the insights of scientific research and the possibility of supernatural phenomena. Desiring to head off thoroughly materialistic accounts of reality without losing hold of the authority offered by scientific investigation and logic, he defended the reasonableness of religious views in general while challenging believers who claimed an ability to "define in detail an invisible world, and to anathematize and excommunicate those whose trust is different."[31] James speculated that "if there be higher spiritual agencies that can directly touch us, the psychological condition of their doing so might be our possession of a subconscious region which alone should yield access to them. The hubbub of the waking life might close a door which in the dreamy Subliminal might remain ajar or open."[32]

In his discussion of the origins of popular psychology in the United States, Andrew Heinze presents James as the most prominent early advocate for a form of psychology rooted in transcendentalist assumptions and closely aligned with metaphysical movements such as New Thought. He contrasts this strain of popular psychology with behaviorist approaches that resisted spiritualized views of the psyche and stressed a person's environment as the key determining factor in each person's psychological development.[33] Although practitioners of inner healing posited the mind as a crucial gateway enabling the believer to access divine power, and therefore stood much closer to Heinze's transcendentalist category, as opposed to the behaviorist school of thought, healers such as Stapleton did not endorse a drift away from more traditional notions of the Christian God. To the contrary, as advocates of inner healing sought to combine psychological and spiritual healing, they frequently prescribed heavy doses of visualization in the tradition of Sanford while specifically avoiding Sanford's deliberate adoption of New Thought terminology. Where Sanford spoke of Jesus lowering his "thought-vibrations to the thought-vibrations of humanity," her successors in the charismatic movement taught individuals simply to imagine Jesus intervening in painful situations from their pasts.[34]

Stapleton, for instance, combined what she labeled as "faith-imagination therapy" with more standard psychological fare, frequently utilizing the language of the "inner child" borrowed from the writings of W. H. Missildine. Faith-imagination therapy involved counselors and prayer partners who helped individuals actively recall painful experiences in their lives and then imagine Jesus transforming those past situations.[35] For Stapleton, faith-imagination therapy offered more than just a way to reorient an individual's mind and emotions in relation to painful memories. Rather, she viewed these sessions as creating objective experiences that reshaped a person's past history.[36]

In the same way, other leaders mirrored Sanford's stress on the role of the imagination and visualization in the healing process while leaving aside some of her other New Thought terminology. Rita Bennett spoke of the ability of Jesus to transform past memories and to create new ones where none existed. (The first Bennett termed "reliving the scene with Jesus"; the second she labeled "creative prayer.")[37] According to the charismatic Jesuit priests Dennis and Matthew Linn, the faithful needed to learn to revisit painful experiences and have Christ "enter the scene where you were hurt and watch him. What does he say and do to you to heal you?"[38] David Seamands, whose book *Healing of Memories* eventually sold over a million copies, encouraged believers to make "use of our sanctified imaginations," pray "as if we were actually there" when a painful past memory occurred, and allow "God to minister to us in the manner we needed at that time."[39]

Illustrative of the actual mechanics of visualization, the Episcopalian healer Leanne Payne told of the healing of a woman who battled imagery from her sexual past whenever she made love with her husband. Payne instructed the woman to "look and see Jesus with the eyes of her heart and stretch out her opened hands to receive from Him." As the unwanted images surfaced in the woman's mind, Payne asked her to "reach her hand to her forehead and take each one as it comes up from her mind, and then hand it to Jesus, whose outstretched hands she visualizes." With this process complete, the final step involved seeing "what Jesus is doing with the old pictures" as he disposed of them.[40]

In very similar fashion, when Stapleton counseled a young man who had trouble connecting with his father when he was young, she walked the counselee through an imaginative experience of playing a baseball game with Jesus and also going fishing. Stapleton "verbally took six-year-old Jody through an entire ball game, strike by strike, hits, foul balls, errors, everything. Batting time alternated between Jody and Jesus in a setting that is duplicated ten million times a spring Saturday throughout the country." The exercise proved "exhausting for both of us." Stapleton then moved on to re-create a fishing scene when Jody was nine. "Step by step we prepared for the fishing trip," she wrote, "and off to the creek we went."[41]

Not all advocates of spiritualized forms of psychotherapy stressed visualization and the "healing of memories"; despite the prevalence of the practice among some of the most recognizable names in the inner healing movement, myriad other techniques were also used, ranging from group prayers to more standard forms of counseling, the use of physical substances such as holy water, and even exorcisms.[42] Nor did all proponents of spiritualized forms of psychotherapy find their way due to the influence of Sanford or her disciples. Richard Dobbins's interest in this type of ministry, for example, surfaced after his wife's battle with "severe and clinical bouts of post partum depression left him desperate to understand the exact nature of the condition ailing his wife." Shortly thereafter, Dobbins, an Assemblies of God minister, pursued training in psychology, and in 1976 he founded Emerge Ministries in an effort to minister to individuals who could be helped by a combination of prayer with psychological insights. He frequently traveled around the country conducting "family rallies" meant "to provide training for marriage, parenthood and family living."[43] Like Dobbins, the licensed clinical psychologist Fred Gross, who had close ties with Jim Bakker in the 1980s and established the Fred Gross Christian Therapy Program, similarly sought to merge prayer with more traditional forms of psychotherapy.[44]

Exceptions notwithstanding, Sanford's teachings proved crucial for the initial emergence of a distinctive inner healing movement among believers by the 1970s, and her influence was especially evident in the central role of visualization and the imagination in several of the most prominent healers' ministries.

The Bennetts referred to Sanford as "that great lady who has helped so many understand healing, both physical and psychological," adding that "many leaders in the healing movement today owe their start to Agnes Sanford's inspiration and teaching." Payne likewise described Sanford as a "magnificent trailblazer in the art of healing prayer," while Stapleton called her "one of the pioneers of the healing ministry in the major denominational churches."[45] In large part due to the influence of Sanford and that of her protégés in pentecostal and charismatic circles, numerous adherents learned to accept a New Thought–style focus on the role of the mind in mediating divine power to the individual.

Dramatic Transformations

Put in historical perspective, proponents of inner healing were by no means the first to call for a fusion of Christianity with psychotherapy. If individuals in the pentecostal-charismatic movement were not alone in their efforts to find common ground between Christianity and psychology, two factors set them apart from many of the other prominent attempts to merge psychotherapy and religion. First, despite the clear overlap between ministers of inner healing and mainstream psychological counselors, the majority of inner healing practitioners lacked formal training in psychology or psychotherapy. "We're not training people to be therapists or psychologists—we're teaching about prayer," Rita Bennett explained. "We're not in competition with [professionals in these fields]. But the great thing is, this is a *lay movement*. You don't have to be ordained, or be a therapist, or have a Ph.D. God can use anybody." Exceptions did exist, such as Richard Dobbins and Fred Gross. By and large, however, Dobbins, Gross, and others like them were far outnumbered by the army of nonprofessional practitioners of inner healing, many of whom were women.[46]

In addition to the lay character of the inner healing movement, continued confidence in the possibility of dramatic transformations, long a staple among pentecostals and charismatics, also set these healers apart from many fellow evangelicals who embraced psychological forms of healing. Inner healing practitioners' attitudes toward homosexuality epitomized such emphases. Unwilling to abandon the traditional Christian condemnation of homosexuality yet eager for an alternative option to the increasing acceptance of homosexuality among medical professionals and the U.S. public more generally, a growing number of believers began recommending inner healing methodologies as a means to transform homosexuals' sexual orientation.[47] Despite the fact that mainstream psychiatrists and psychologists by the 1970s and 1980s recoiled at pentecostals' and charismatics' condemnation of homosexuality, advocates of inner healing frequently associated homosexuality with psychological wounds amenable to prayer and spiritualized forms of psychological therapy.

In articulating their approach to same-sex attraction, practitioners resisted the inclination in pentecostal and charismatic circles to automatically link same-sex attraction with demonic activity. "Too often we've seen Pentecostal churches trying to cast out the demon of homosexuality, while non-charismatics promise that by believing the right thing, it will go away," stated Andy Comisky, a one-time pastor in the Vineyard Christian Fellowship and prominent ex-gay minis-ter.[48] As another proponent explained, homosexuality reflected "the outworking of any number of breakdowns and dysfunctions in the early formation of indi-vidual identity. Most often these reach back to basic parent/child relationships and result in a warped or underdeveloped sense of one's own gender, perhaps the most fundamental building block in personality development." By exten-sion, with these wounds in place, individuals proved "unsure of their sexual identity" and instead searched for "assurance [of their sexual identity] through same-sex 'bonding,' expressed sexually." Through the ministry of inner healing, though, ministers held up the possibility of healing these wounds from the past—and by extension changing a person's sexual orientation—through iden-tification with Christ.[49] According to Ruth Carter Stapleton, homosexuals needed "our love, plus more searching self-knowledge, plus the opportunity to meet the Christ who loves homosexuals and who died to give them life and wholeness, just as he did for the 'less condemned, just-as-guilty, respectable' people."[50] Stapleton's compassion offensive underwhelmed proponents of gay rights in the United States. Nevertheless, the changing approaches to homo-sexuality on the part of some adherents reflected a decided move away from demonic explanations of conditions believers deemed sinful even as they re-tained the pentecostal and charismatic aspiration for dramatic transformation.

Controversy

To be sure, references continued to appear in pentecostal and charismatic litera-ture claiming transformations of believers' sexuality without attributing them to anything resembling inner healing or psychological therapy. Testimonies such as these stood much closer to early models of healing in the pentecostal movement, and often appeared among individuals who had much closer ties to traditional pentecostalism and formal pentecostal denominations. "Philosophy, psychology, religious creeds and doctrines were all slippery rocks that could not be grasped," wrote one believer who turned to David Wilkerson's pentecostal Teen Challenge ministry in the early 1970s for help to remove his sexual attraction to other men. "I needed a foundation. I found it in the Word of God."[51] The author's total reli-ance on divine assistance to the exclusion of other methodologies mirrored the assumptions articulated by Teen Challenge's founder. "The same Christ who cures heroin addicts also cures and delivers prostitutes, homosexuals, lesbians, and all demon-harassed souls," Wilkerson wrote in 1973. "All social agencies combined, with their money and knowledge, cannot deliver a single soul from the bondage of sex, drugs or alcohol."[52] As Wilkinson's comments illustrated, the divergent approaches to homosexuality in the pentecostal-charismatic movement signaled a much broader rift regarding the compatibility of divine healing with more secular forms of healing such as psychotherapy.

Opposition to the influence of psychology and psychotherapy in pentecostal and charismatic circles drew national attention in the early 1980s when the Maryland-based charismatic pastor Larry Tomczak faced a libel suit for $19.5 million brought by Thomas Harris, author of the widely popular *I'm O.K.—You're O.K.* In a 1979 service that was broadcast via radio, Tomczak repeated a widespread rumor that Harris had killed himself. Drawing on the long history of ambivalence in pentecostal and conservative evangelical circles toward psychology, Tomczak warned his audience to "beware of 'any philosophy which could undermine the Scriptures.'" "Years ago, there was a book on the market called *I'm OK—You're OK,*" he explained. "People said, 'That's a wonderful new book—new psychology, new things to follow.' Most people today don't know that the author of that book committed suicide about two years ago, and yet people are still practicing some of his philosophies." A *Charisma* article detailing the situation noted that Tomczak had characterized psychiatry as an "unbiblical form of relief" in an earlier book, though "the evangelist says he does not believe that all forms of psychiatry are intrinsically evil." "I personally am not an enemy of psychiatry," the author quoted Tomczak as saying. "The key to psychiatry, as in anything must be Jesus Christ."[53] Tomczak's backtracking notwithstanding, the fact remained that his initial comments would have resonated only with an audience who considered psychology and psychiatry suspect, at least, if they did not reject it out of hand.

Tomczak and other pentecostals and charismatics distrusted attempts to integrate divine healing with psychology for a variety of reasons. In her 1976 survey of the burgeoning inner healing movement for *Charisma*, Sherry Andrews chronicled the numerous objections that arose to these ministries, such as their tendency to create "junior psychiatrists," to focus on the old and not the new, and to blame the past for everything.[54] Ten years later, in 1986, another writer for *Charisma*, David Hazard, cautioned readers that "beneath the surface of this growing ministry lies [sic] some potential dangers." He recounted his observations of a charismatic house meeting at which a husband-and-wife team had discussed their problems. Hazard was a bit unnerved when the group leader, "with the casual but detective air of a practiced therapist . . . leaned back in his chair and said, "Don, tell me about your relationship with your father." To clarify what he thought his experience said about changes in the pentecostal-charismatic movement, Hazard described how in the 1970s, "life-controlling sins and weaknesses were chalked up to demon interference. A prayer of deliverance would follow. Now, it seems, we say that many problems can be traced to childhood trauma, or, a few feel, even to turmoils experienced in the womb." Though Hazard cautiously approved of ministries of inner healing, he, too, highlighted detractors' accusations, for example claims that inner healing could lead individuals to become "navel-starers" and substitute a "pity party" for genuine healing. Others, he added, believed these trends represented no less than the infiltration of the movement by "Eastern mysticism and even necromancy."[55]

Many of the criticisms leveled at the new form of ministry mirrored earlier pentecostal reservations regarding psychologists' tendency to explain away sin and undermine biblical standards of morality. One of the most high-profile critics of psychology in fact was a man with impeccable pentecostal credentials, Jimmy Swaggart. Best known by many Americans for his rapid fall from grace during the 1980s over charges of sexual indiscretion, for years Swaggart's ministry—one of the largest Christian ministries in the world—was associated with the Assemblies of God. Swaggart consistently rejected what he called the "psychologizing of the church." As he articulated his opposition to such trends, Swaggart drew many of his ideas from evangelical writers, including Dave Hunt, and Martin and Deidre Bobgan, who made it their mission to expose "psychoheresy" and the impact of metaphysical "cults" on trends in U.S. Christianity epitomized by the inner healing movement and Word of Faith themes. Though Hunt's book *The Seduction of Christianity*, which he coauthored with T. A. McMahon, in particular provoked a sharp backlash among believers who were defensive of the pentecostals and charismatics attacked in the book, Swaggart found it thoroughly persuasive. In an article in which Swaggart quoted Hunt and also gave credit to the Bobgans' 1987 book *Psychoheresy: The Psychological Seduction of Christianity*, he railed against psychological explanations of the human condition. "Sin has suddenly become 'a mistake," he lamented. "Sinners are no longer called 'sinners,' they're just individuals uninformed on how 'good' they are." Instead of being called to repentance, people instead "are told they need to seek 'psychological rehabilitation.'" Just a few months before he found himself in an unwelcome national spotlight, Swaggart vehemently denied that a mind could become sick. "This would be the same as saying a thought could be sick or a color could be sick," he argued. When it came right down to it, psychology not only was inherently anti-Christian, according to Swaggart, but also was a "pseudoscience—defined in the dictionary as 'a system of theories, assumptions, and methods erroneously regarded as scientific.'" Thus, Christians who embraced psychology in actuality embraced a "pseudoscience, or pseudoscientism," that arrogated a "scientific label to protect and promote opinions which are neither provable nor irrefutable." Swaggart concluded that "practically all the fads sweeping the church today (such as visualization, inner healing, self-esteem, possibility thinking, dream-your-own-dream, positive mental attitude, and creative confession) are offshoots of secular psychology."[56]

To those who challenged Swaggart with the claim that Christians throughout the centuries had utilized numerous technologies and ideas in their daily life that could not be found in the Bible, Swaggart had this response: "The Bible does not claim to be a handbook on engineering, science, etc. (Although, whatever it does say on these subjects is 100 percent accurate.). . . . However, the Bible *does* claim to be a handbook on the 'human condition,' and it *does* claim to hold all the answers in this particular human area."[57]

Bob Gass's 1983 comments in *Christ for the Nations* (previously known as the *Voice of Healing* and edited by Gordon Lindsay) neatly summarized the impatience many pentecostals felt with psychology: "Smith Wigglesworth [a British healer whose ministry influenced many U.S. pentecostals] was a powerhouse for God, but he was no psychologist. He had never read 'How to Win Friends and Influence People.'" According to Gass, Christian psychologists complicated what should be a very simple process. When dealing with hurts in the past, he instructed readers: "Forget those things which are behind you! You don't need to know any more than this to be healed from yesterday."[58]

The inner healing movement clearly did not find acceptance among all pentecostals and charismatics, and some of its most vociferous critics were people with strong ties to traditional pentecostalism who sought to protect the ethos of the early movement. These detractors demonstrated the durability of early pentecostals' ambivalence toward any incorporation of psychology into pentecostal and charismatic healing. It was no accident that the majority of the leaders of the inner healing movement hailed from nonpentecostal denominations. Ministries of inner healing survived these internecine quarrels, though, and managed to establish themselves as a permanent fixture on the map of pentecostal and charismatic healing.

Word of Faith

If more conservative pentecostals and charismatics could not tolerate their colaborers' cessation of hostilities with psychotherapists, this did not preclude many from reaching conclusions very similar to those of inner healing advocates regarding the centrality of the mind in the healing process. Beginning in the late 1960s and 1970s, the same period in which inner healing came into its own, Word of Faith healers popularized the teachings of E. W. Kenyon for a new generation of believers. Though Word of Faith leaders stood much closer to the original pentecostal ethos than their counterparts in the inner healing movement, they, too, zeroed in on the mind as the key to healing.

Led by Kenneth Hagin, Kenneth Copeland, Frederick K. C. Price, and other figures, Word of Faith ministries caught fire by the 1970s with a vision of healing fundamentally in sync with many Americans' consumption-oriented, therapeutic instincts. These proponents of "positive confession" demonstrated a full-fledged commitment to Kenyon's stress on the power of words, tirelessly instructing their followers to respond to negative circumstances with a steady stream of positive statements that flowed from a unflinching confidence in the promises contained in God's Word.[59] Considered the father of the Word of Faith movement, Kenneth Hagin did more than anyone else to transmit Kenyon's teachings regarding the power of positive confession directly to pentecostal audiences (though not exclusively to pentecostal audiences). First a pastor in the Assemblies of God and then an itinerant evangelist, Hagin's influence increased dramatically when he began a regular radio broadcast in 1967 and published a ministry periodical, the *Word of Faith*, beginning in 1968. Hagin repeatedly denied Kenyon's influence on his teachings, yet comparisons of Hagin's writings with Kenyon's reveal numerous passages that are nearly identical.[60]

Part of Hagin's unwillingness to acknowledge his debt to Kenyon likely stemmed from a recurring theme among Word of Faith ministers regarding the newness of their teachings. Though Word of Faith ministers certainly utilized verses from the Bible to back up their claims, they also placed a premium on their ability to hear directly from God and receive new revelations and insight into the "true" meaning of scripture. When Hagin described the way he initially learned the principles of divine healing, he made it very clear that his teachings derived solely from illumination provided by the Spirit as he read the Bible.[61] Along similar lines, his emphasis on the "spoken word," as seen in his repeated references throughout his ministry to the transliterated Greek term "rhema," often was meant to highlight the importance of direct, immediate revelations spoken by God for the present moment.[62]

In view of Word of Faith adherents' commitment to "new revelation," it is not surprising that those who participated in Word of Faith services encountered a modified conception of faith that differed in important respects from the type of faith promoted by early believers. Put simply, Word of Faith leaders depicted faith as the natural byproduct of the rightly calibrated mind. Early pentecostals certainly taught believers at times to ignore their symptoms and confidently go about their daily lives as a sign of their faith, yet the saints' admonitions for faith lacked the persistent emphasis on positive self-talk that permeated Word of Faith teachings. Early adherents typically did not zero in on the need for believers to constantly program their minds to reaffirm the truths they had learned regarding God's promises. Instead, faith represented an internal state of confidence that took God at his word. In 1938, the English pentecostal healer Smith Wigglesworth, whose ministry and writings were well known in North America, distinguished between natural faith and supernatural faith: "As I saw in the presence of God, the limitations of my faith," he wrote, "there came another faith that took the promise, a faith that believed God's Word. . . . God gave a faith that could shake hell and anything else."[63] The early pentecostal healing evangelist John G. Lake quoted a member of his team who frequently told believers to "stop praying for five minutes and BELIEVE GOD, and see what will happen." "It is perfectly amazing the things that will happen when people will believe God," Lake concluded.[64] "If we pray believing," the Pentecostal Holiness minister F. M. Britton confirmed in his 1919 book *Pentecostal Truth*, "we shall have what we ask for."[65]

Proponents of positive confession would have agreed with descriptions of faith as an unshakable confidence in God and his promises, but the mind and speech proved central in their teachings to a degree not seen among early believers. The sociologist Milmon Harrison neatly summarizes the Word of Faith credo: "Not just verbal confessions but, movement members are taught, also their thoughts and self-talk are to be guarded, governed, and kept positive and 'scriptural.' Believers are encouraged to be diligent in maintaining a positive mental attitude and inner dialogue. Mental discipline, mental 'hygiene,' or self-censorship, should be an ongoing practice as demonstration of one's faith. . . . As in other religions with their basis in New Thought or Mind Science, for members of the Word of Faith Movement, there is indeed power in positive thinking."[66]

Hagin's response to a woman who came to him for healing of a malignant growth on her face epitomized Word of Faith healers' assumptions regarding healing. He instructed her to "just say, 'According to the Word of God, I am healed. I believe this cancer is healed.' According to the Word, it is healed. Go to bed saying it, get up saying it. Say it sweeping the floor, say it washing the dishes. Say it everytime you think of it."[67] Kenneth Hagin, Jr., followed in his father's footsteps when he instructed readers in 1980 to spend their time "taking care of your part of the contract. Set a time for your healing, a time when you state, 'I believe that I receive *now*.' Keep saying it. That's the way to receive your healing."[68] As the Hagins' comments suggest, Word of Faith healers mimicked E. W. Kenyon's inclination to define the prayer for deliverance and healing less as a petition than as a simple exercise of "our Legal Rights." "You have as much right to demand healing," Kenyon promised his readers in 1916, "as you have to demand the cashing of a check at a bank where you have a deposit."[69]

Kenyon's successors liked the analogy—so much so that most Word of Faith healers promised the faithful equally powerful financial healings to accompany the restoration of their bodies. Here Word of Faith teachings cultivated inclinations already apparent among several of the midcentury healing evangelists. Oral Roberts, for example, offered "Blessing Pacts" and "Prayer Pacts" early on in his ministry, encouraging his audience to pray explicitly for prosperity. By the early 1970s, he was packaging such emphases under the banner of "seed-faith."[70] A contributor to A. A. Allen's ministry periodical confirmed the tangible, material rewards accompanying the life of faith: "God Gave Me a New 1961 Cadillac!" The writer also voiced appreciation for a God-given upgrade from a "little rooming house" to a "nice brick house" that "I can call my own until Jesus sees fit to change that." With results like these, it is not difficult to see why Allen's supporter was "more determined than ever to stick with the people of God."[71]

In promising financial blessing, Word of Faith figures picked up where mid-century healing evangelists such as Allen left off. As Kenneth Copeland, one of the most prominent proponents of positive confession, explained in 1985, the path to divine blessing and divine healing was a simple and straightforward one: "Analyze your needs. Analyze your wants. Go to the Word of God that covers your needs and wants. Don't relent. Speak faith-filled words." Anyone wondering if such a simple formula worked need only look to Copeland's life for assurance; among other luxuries, his ministry in Fort Worth, Texas, included a private airport.[72] "God is not telling you to be a pauper. He does not want you to be poor," the Los Angeles–based televangelist Frederick K. C. Price explained. Quite the contrary, God "wants all of us to be rich. There is nothing wrong in that. He is rich."[73] Not surprisingly, spiritual guarantees of wealth attracted a ready following, as well as no small number of critics (not the least of whom was Dave Hunt). Aware of the chorus of accusations that Word of Faith teachings derived from metaphysical sources and equated Christianity with self-centered wish fulfillment, advocates qualified their "health and wealth" guarantees by insisting that the believer's desires must please God and align with scripture.[74] The basic message, however, remained a clear crowd-pleaser.

Apart from their feel-good message, another key source of the success of Word of Faith involved ministers' adroit use of mass communication outlets that created a context in which numerous individuals could embrace components of Word of Faith emphases while remaining in their more established denominations, pentecostal or otherwise. As a testament to the importance of mass communication in spreading the message of positive confession, the Trinity Broadcasting Network, headed by Paul and Jan Crouch, claimed to be the largest Christian television network in the world as it provided a constant stream of Word of Faith teaching accessible in the United States and abroad.[75]

Significantly, the broad exposure facilitated by TBN helped Word of Faith leaders transcend a racial divide that had persisted in pentecostal circles during the later decades of the twentieth century and was particularly evident in pentecostal political culture. African-American pentecostals proved "far more supportive of Great Society–style intervention on behalf of the needy and oppressed," for instance, than white pentecostals and charismatics, who in large numbers joined an evangelical exodus from the Democratic Party, beginning especially in the 1970s.[76] Word of Faith emphases managed to rise above these barriers.

Here, the strong continuities between the message of midcentury healing evangelists and Word of Faith leaders, not to mention the widespread enthusiasm regarding the power of positive thinking pervading much of U.S. society, played an important role in establishing a broad base of support. Among black pentecostals and charismatics, several widely known religious leaders in the African-American community throughout the twentieth century laid the groundwork for Word of Faith teachings by offering their listeners a potent healing mixture of New Thought–inflected themes, traditions with roots in African forms of spirituality, as well as pentecostal emphases. These figures ministered to black Americans—many of whom were recent transplants to the North as a result of the "Great Migration" during the 1910s, 1920s, and 1930s—navigating what was often a very unfamiliar urban landscape. Prominent African-American leaders broadcasting metaphysical-style themes in the first half of the twentieth century included Prophet James Jones and Father Divine, while later ministers who popularized such themes among predominantly black communities included Frederick J. Eikerenkoetter II ("Reverend Ike") in New York City and Johnnie Coleman in Chicago. Representative of the pentecostal contributions that helped shape these individuals' ministries, Reverend Ike initially pastored a pentecostal church before going on to greater fame, and he acknowledged Oral Roberts as a significant influence and role model.[77]

African-American Word of Faith figures built on this metaphysical current evident in the black community during the twentieth century. Price, a student of Hagin, is frequently credited with introducing Word of Faith emphases to largely black audiences, and he soon was joined by other high-profile African-American ministers such as Leroy Thompson and Creflo and Taffi Dollar. The Dollars associated closely with Copeland and took an increasingly visible role in the mid-1990s, after Price and Hagin had a falling-out over racist remarks in which Kenneth Hagin, Jr., condemned miscegenation. Drawing on Copeland's teaching that human beings directly shared in God's nature, in classic metaphysical style, Creflo Dollar collapsed the distance between God and nature, and in particular between God and human nature. "I am going to say to you right now you are gods, little g," he promised his listeners in 2002. "You came from God and you are gods." You are not just human, the only human part about you is this physical body that you live in." Here Dollar illustrated what Jonathan Walton has referred to as "metaphysical physicality," wherein "being in sync with the Word of God affords persons a metaphysical existence in the physical realm."[78]

While the precise scope of the Word of Faith movement's influence is difficult to assess, Kenyon's emphasis on the ability of faith-filled speech and thoughts to shape a believer's reality clearly reached a significant proportion of the pentecostal and charismatic populace during the later decades of the twentieth century. In the process, Word of Faith leaders channeled to the faithful what was in significant respects a New Thought style of spirituality, albeit repackaged and reformulated to appeal to a conservative Christian audience.

Word of Faith and Inner Healing: Hybrid Approaches

Despite the shared connections to New Thought linking Word of Faith healers with practitioners of inner healing, ministers in Word of Faith ministries stood right alongside individuals such as Swaggart in protesting inner healers' open embrace of psychology and psychotherapy. Kenneth Hagin, Sr., told his readers that the "concept of *spiritual* healing came into being when some psychologists got saved and filled with the Spirit and tried to mix psychology in with the Word." According to Hagin, these well-meaning individuals simply misunderstood the true nature of healing. "They were born again, all right, and were really filled with the Holy Spirit," he conceded, "but they got confused." To the contrary, true divine healing, "God's kind of healing—is not *mental*, as Christian Science, Unity, and other metaphysical teachers claim. Neither is it just *physical*, as the medical world teaches." Repeating arguments identical to those preached by E. W. Kenyon, John Alexander Dowie, and other figures at the turn of the twentieth century, Hagin insisted that God always healed "*through your HUMAN SPIRIT.*" On the other hand, when "man heals (and man can heal, whether you realize it or not), he must do it either through the mind, or through the physical senses."[79] By definition, then, any incorporation of psychology into pentecostal and charismatic healing sullied the purity of true divine healing. Hagin's fellow Word of Faith leader Kenneth Copeland expressed a similar impatience with psychological methods. "If depression has driven you into a spiritual nose dive," he wrote, "all you have to do to break out of it is to get your eyes off the past and onto your future—a future that's been guaranteed by Christ Jesus through the exceedingly great and precious promises in His Word."[80]

Word of Faith critiques of the types of teachings promoted in the inner healing movement serve as an instructive illustration of the important differences between the two groups. Healing claims made in the Positive Confession branch of the pentecostal-charismatic movement often retained the instantaneous character of early pentecostal testimonies, and figures such as Hagin described healing as a purely spiritual affair, despite an evident prioritization of the mind's role in the process. Proponents of inner healing, on the other hand, offered a model of healing much further removed from the template established by early pentecostals, especially given these proponents' explicit appropriation of psychological terminology and emphasis on the imagination and visualization in the healing process.

Despite the apparent gulf separating promoters of Word of Faith from inner healing leaders, some of the most high-profile pentecostal and charismatic figures of the 1990s and early 2000s were individuals who managed to fuse themes from the two camps without clearly identifying with either. Exploiting the natural connections to the broader therapeutic culture inherent in both the Word of Faith and inner healing movements, such hybrid approaches synthesized the two into a new amalgam that proved highly popular among the faithful.

On the one hand, Joyce Meyer, who appeared alongside the Oneness pentecostal minister T. D. Jakes in *Time*'s 2005 list of the twenty-five most influential evangelicals, offered quintessential Word of Faith principles to readers of her writings on healing. She asked, "How do you stand against sickness?" "For starters," she continued, "*plead the blood* of Jesus against the sickness and over every part of your body—your immune system, your organs, your blood cells, and so on. Then *speak the word* over your body." Believers should affirm: "Father, I believe it's Your will that I be in health. I believe that by the stripes of Jesus, I am healed. Your Word is health and life to my body, and it *will* accomplish that which You please and purpose." In another revealing example of the influence of Word of Faith emphases, Meyer continued: "Once you've done this, avoid going around and saying things like, 'Man, I feel bad, I am so sick,' or 'I know I'm going to be sick because everybody else is getting it.' This puts your mouth in agreement with the sickness. Instead, ask God to help you keep your mind and mouth in agreement with His Word."[81]

Many of Meyer's instructions for dealing with emotional ills and not just physical ills could have been plucked right out of a Word of Faith handbook as well, given her clear stress on the power of the spoken word and of a positive mental outlook. In a handbook on dealing with insecurity, Meyer counseled readers to "speak, on purpose, good things about yourself." In her own life, she found that she had to "convince myself I was okay before God could really do anything through me." Meyer went on to model the type of prayer she recommended for believers: "I am the righteousness of God in Jesus Christ. I prosper in everything I lay my hand to. I have gifts and talents, and God is using me. . . . I eat right, I look good, I feel good, I weigh exactly what I should weigh."[82]

For all of her stress on the power of thought and speech to shape a believer's physical and emotional reality, individuals reading Meyer's many books encountered much more than just Word of Faith principles. In addition to her appropriation of Word of Faith themes, Meyer also demonstrated a ready familiarity with the language of popular psychology, frequently interjecting discussion of her own battles to overcome the effects of childhood abuse. "I believe that most people are abused in one way or another during their lifetime," she wrote in the opening chapter of *Beauty for Ashes: Receiving Emotional Healing*. "Some common forms of abuse are: physical, verbal, emotional and sexual. Whatever form it may take, abuse causes a root of rejection."[83] In a revised and expanded edition, she made the psychological connections even more explicit. Those traumatized by abuse were "psychologically deficient" and in danger of being thrown "into a state of psychological damage that prohibits them from functioning properly in relationships with others." Ensuing chapters titled "Behavior Addictions Caused by Abuse," "Self-Rejection or Self-Acceptance," and "The Confidence to Be Yourself," among others, made clear her intent to baptize the tropes of U.S. therapeutic culture in biblical waters.[84]

Much like Meyer, the pastor and evangelist T. D. Jakes mixed a strong dose of Word of Faith themes, as well as popular psychology, into his discussion of emotional healing. Much of the advice scattered throughout *Woman, Thou Art Loosed!*, a bestseller first published in 1993, illustrated his interest in the power of positive confession: "Quit telling yourself, 'You're too fat, too old, too late, or too ignorant.' Quit feeding yourself that garbage." According to Jakes, too often women in particular tended to "speak against their bodies, opening the door for sickness and disease." Instead, he directed his readers to "speak life to your own body." Faith-less speech had the ability to "keep you bent over and crippled." The devil "would love to destroy you with your own words. Satan wants to use *you* to fight against you."[85]

Also like Meyer, Jakes incorporated common psychological tropes right alongside Word of Faith themes. As it happens, his mother studied psychology in graduate school, and Jakes himself identified psychology as his major while he attended West Virginia State College for one year.[86] In *Woman, Thou Art Loosed!* Jakes eventually described psychotherapists as "practicing an uncertain method on people as they ramble through the closets of a troubled person's mind," but the book showed more than a little resemblance to popular psychology. It was marketed as an answer for those who had been "wounded by a childhood tragedy, a sordid memory, a failed relationship, or even choices and decisions that are now sources of regret." According to Jakes, many women "wrestle with infirmities in emotional traumas," as opposed to strictly physical ailments. These "emotional handicaps" had the potential to "create dependency on many different levels. Relationships can become crutches." Individuals in such relationships needed to "break the habit of using other people as a narcotic to numb the dull aching of an inner void." He concluded the book by reminding his readers that Christ wanted the "potential within you to be unleashed so you can become the person you were created to be."[87] Lest any doubt remained regarding the psychological overtones in Jakes's writings, beginning in 2007 he appeared alongside the U.S. television personality and psychologist Phil McGraw on the *Dr. Phil* show.[88]

Shortly after Meyer and Jakes emerged on the national stage in the early 1990s, others soon followed who mastered a nearly identical formula for success. Paula White, who copastored with her husband one of the largest churches in the United States, Without Walls International Church in Tampa, Florida, related to her readers the types of "admonishments and declarations" she made to herself. In her 2007 book *You're All That! Understand God's Design for Your Life*, she quoted the positive confessions penned in her personal journal: "I admonish you right now, Paula, to believe with all your heart, mind and soul that you are: blessed, valuable, beautiful, strong, smart, favored, okay!" "Speak in the first person," she explained. "Tell yourself who you are and who you are becoming in Christ."[89]

Figure 4.1 T. D. Jakes prays for a member of his Dallas church, The Potter's House. James Mitchell/ Ebony Collection via AP Images.

Despite the clear overlap between White's discussion of positive confession and Word of Faith themes, individuals who subscribed to Hagin's sharp differentiation between psychological healing and spiritual healing must have been dismayed at her simultaneous references to methods of emotional healing in the tradition of inner healing. She specifically taught her readers to recall painful memories "as vividly as possible, with as many details as possible," and then imagine "Jesus as being part of the scene in which you experienced deep emotional pain." "Take Jesus to the place where your heart was broken," she instructed. "Take Him to the place where you sat in abandonment after being rejected." Mimicking the basic principles promoted by other believers who sought to spiritualize psychotherapy, White promised that Jesus transcended time and "is just as real in the past as He is today"; as such, the believer could have confidence that he "is just as real in your past memory as He is in your present thinking and feeling."[90]

The widely popular pastor and evangelist Joel Osteen of Houston disseminated a similar, relentlessly positive message regarding the power of optimistic faith, though with much less enthusiasm for dredging up the memories of the

past. To a significant degree, Osteen's national television audience, as well as
the nearly 30,000 attendees of his charismatic church, learned about the importance of dealing with the emotional wounds of the past in a manner quite
distinct from the spiritualized forms of psychology embraced by pentecostals
and charismatics associated with the inner healing movement. Life provided
two distinct file cabinets, he taught, one with memories of joy, happiness, victories, and accomplishment, and another "with the hurts and pains of the past,
all of the negative things that have happened to us." Those who wanted freedom
from the controlling wounds of the past needed to make a simple choice: "If you
want to be free, if you want to overcome self-pity, throw away the key to file
number two." Like other healers, Osteen was convinced of the power of the
mind and the imagination to take us back to past events, but he considered this
a very dangerous proposition. By reliving painful experiences and seeing them
in the imagination, sufferers tore open old wounds that "will never properly
heal until we learn to leave it alone." "Don't waste another minute trying to
figure out why certain evil things have happened to you or your loved ones," he
concluded.[91]

Whereas Osteen confirmed the continued ambivalence toward psychological
forms of healing in certain pentecostal and charismatic circles, in other respects
his writings revealed an indebtedness to the common themes and emphases associated with U.S. self-help culture that was no less pronounced than the indebtedness to the same tropes evident in the ministries of Meyer, Jakes, and White.
One need look no further than titles of Osteen's books to discern the centrality
of self-realization in his articulation of the Christian life. *Your Best Life Now*, he
promised in 2004. Three years later, readers learned the keys to *Becoming a Better
You*. Osteen instructed the faithful in the importance of "understanding your
value," "letting go of emotional wounds," and "learning to like yourself."[92] The
common denominator throughout both books involved a basic commitment to
the power of positive thought and speech to determine one's destiny, so long as
those thoughts and speech accorded with the promises mentioned in God's
word.

As Meyer, Jakes, White, and Osteen illustrated, by the turn of the twenty-
first century Word of Faith healers and inner healing practitioners' prioritization of the mind had spilled over to shape a much broader pentecostal and
charismatic audience, not to mention numerous other Americans who encountered these teachings via various media outlets. Diehard traditionalists, including numerous Word of Faith healers, remained wary of the importation of
psychological concepts and terminology. At the same time, many who were attracted to key aspects of the Word of Faith message showed little interest in
absolutist renunciations of psychology. Distinctions aside, believers from a
wide variety of backgrounds grew accustomed to hearing about the power of
positive thinking, as pentecostal and charismatic healers incorporated themes

from both the New Thought tradition and the ubiquitous popular psychology saturating U.S. culture. Adherents would not have admitted as much, but metaphysical-like depictions of physical and emotional healing predicated on the mind's ability to transmit the Spirit's power—directly to the believer and in a predictable and reliable fashion—were here to stay.

Perfect Bodies, Plentiful Profits

For all of the attention pentecostals and charismatics paid to the role of the mind in the healing process since the 1970s, they never lost sight of the body. Once again, Oral Roberts was in the middle of the action. Beginning in 1976, students attending ORU encountered a newly instituted policy insisting that overweight students shed their extra pounds. Toward that end, the university implemented an aerobic exercise program requiring physical education courses coupled with careful monitoring of students' weight and extracurricular activities. Paul Brynteson, chairman of the health, physical education, and recreation department at the school, indicated that "an acceptable body fat level is 20 percent for women and 15 percent for men. A woman having more than 35 percent body fat, or a man having more than 25 percent, is considered obese." Those who were overweight were required to sign a contract with the university committing to lose the extra weight at the rate of one to two pounds per week. Failure to do so led to probation, and potentially suspension from classes. According to one student quoted in the *New York Times*, the school required him to reduce down to 160 from 215 pounds. Despite his 3.7 grade-point average, he eventually received a letter over his summer break indicating that "before you will be able to complete registration this fall, you must report for your weight check. To be readmitted your weight must be at or below 198 pounds." After receiving the letter, the student left the university. (Two years after ORU implemented its aerobic exercise program, four students had been suspended for failing to lose enough weight; others simply withdrew and applied elsewhere.)[1]

Critics took aim at ORU's weight reduction program and also targeted the school's policy of refusing admittance to students in wheelchairs (the school claimed that the buildings on campus were not built to accommodate the disabled). In 1977, the American Civil Liberties Union and the Oklahoma Coalition of Citizens with Disabilities sued the university over its treatment of obese and handicapped students, though they later dropped their complaint regarding the weight reduction program in order to focus solely on ORU's treatment of the disabled. By 1978, the school had changed its policy toward those in wheelchairs, avoiding a protracted legal battle over the issue. The weight reduction program remained in place.[2]

The lengths to which ORU was willing to go to keep its campus full of thin, healthy students—to the point of requiring annual checkups for body fat percentage, coupled with threats of suspension from classes and restrictions regarding the acceptance of students in wheelchairs—offers a telling illustration of the growing connection between diet, health, and healing in believers' minds, and of the extent to which many participated in the avid pursuit of perfect bodies prevalent in U.S. society. No longer content with the mere eradication of disease, the faithful increasingly went after bigger game: the ideal body promoted in mainstream U.S. diet culture.

The careful regulation of the body served as a perennial theme, of course, throughout the history of pentecostalism. As an aspiring pentecostal poet wrote in 1931 regarding the spiritual benefits of asceticism, the disciples of Jesus who waited for the Holy Spirit after his ascension "were not feasting, they were fasting. . . . They were filled by the Holy Ghost, not stuffed with a stew or roast. . . . Put out the fire in the kitchen and build it on the altar. More love and more life, fewer dinners and get after the sinners."[3] From the beginning, overindulgence was held as sinful because it distracted individuals from their all-important pursuit of spiritual satisfaction and power. Franklin Hall and other midcentury figures carried forward the traditional pentecostal focus on asceticism even as they solidified the connection between healing and fasting. It was not until the later decades of the twentieth century, though, that pentecostal and charismatic healers assimilated mainstream trends in U.S. culture by exhorting their followers to discipline the body in pursuit of an outward, visible physical perfection and offering a wide range of dietary products that effectively commodified pentecostal healing.

Diet and U.S. Therapeutic Culture

In many respects, the commodification of pentecostal healing since the 1970s followed a well-worn pattern charted much earlier by entrepreneurial figures at the turn of the twentieth century who helped shape the burgeoning therapeutic culture in the United States. The growing idealization of thin bodies coupled with advances in nutritional science during the early 1900s produced an environment ripe for products promising to help users improve their health and shed extra pounds. The various goods helping consumers achieve a rapturous state of health, vitality, and weight loss ranged from Kruschen Salts ("The Modern Safe Way—Right Way to Lose Fat") to Ex-Lax (the key "toward helping nature give you a clear, healthy complexion and bright sparkling eyes") to Cascarets (the "Candy Cathartic").[4]

Others found great success peddling a much cheaper device: food abstinence. Edward Hooker Dewey's "fasting cure" and "no breakfast plan" were believed to cure a whole host of ills.[5] Bernarr Macfadden built a publishing empire focused on the benefits of physical exercise and fasting.[6] Upton Sinclair likewise promoted fasting as the key to wellness after writing his now better known exposé of the U.S. meat packing industry.[7] Francis Humphris advocated careful dietary restrictions coupled with electrical stimulation.[8] Though Horace Fletcher, the "Great Masticator," was not enamored with the "fasting cure," his insistence that his followers should chew each bite at least twenty times in order to extract the full nutrition undoubtedly cut more than a few meals short as well.[9]

In terms of nutritional science's role in cementing the emerging correlation between diet, slimness, and health in the U.S. psyche, as early as the 1880s Wilbur Atwater, a chemist at Wesleyan University, became interested in establishing ideal caloric values for individuals. It took time for the U.S. medical profession to warm to the idea that obesity posed a significant health risk, but by the first decade of the twentieth century more and more physicians had seen the light, spurred in part by actuarial studies conducted by life insurance companies establishing a clear connection between excess weight and increased mortality. In addition, by 1905 European scientists had confirmed the importance of trace nutrients—eventually dubbed vitamins—whose deficiency in the diet led to diseases such as beriberi, scurvy, and pellagra. (U.S. researchers added to this growing body of knowledge during the 1910s.)[10]

Despite the importance of such strides in nutritional research, Americans' budding interest in the interconnections between diet, thinness, and health at the turn of the twentieth century cannot be attributed solely to the impact of research on nutritional science or to medical castigations of obesity. Though the medical community helped establish the emerging diet culture in important respects, broad-based awareness of the progress in nutritional science had not yet had sufficient time to percolate throughout U.S. society, and other factors likely played a more fundamental role.

The historian Peter Stearns argues that the U.S. diet culture arose primarily as a response to the increased influence of consumer capitalism at the turn of the century. Here, explicitly "religious jeremiads" attacking consumerism lost their reformatory power as growing urbanization and a changing economy characterized by an overabundance of supply set the stage for Americans to increasingly shed their Victorian sensibilities. During this period, "constraint, including the new constraints urged on eating and body shape, was reinvented to match— indeed, to compensate for—new areas of greater freedom." Whereas previous generations attempted to counteract the perceived dangers of wealth and luxury by encouraging expressions of self-denial rooted in a "traditional religious sternness," increasingly these restrictions were replaced by "a more subtle set of moral compensations." According to this logic, Americans' acceptance of new constraints in areas such as diet gave them a moral license of sorts to more fully embrace the "acquisitiveness" associated with consumer culture.[11]

Stearns's analysis does not help explain the development of early pentecostal healing. Despite the saints' stress on fasting, the holy trinity of U.S. diet culture—nutrition, thinness, and health—simply did not coalesce within the plainfolk culture that permeated the early pentecostal movement. Some leaders commented on the importance of a proper diet for health, yet physical appearance rarely, if ever, seemed to factor into the equation. Likewise, when Franklin Hall wrote on the subjects of proper diet and fasting in 1947, he did not immediately assume that readers would want to fast in order to lose weight. To the contrary, Hall seemed more concerned with those who were *under*weight. "Many thin people are thin because their functional glands and organs are so burdened and overworked from food over-indulgence they cannot take on weight no matter how much they eat," he wrote. "I have seen many thin and underweight people gain weight and become of normal weight after a fast of ten days or more followed by weeks of careful eating. In many instances all that was wrong was that they needed to give their organs a much needed vacation and their belly a holiday." Hall's sales pitch for fasting would have fallen on deaf ears among pentecostals and charismatics later in the century: "Daniel's diet made him appear 'FATTER AND FAIRER' than the children of the world."[12]

Whereas Stearns's argument does little to illuminate early pentecostal healing culture, and despite his tendency to overlook various religious groups' contributions to the emerging twentieth-century diet culture, his description of Americans' turn to "a more subtle set of moral compensations" nevertheless fits quite well with the choices that later pentecostal and charismatic figures made as they worked to move the dials on their bathroom scales in a decidedly different direction from that of their forebears.[13] It is no coincidence that prominent pentecostal and charismatic leaders began to alter their discourse to fit with the U.S. diet culture beginning in the 1970s—precisely a time when adherents were enjoying the fruits of U.S. consumer culture as never before. With solidly middle-class families swelling the ranks of the faithful, healers learned to open up room for the saints' growing obsession with physical appearance and bodily perfection; in time, they also commodified pentecostal healing to an unprecedented degree by providing the faithful with more and more healthy ways to spend their new-found wealth.

Spirit-Led Diet and Exercise

The initial signs of pentecostals' and charismatics' widespread interest in dietary healing corresponded with a revival of interest in diet and fitness in the United States more broadly during the 1960s and 1970s, as a wave of healthy-minded enthusiasm swept across the country. Americans' new-found love affair with jogging and aerobic exercise and the growing popularity of organic foods epitomized these changes. Indicative of pentecostals' and charismatics' attunement to these developments, a significant relationship developed between Oral Roberts and the Texas-based Christian physician Kenneth Cooper, who coined the term "aerobics" in 1968. Roberts enthusiastically adopted Cooper's aerobics program in 1972, which eventually became the model for ORU's controversial school-wide aerobics program, and by 1974 Roberts had unveiled the $2 million state-of-the-art Kenneth H. Cooper Aerobics Center on campus. Appropriately enough, Cooper spoke at the dedication.[14]

Several others joined Roberts in guiding pentecostals' and charismatics' interest in the power of food and exercise from the periphery to the mainstream of the movement. A decade before Roberts's conversion to Cooper's aerobic regimen, Frank Ford founded Arrowhead Mills, an organic food distribution company. At the time, Ford had no connection to the charismatic movement, but in the early 1970s, following a profound spiritual experience, he enthusiastically supported the charismatic cause and began advertising his products to charismatic audiences.[15] One promotion for his *Simpler Life Cookbook* asked: "If the Lord has been quickening you to cleanse the temple of the Holy Spirit by cleansing your body of the foods of 'Babylon'—highly refined foods full of preservatives, nitrates, coloring agents, hydrogenated fats and refined sugar—we would like to hear from you." The ad criticized "this diet handed to us by modern food processing" and reported that "many believers are returning to eating foods the way God made them." The promotion simultaneously drew on the nomenclature of the holistic health movement as well as the apocalyptic fears imbibed by pentecostals and charismatics as they read works such as Hal Lindsey's *Late Great Planet Earth*: "We here at Arrowhead Mills believe we have neglected the whole person that God wants us to be in the difficult times which lie just ahead. . . . People who know how to raise a garden and cook properly with whole grains, beans and seeds will be able to help others in the natural realm to improve the health of their families and to enjoy the foods which God created for our use before humanistic arrogance, through technology, changed them into something harmful to our health."[16] Ford's explicit differentiation between natural foods linked with God's creative power and "manufactured" foods stripped of this power by modern technology permeated the writings of high-profile figures in the pentecostal-charismatic movement by the end of the twentieth century.

In addition to her much more visible efforts to spread the message of inner healing, Ruth Carter Stapleton also called attention to the importance of a natural diet and lifestyle in 1978 when she founded a spiritual retreat center, named Holovita, near Denton, Texas. Describing her vision for the center just prior to its grand opening, the Southern Baptist charismatic explained: "The whole thing is going to be an expression of my philosophy. You can't miss the message. See, everything is getting back to basics, to cotton and natural wood. Simplicity." Like Ford, Stapleton stressed a natural diet as a key element in her program. In the words of one reporter, the typical weekend Stapleton had planned for this "charismatic's Esalen" would include much more than just lectures: visitors would "hear live evening concerts out on the lawn, eat meals prepared from Holovita's own garden, smell the flowers from its small greenhouse, just outside [the visitor's] own bedroom window." Stapleton's commitment specifically to a natural diet only intensified in the early 1980s when she was diagnosed with pancreatic cancer. Eschewing more conventional treatment, Stapleton instead combined a regimen of prayer and meditation with a macrobiotic diet promoted by the diet guru Michio Kushi of Boston. Though Stapleton lost her battle with cancer in 1983, her exploration of natural, dietary forms of healing garnered national attention, including an article in *People*, and undoubtedly came to the attention of more than a few pentecostals and charismatics.[17]

Much more than natural foods, a widespread crusade against fat proved the most influential gateway to dietary conceptions of healing during the 1970s and early 1980s as caloric charts, nutritious-but-tasty recipes, admonitions to exercise, and weight-loss grade cards inundated believers. For instance, the charismatic healing evangelist Francis Hunter often injected a healthy dose of self-deprecating humor into her enormously successful *God's Answer to Fat . . . Loøse It!* But she left no doubt regarding the very serious link between fat and sin. Drawing on the sixth chapter of Romans, she taught readers how to read the text specifically with diet and weight loss in mind. She quoted specific verses and inserted her own commentary in italics: "The sixth chapter of Romans really spoke to me concerning dieting," she wrote. "'Do not let sin (appetite) control your puny body any longer; do not give in to its sinful desires.'. . . 'Don't you realize that you can choose your own master? You can choose sin (*food*) (with death) (*fat*) or else obedience (with acquittal) (*or obedience with a weight loss*)."[18]

Another believer went so far as to instruct his overweight readers in 1981 "to get disgusted with yourself. When clothes don't fit, you look in the mirror and say, 'Oh, you stuffed sausage, what's wrong with this?'" Calling for "an attitude of abhorrence" when it came to issues of fat, the author cited a scripture from Romans commanding believers to "abhor that which is evil, cleave to that which is good." "Gluttony or overeating is one of the *acceptable* sins among Christians," he lamented, when in actual fact, "portly, generously endowed" bodies were sinful bodies. In comparison, other writers avoided explicit calls for self-hatred, yet the same underlying logic connecting fat with sin pervaded books published by pentecostals and charismatics, including Joan Cavanaugh's *More of Jesus, Less of Me*, Patricial Kreml's *Slim for Him*, and Neva Coyle and Marie Chapian's *Free to Be Thin*.[19]

Pentecostal and charismatic writers highlighted more than just the physical benefits of a trimmed-down body, of course; they accentuated the spiritual rewards as well. "The Lord Jesus Christ did not die to give those who believe in Him as Saviour liberty to cater to their sensual appetites," Ann Thomas admonished in a Bible study directed toward pentecostal and charismatic women. "He died to give Christians the power to keep their own desires in control in order to serve Him and other people." Thomas's dietary program was neatly summed up in two of her chapter titles: "Devaluate Physical Food" and "Eat Lots of Spiritual Food."[20] In similar fashion, in her widely popular book written with Marie Chapian, the pentecostal Neva Coyle indicated in 1979 that conquering sinful eating habits opened the door for believers to say "I am totally victorious over food. . . . Jesus alone satisfies me. Jesus alone gives me strength to handle anger, frustration, and to live up to my daily responsibilities. I need no other reward than to walk in a covenant of obedience with Him."[21]

Despite these spiritual disclaimers, in the end all of the pentecostal and charismatic figures who tapped into the popular U.S. diet scene offered a vision of health and thinness that freed adherents to embrace the therapeutic and physical ideals permeating U.S. culture. As a result of participating in a weight loss program created by Coyle and Chapian, one woman exulted, "I feel much better about myself. I've learned how much He cares about me because I spend time with Him every day. . . . The change in me personally is far greater than the weight loss." "The Lord Jesus has promised to be your teacher, friend and guide," Coyle and Chapian added. "Trust Him to speak to you and help you discover yourself."[22]

Pentecostals and charismatics, of course, were not the only U.S. Christians participating in the burgeoning fitness culture; their celebration of the holiness of thinness and the sinfulness of fat corresponded to similar appropriations of the U.S. diet culture by Christians of all stripes during the same period. Contemporary Christian diet culture initially emerged in the 1950s and 1960s in the writings of the Presbyterian Charlie Shedd and the Episcopalians Deborah Pierce and H. Victor Kane. As observed by the historian R. Marie Griffith, these individuals paved the way for later developments in the genre by mediating New Thought themes of the power of positive thinking and the perfectibility of the body to a Christian audience and by explicitly linking fat with sinfulness.[23]

Specifically in pentecostal and charismatic circles, the popularity of Word of Faith teachers from the 1960s contributed to believers' growing enthusiasm for physical, material evidence of the Spirit's work such as weight loss. Proponents of positive confession insisted that financial and physical blessings automatically accrued to those living the life God intended, and beautiful bodies fit this schema perfectly. As the freelance charismatic writer Lona White explained in a 1982 *Charisma* article, "our confession can work against us if we allow it. I discovered that often when I get into a situation where food is being served, I babble endlessly about my 'terrible weight problem' and that 'I really shouldn't be eating this,' and on and on." The problem, according to White, was that as she confessed this, she was "feasting not on the Word of faith and hope but of failure. I am drinking vinegar instead of new wine. The moral here: Stop your mouth when it is about to murmur and complain."[24]

Even apart from the influence of Word of Faith emphases in the pentecostal-charismatic movement, any good pentecostal or charismatic convinced of God's healing power and of the availability of a disease-free body already was primed for the fascination with perfectly fit bodies evident in the U.S. diet culture. Thus, it is not surprising that pentecostals and charismatics quickly assimilated the tools of the trade with great success; pentecostal and charismatic authors not only joined the conversation in the 1970s, but soon functioned as some the most prominent proponents of Christianized approaches to weight loss in the United States.

While the pentecostal and charismatic diet culture clearly overlapped with emphases promulgated by nonpentecostal, noncharismatic Christian writers, distinctive patterns emerged in the pentecostal and charismatic literature that resonated in particular with pentecostal and charismatic audiences. What typically distinguished pentecostals and charismatics from their counterparts in the broader evangelical world involved a very vivid sense of the availability of supernatural resources in their struggles.

In at least a few instances, pentecostals and charismatics in the later decades of the twentieth century held out the possibility of direct miraculous intervention in their pursuit of the perfect body (even if they never quite matched the attendee at one of A. A. Allen's services who claimed she instantly lost 200 pounds).[25] Hunter, for example, recounted how she came to a point of desperation. "GOD, IF I NEVER GET TO EAT ANOTHER THING THAT I REALLY LOVE, I'LL DO IT FOR YOU. I GIVE YOU MY APPETITE." After this engagement of her will, God did a miracle: "HE COMPLETELY TOOK AWAY MY DESIRE FOR FOOD!"[26] Hunter's experience proved the exception rather than the rule; nonetheless, it demonstrated the persistence among pentecostals and charismatics of a keen sense that God could and would act immediately on behalf of his chosen people, even in relation to weight loss.

More typical instances of adherents' adapting the Christian diet culture to fit with their highly spiritualized worldview revolved around the possibility of divine guidance in the weight-loss process. The weight-loss writer Patricia Kreml described the Holy Spirit in 1978 as the "best authority on proper nutrition, compulsive eating, etc." As such, dieters need to enroll in "His school" and learn to "listen, ask questions, receive answers, and be taught according to [the Holy Spirit's] perfect will."[27] Similar themes appeared in the works of Coyle and Chapin. "One certain need is to hear [God] concerning your goal weight," the authors wrote in 1984. "You also need His guidance concerning how many calories you should be eating daily. He is Lord of your body. He knows your frame and exactly how you should take care of it." As with Kreml, Coyle and Chapian understood this guidance as an ever-present resource for those craving an ideal body. They told the story of a woman who stood in front of the baked goods at the supermarket. She was "quite hungry and knew she could polish off a package of caramel Danish pastries on the way home." In the midst of this temptation, however, she "heard the Lord gently speaking to her spirit: 'Don't do it.'" Strengthened by this guidance, she "turned and walked to the produce department where she chose a bag of apples."[28]

Alongside direct instruction from the Holy Spirit, at other times a simple awareness of the Spirit's convicting presence would suffice. "Do you realize that the Spirit is right there when you sneak that scoop of ice cream?" Kreml asked her readers in 1978. "He's there when you cheat on your diet. He's there day and night," she continued. The Spirit stood by when dieters went to "open the refrigerator" or "eat that cookie." "How sad He must be at those times; how disappointed He is that we don't reach out to Him for help."[29]

Other pentecostals and charismatics extended the spiritualization of U.S. diet culture by discerning the activity of demonic powers in believers' struggle with weight. For Cavanaugh, the sheer subtlety of the various temptations to make poor food choices, coming at times through the influence of friends and family, convinced her that an evil power was at work. When temptations appeared "so subtle as to seem diabolically planned," she concluded, "they are."[30] Francis Hunter likewise described Satan as a shape-shifting power who could manipulate food for his purposes. The devil can "disguise himself as a candy bar," she wrote in 1975. "He can be a cake, with gooey frosting on it. He can be a pudding. . . . The devil tries to tell us if we eat a little something sweet it will satisfy us." Far from a merely physical issue, for Hunter achieving an ideal body engaged the believer in spiritual warfare; demonic temptation to eat required a spiritual battle plan for resisting Satan's very personal onslaughts.[31] Along similar lines, when Melba Ward, a charismatic dieter who lost over 100 pounds, wrote on weight loss in 1975 for *Aglow*, she tempered her focus on the supernatural by stressing her need for "deliverance from weight" more than just deliverance from evil powers; at the same time, direct references to Satan remained in her instructions. She directed readers to "recognize how deliverance from overweight works: you sow seeds (cut calories) and Jesus delivers you of pounds." "When Satan attacks," she continued, "admit your weakness" and "command him to leave in Jesus's name, by the power of the Blood." Though Ward focused on deliverance from calories more than the believer's battle with the devil in her article, Satan remained a potent foe.[32]

Clearly, the increasing fascination with bodily perfection among pentecostals and charismatics did not preclude a continued role for spiritual warfare. Though much of the advice given by these authors dovetailed with the type of advice given in most every dietary self-help book published in the United States, if there was a recurring theme that set pentecostal and charismatic diet literature apart from many of their counterparts', it involved the tangible role supernatural powers played in adherents' war on weight. The Holy Spirit stayed by believers' sides, guiding them with specific directions in their times of need. The Spirit also enabled adherents to repel the demonic temptations brought by evil spirits seeking to short-circuit the saints' efforts to obediently discipline their bodies. Good and evil spirits alike appeared very concerned with believers' struggle for a beautiful, healthy body during the final decades of the twentieth century.

Throughout the 1980s and 1990s, the pentecostal and charismatic diet culture showed few signs of abating. New voices joined the chorus, and new products appeared that aided believers in their pursuit of healthy, beautiful bodies. One such up-and-coming star during the 1980s was Stormie Omartian, a singer, dancer, and television actress prior to her embrace of pentecostal-style Christianity. Following serious bouts with depression and suicidal thoughts, Omartian embraced pentecostalism after meeting Jack Hayford, the influential pastor of a large pentecostal Foursquare church in California. Soon thereafter, Omartian put her talents to use for Christian audiences, writing various books aimed especially at evangelical women and producing fitness products such as *Stormie Omartian's First Step Workout Video*, which featured "an all-new, 28-minute, easy workout featuring tension releasing, toning and stretching, firming and strengthening, and non-impact exercises."[33]

In another important indicator of the growing appeal of dietary healing among pentecostals and charismatics, by the 1990s and early 2000s several prominent pentecostal and charismatic African-American leaders had spread the gospel of physical perfection to new audiences.[34] *Lay Aside the Weight*, published by the widely popular minister T. D. Jakes in 1997, detailed his own struggle with weight loss, chronicling his dramatic excision of over 100 pounds in a little over a year. Though race was not the focus of the book, Jakes briefly addressed the connection between black culture and food. "One of the things that helped me to get an understanding was the effect of my culture on my eating habits," he wrote. "African Americans, like many other cultures in our society, celebrate most major events with food. We bring food when babies are born; we bring food when people die. We celebrate every holiday with food, and most of our family outings and events are surrounded by lots of fat-filled, sugar-loaded, festive-type foods." One of the keys to transforming his weight, then, involved transforming the African-American culture regarding food. "My first challenge," he continued, "was to develop good times that were not inundated with fatty foods."[35] A few years after the book's publication, Jakes demonstrated his continued interest in the subject by inviting the fitness expert Donna Richardson, who produced best-selling fitness videos, including *Sweating in the Spirit* and *Body Gospel*, to speak at his God's Leading Ladies conferences.[36]

Kara Davis, an African-American physician in the Chicago area and copastor of a charismatic church, similarly targeted obese African-American Christians.

While serving as an assistant professor of clinical and internal medicine at the University of Illinois College of Medicine, Davis "noticed that an unusually high number of African-American women were obese." Following this observation, she took an "aggressive step toward educating women of color about emotions and lifestyles that trigger overeating."[37] In her weight-loss regimen, Davis stressed the fruits of the spirit, such as love, joy, peace, and gentleness, as pre-requisites for weight-loss. For those readers who lacked the type of spiritual and emotional strength required to immediately implement the program, Davis did allow for pragmatic concessions. Given the fact that spiritual growth "takes time—sometimes years, decades or even a lifetime," she permitted "assistance in the form of medications and operations *while* [Christians struggling with obe-sity] mature in their faith." The implication of her philosophy was clear: spiritual maturity naturally correlated with a fit body, while spiritual weakness corre-sponded to obesity.[38]

Other African Americans cheering pentecostals and charismatics toward health and fitness at the turn of the twenty-first century included Lee Haney and LaVita Weaver. Haney, an eight-time Mr. Olympia, hosted *Totalee Fit* for the Charismatic TBN Network, "bringing a balance of exercise, diet and spir-itual well-being to us."[39] Weaver, who appeared as a cohost with Haney on *Totalee Fit*, wrote her own Christian health manual, *Fit for God*, which she billed as "The 8-Week Plan that Kicks the Devil Out and Invites Health and Healing In."[40] As these examples suggest, by the 1990s and early twenty-first century, the stress on perfectly fit bodies had transcended racial divisions in the pentecostal-charismatic movement.

In elevating the importance of physical appearance in the discourse sur-rounding health and healing, pentecostal and charismatic diet and exercise gurus radicalized previous believers' emphasis on palpable manifestations of God's presence and power. Earlier pentecostals' warnings regarding a vain preoc-cupation with exterior appearance gave way to an expectation that the visible world and especially the human body should mirror the perfection of the spiri-tual world. Early pentecostals often saw fasting as a means to procure God's healing touch, yet asceticism had never been linked so thoroughly to exterior beauty. Similarly, early pentecostals' stress on divine healing assumed a direct correlation between the Spirit's activity and a healthy body, yet physical appear-ance had never before served so clearly as an index of the operation of the Spirit.

Natural (Yet Divine) Healing

Whereas most of the pentecostal and charismatic writers who addressed issues surrounding diet beginning in the 1970s and 1980s focused disproportionately on issues surrounding weight, soon a new type of healer emerged to carry the banner of dietary healing. As Ruth Carter Stapleton did in her battle with cancer, these figures zeroed in on the curative properties associated with various foods, importing a distinct naturopathic sensibility that stressed God's divine blessing on natural substances and aligned believers more closely than ever before with the holistic health movement. Pentecostal and charismatic weight-loss gurus' metaphysical-like inclinations to treat the physical world as a microcosm of the spiritual world and to correlate perfection in the spiritual realm with bodily perfection in the physical realm were still very much present, but more and more, such emphases were transposed into a decidedly new key.

In addition to Stapleton, a key early player in pentecostals' and charismatics' turn to natural foods in their pursuit of dietary healing was Maureen Salaman. Whereas Salaman's visibility in the pentecostal-charismatic movement dramatically increased beginning in the mid-1980s due to her television program *Maureen Salaman's Accent on Health*, her turn to holistic healing methods rooted in naturopathic principles occurred years earlier. As Salaman recounted the story, her initiation into the world of alternative healing began with the illness of her spiritual mentor, Helen Sweet. After learning that Sweet was dying of cancer, Salaman took personal responsibility for her friend's care, shuttling her back and forth for chemotherapy. Dismayed by the side effects associated with the treatments, Salaman searched in earnest for an alternative. "Each journey to a health food store was an adventure into a new land of strange and unfamiliar products," she recalled.[41]

Despite Salaman's efforts, Sweet eventually succumbed to cancer. Devastated by the loss, Salaman tried to make sense of everything. "I thought often of Helen's case," she recounted, "and wondered if it hadn't originated from a poor diet such as the one I had been on. Helen had been faithful to God's word in everything but diet." Salaman continued to sort out the link between diet and health, setting aside time at Lake Tahoe to recuperate from the ordeal. There she received a revelation regarding the spiritual significance of natural dietary choices. "As I meditated looking into the incredibly clear water," she explained, "I suddenly understood the power of God. . . . It occurred to me clearly that along with my spiritual connection with God, I had to maintain a physical connection through eating food as close as possible to the way God made it." "Anything less than that," Salaman concluded, "was a compromise that broke my connectedness with God and Godliness."[42]

Salaman's intuitions regarding the inextricable relationship between natural foods and divine power harmonized neatly with the metaphysical underpinnings supporting much of the holistic health movement. Her staunch advocacy of holistic alternatives to conventional medicine, though, derived especially from her involvement with a specific cancer treatment, known as laetrile, that she discovered in the midst of her quest for unorthodox cancer therapies on behalf of her friend. (While laetrile technically referred to a synthetic compound, it was often used interchangeably with a closely related natural substance, amygdalin, that could be found in apricot pits and other sources.) The first seizure of laetrile by the U.S. government occurred in 1960, and in 1963 the Food and Drug Administration (FDA) rejected an application requesting approval of laetrile as a new drug, citing a lack of evidence regarding the substance's efficacy and safety. As the FDA stepped up enforcement throughout the 1960s and 1970s, the issue turned intensely personal for Salaman; the California physician she and Sweet consulted regarding the controversial treatment, John Richardson, was arrested in 1972 for continuing to administer the substance. Infuriated by Richardson's "humiliating treatment," Salaman embarked on what would become a lifelong battle against the enemies of "freedom of choice in medical care." Following on the heels of Richardson's arrest, both she and her husband, Frank Salaman, became involved with the Committee for Freedom of Choice in Cancer Therapy, ultimately renamed the Committee for Freedom of Choice in Medical Care.[43]

In a development crucial to Salaman's career and eventual visibility in holistic healing circles, the newsletter she started to spread awareness of Richardson's plight caught the attention of individuals associated with the radio station KEST in San Francisco. Soon she began hosting the *Totally Yours Show*, dedicated to providing a voice for "alternative opinion" associated with "many revolutionary breakthroughs in preventing illness and healing disease, nutrition, and weight loss and control."[44] (Though ownership of KEST had long since changed hands, the station had begun in 1925 as an outreach of Glad Tidings Temple, a pentecostal church that had hosted the meetings of early healing stalwarts such as Aimee Semple McPherson and Charles Price.)[45]

Indicative of the prominence Salaman achieved among advocates of "health freedom" as well as the broader world of holistic healing, in the early 1980s she became the president of the National Health Federation (NHF), which billed itself as the "world's oldest health-freedom organization." Detailing her work with the NHF, Salaman described her "struggle to keep the American Medical Association, the Food and Drug Administration, and the multibillion dollar pharmaceutical industry—the Unholy Trinity—from making vitamins and minerals prescription items." She also lauded the NHF's role in "stopping an Orwellian thought-police bill sponsored by the late Senator Claude Pepper" that, she argued, would have stifled freedom of choice by restricting the dissemination of information that went against the grain of mainstream scientific and medical opinion.[46] As a testament to the intensity of Salaman's resistance to any form of interference by the U.S. government in the choices of citizens, in 1984 she ran as the vice-presidential nominee of the newly formed (far right) Populist Party.[47]

While it is difficult to assess how many pentecostals and charismatics supported—or even were aware of—Salaman's political activities, by the mid-1980s her message of healing through nutrition began to reach pentecostal and charismatic audiences via her television program *Maureen Salaman's Accent on Health*. (It is likely around this time that Salaman began attending the charismatic Cathedral of Faith in San Jose, California.)[48] The program initially appeared on the California-based Family Christian Broadcasting Network, founded by the pentecostal minister Ronn Haus. Even greater exposure followed the syndication of Salaman's show on TBN beginning in the late 1980s. While Salaman's numerous books, including *Nutrition: The Cancer Answer* (1984), *Foods That Heal* (1989), *The Diet Bible* (1990), and *All Your Health Questions Answered Naturally* (1998), were marketed to audiences that extended well beyond pentecostal and charismatic circles, undoubtedly these titles found their way to more than a few of the bookshelves of pentecostals and charismatics, as more and more believers encountered the "First Lady of Nutrition."[49]

Salaman's broadsides against the medical establishment and "big pharma" notwithstanding, it is important to note that individuals who read her books encountered more than just antimedicine rage. Interspersed throughout her promotion of various nutritional and unorthodox therapies, she included numerous references to respected mainstream physicians and research studies that supported her basic conclusions regarding the importance of diet for health. That said, the sheer intensity of Salaman's frequent antimedical diatribes ensured that her message would only reach a particular subset of the pentecostal-charismatic movement. Other healers in the movement, and especially figures who appeared on the scene in the 1990s, sidestepped this limitation in important respects. In the process, these individuals—many of whom were professionals with M.D., D.O., and N.D. after their names—spread a vision of healing quite similar to Salaman's to a much larger segment of the pentecostal and charismatic population.

The timing of the emergence of professional healers in the pentecostal-charismatic movement who stressed the benefits of nature-based methodologies was no accident. By the late twentieth century, the relationship between M.D.s and their alternative counterparts had thawed considerably, and the growing appreciation of holistic methodologies among believers corresponded closely to the new-found levels of respect other alternative healers increasingly enjoyed. Of course, orthodox physicians throughout much of the twentieth century typically cast scorn on everything from osteopathy to chiropractic and naturopathy, dismissing them, in the words of a 1924 medical manual, as "medical cults" that "feed on human hope as well as on human ignorance and credulity."[50] While this ostracization provoked a variety of responses among unorthodox healers, many increased their respectability, as well as their market share in the healing marketplace, by accentuating their compatibility with mainstream science. Some alternative practitioners submitted to licensing laws requiring basic levels of training in various scientific disciplines, and others learned to distance themselves from the explicitly religious frameworks espoused by the founders of their various approaches to healing.[51]

By the late twentieth century, well-known physicians such as Andrew Weil and the surgeon Bernie Siegel symbolized the emerging dialogue between alternative healers and mainstream physicians. Weil, a Harvard-trained physician who rebelled against the medical establishment in favor of alternative medicine in the early 1970s, eventually began to advocate a form of "integrative medicine" combining the best of both worlds. In an attempt to practically implement his ideas, Weil founded the Program in Integrative Medicine at the University of Arizona in 1994 (which eventually became the Arizona Center for Integrative Medicine) with the aim of encouraging orthodox physicians to become well versed in alternative therapies so that they could direct patients to the various available holistic methodologies.[52] In his own attempt to combine standard medical training with a spiritualized approach to healing, Siegel, the author of *Love, Medicine, and Miracles*, described God in 1986 as "the same potential healing force—an intelligent, loving energy or light—in each person's life. . . . God is a resource. The energy of hope and faith is always available."[53]

The surest sign of alternative medicine's growing acceptance throughout U.S. culture in the late twentieth century was the growing willingness of mainstream physicians and governmental agencies to acknowledge the viability of some alternative methodologies. In 1991, the U.S. Senate directed the National Institutes of Health (NIH) to establish a panel (eventually referred to as the Office of Alternative Medicine [OAM]) to begin assessing the potential efficacy of various alternative practices. The Appropriations Committee only allocated $2 million toward the effort—a small fraction of the NIH's budget—but this formal recognition of alternative therapies and their potential benefits provided a new degree of legitimacy to unorthodox methods. Throughout the 1990s and into the twenty-first century the funding appropriated to the OAM steadily increased, and in 1998, the OAM became the National Center for Complementary and Alternative Medicine—the addition of the term "complementary" providing one more indication of alternative medicine's transition away from the fringes of mainstream medicine.[54]

No doubt emboldened by the increased respectability associated with alternative medicine, several pentecostal and charismatic healers emerged during the late twentieth century who, like Salaman, promoted various unorthodox therapies rooted in diet while simultaneously highlighting their scientific training and degrees. One of the earliest harbingers of the ascendancy of professional pentecostal and charismatic healers, it turns out, played a crucial role in Salaman's rise as a significant voice for healing among pentecostals and charismatics. Donald Whitaker brought the relentless campaigner for medical freedom to the attention of TBN's leadership, Paul and

Jan Crouch, through her appearance in the late 1980s as a guest on his show *Calling Dr. Whitaker*, also shown on TBN. Trained as an osteopathic physician, Whitaker advocated nutritional pathways to healing and marketed his own line of nutritional supplements.[55]

In the 1990s, several other trained physicians followed in Whitaker's footsteps and helped spread a healing gospel premised on the healing power of nature to a much larger pentecostal and charismatic audiences. A physician trained in preventative medicine, Reginald Cherry, for example, crafted a message that aligned neatly with the burgeoning popularity of alternative medicine, and, in particular, a generalized form of naturopathy tied to the use of natural foods and substances. Disseminating his ideas beginning in the 1990s through several books on biblical healing and his TBN television program *The Doctor and the Word*, Cherry, a onetime associate of Kenneth Cooper, lamented the fact that "for much of this century, merchants of 'natural' health products and practitioners of alternative therapies had been shunned by the medical community." He acknowledged there "often has been good reason for skepticism of some of the fads, the excessive claims, and the emphasis on New Age mysticism associated with health food stores" but also insisted that "no one can deny the genuine healing qualities of many natural substances." Cherry went on to describe various evidence that suggested the ameliorative impact of gingko, selenium, lycopene, and so forth on a variety of illnesses, including Alzheimer's disease, diabetes, and cancer.[56]

Indicative of Cherry's attraction to nature-based healing methods, he explained that at times that the Holy Spirit instructed him to turn from traditional medical advice and instead utilize specific dietary regimens, as opposed to surgery or medicines. When tests showed three blocked arteries in one of his middle-aged patients, for instance, Cherry acknowledged that in similar past situations he had "been led [by God's guidance] to recommend surgery for patients, and they, in fact have done very well." Nevertheless, like his patients, he did not "feel peace" about going ahead with the surgery. After praying and "petitioning God for His specific pathway of healing for this patient," he received a "unique program" given him by God for this man's condition. The regimen consisted of vitamin E to prevent fat buildup; garlic and low-dose aspirin to reduce blood clots; and "other substances such as Co Q-10" to strengthen heart contractions, combined with frequent exercise. Cherry reported that the "patient's chest pain is totally gone."[57]

Despite his stress on the power of nature to heal, Cherry did not entirely disavow his training as an M.D., and he never relinquished the benefits of a close association with the medical establishment. Natural methodologies simply functioned as valid alternatives that worked just as well as standard medical care. In his 1996 book *The Doctor and the Word*, in fact, Cherry dedicated an entire chapter to "Why a Christian *Should* See a Doctor."[58] That said, Cherry criticized the medical establishment's resistance to alternative medicine. He specifically tried to counter physicians' objection that "phytochemicals, herbal substances, and vitamins . . . 'have not been studied enough.'" In response to these claims, he pointed to the World Health Organization's statement claiming that "historic use of an herbal is a valid form of information on safety and efficacy in the absence of scientific evidence to the contrary." Cherry highlighted herbs such as saw palmetto that have "been used by Native American Indian tribes for centuries for prostate problems." Regarding the lack of double-blind placebo studies for many herbal supplements, he simply indicated that such studies often could cost over $20 million.[59] In the end, for Cherry the ideal doctor inspired by the Spirit simply knew "when and how to use modern technology or when to back away from technology to allow God to heal supernaturally." This vision of a "God-centered medical practice," constantly guided by the Holy Spirit, allowed Cherry to move comfortably between alternative methodologies, traditional approaches, and prayer for direct divine intervention on a case-by-case basis.[60]

Don Colbert, a graduate of ORU School of Medicine and author of the popular book series *The Bible Cure*, went even further than Cherry in liberally dispensing advice laden with naturopathic assumptions beginning in the late 1990s.[61] Like Cherry, Colbert never renounced his medical training, though he did consistently highlight modern medicine's limitations. In laying out his rationale for the importance of diet for dealing with various toxins and for gaining overall health, Colbert contended that "conventional medicine with its prescriptions many times cannot help. Medical specialists will have to address the root of this problem." Quoting Thomas Edison, he insisted that the "doctor of the future will give no medicine, but will interest his patients in the care of the human frame, in diet and in the cause and prevention of disease."[62]

The most telling indication of Colbert's connections with alternative medicine was his unreserved promotion of naturopathic assumptions regarding the dangers of various toxins and the need for detoxification. In classic naturopathic style, his *Toxic Relief: Restore Health and Energy through Fasting and Detoxification* spelled out the dismal state of worldly existence as humanity entered the twenty-first century: "We live in a toxic world, a toxic planet that is taking a heavy toll upon our bodies every day, whether we know it or not." In three chapters, he then enumerated a whole host of factors that made the reader wonder how humans survived in the modern world at all. Environmentally, Colbert lamented a wide variety of chemicals in the air associated with the manufacture of consumer goods: carbon monoxide, lead, ozone, and sulfuroxides, to name a few. Indoors, another set of dangers awaited: everything from mold to dust mites, formaldehyde from carpets, and the toluene from paints. He went on to detail various organophosphate pesticides used in agriculture and believed to cause memory loss, depression, anxiety, and various forms of cancer. Chlorine used to purify the water supply formed trihalomethanes, which could also lead to cancer. This was not to mention the variety of mass-produced foods overloaded with preservatives or the willfully ingested medicines such as antibiotics that could destroy the balance between good and bad bacteria in the body. For nearly twenty-three pages, Colbert listed danger after danger associated with life in modern societies.[63]

Figure 5.1 Don Colbert featured on the front cover of a 2003 issue of *Charisma*. Colbert's health advice was featured again in "God and Your Health," a January 2007 special issue of *Charisma*. Reprinted with permission from *Charisma*, November 2003 and January 2007. Copyright Charisma Media, USA. All rights reserved. www.charismamag.com.

Figure 5.1 (continued).

Like Colbert, Jordan Rubin, a popular evangelical speaker and writer who appeared before a wide variety of pentecostal and charismatic audiences, repeatedly highlighted technological "marvels" that in actuality involved negative repercussions for health.[64] Far from a modern marvel, the fact that food could "last for *decades* on a store shelf" indicated an ambush by "our technological and marketing skills." Similarly, far from being celebrated, the fact that scientists could "splice together the genes of one species into another to 'custom design' a selected end product" suggested that science was rapidly outpacing the ability of our bodies to adapt. Instead, Rubin indicated, "our bodies are still 'genetically wired' to function best on the foods favored by our ancestors." Whereas God's dietary guidelines "contain no refined or processed carbohydrates and only a very small amount of healthy sweeteners . . . the typical American diet is just the opposite." Humans had turned upside down the natural health mechanisms God put in place. As such, Americans "stray far from God's design with an array of techno-foods rich in empty calories, filled with refined carbohydrates, and woefully inadequate in nutrition." For nearly ten pages, Rubin extolled the superiority of "primitive diets" that preceded the advent of modern life, citing a naturopathic doctor who found that "a number of aboriginal, primitive societies, in Australia, Africa, and South America successfully passed into the twentieth century and enjoyed remarkably low rates of cancer, rheumatoid arthritis, obesity, diabetes, osteoporosis, heart disease, and other 'modern' conditions— *until they switched to modern diets*."[65]

Echoing themes that appeared throughout Salaman's writings, Rubin proved far less cautious than Cherry and Colbert in his criticisms of orthodox medicine. A chapter in his 2004 *Maker's Diet* titled "How to Get Sick: A Modern Prescription for Illness" highlighted the negative impact of "get[ting] all of your immunization shots," of "tak[ing] lots of medications," and of "visit[ing] your medical doctor often." "Conventional medicine sends its troops into battle against disease armed solely with surgery, pharmaceuticals, and invasive therapies (including chemotherapy and radiation)," Rubin wrote. "Anything outside the ironclad realm of a knife, a pill, or an x-ray machine is considered voodoo or worse. The genuine 'maintenance' of health is simply beyond the scope of this 'take-two-tablets-and-call-me-in-the-morning' philosophy."[66]

Rubin never suggested that his readers should totally reject orthodox medicine, yet his continual challenge to the medical establishment reflected his training background. Unlike Colbert and Cherry, Rubin stood entirely outside the medical establishment: he held a doctorate in naturopathic medicine from Peoples University of the Americas School of Natural Medicine and a Ph.D. in Nutrition from the Academy of Natural Therapies. He was also a Certified Nutritional Consultant and a member of the American Association of Nutritional Consultants.[67]

Much like Rubin, Don VerHulst, who appeared as a frequent guest on *The Jim Bakker Show*, indicated to his readers that he "embraces the naturopathic philosophy of health." According to his biography, VerHulst completed medical school but never obtained a license to practice medicine. Though careful to acknowledge that "medicine does some good," his resistance to the medical establishment shone throughout his writings. "I prefer . . . to use medicine in the form of natural remedies," he explained, "which are safer than manufactured drugs." Traditional physicians came in handy when someone "suffers a traumatic injury or is involved in an accident," but where "day-to-day health is involved . . . you'll want to apply the words of Hippocrates, the Greek physician considered the father of modern medicine: 'Let you food be your medicine and your medicine be your food.'"[68]

Despite the appeal of figures such as Rubin, VerHulst, and Salaman among many of the faithful, Cherry and Colbert's more nuanced approach to the medical establishment more accurately reflected the practical bottom line when it came to the typical believer who was interested in alternative methodologies: there is little evidence to suggest that a significant number of pentecostals and charismatics attracted to the message of natural healing intended to reject out of hand mainstream practitioners and their stress on "science-based" medicine. Instead, like many of their fellow Americans, most simply followed up their doctor's visit with a trip to their alternative practitioner.[69]

Natural Substances, Science, and the Bible

Given several prominent pentecostal and charismatic healers' naturopathic inclinations in the late twentieth and early twenty-first centuries, and their descriptions of illness as a neglect of God's natural order, it should come as no surprise that the prescriptions typically offered revolved around various therapies—often associated with diet—considered natural and unsullied by modern technology. The key difference separating pentecostal and charismatic healers from other alternative healers who stressed the intrinsic power of nature involved their repeated appeals to scriptural authority to validate their claims. Whereas naturopaths historically incoporated a divine element into their discussion of healing by stressing the close relationship between nature and a form of cosmic energy, pentecostals and charismatics often added a supernatural dimension to their healing message of nature-based healing by stressing biblical justifications for their practices. In this manner, healers often implied, if they did not always explicitly state it, God's special blessing and power accompanied the use of natural substances. Of course, Christians had been justifying all sorts of activities and decisions through references to scripture since the inception of Christianity. Building on this long tradition, pentecostal and charismatic proponents of various nature-based healing methods formulated elaborate systems linking specific biblical verses with modern understandings of vitamins and nutrition.

Salaman's *Diet Bible*, published in 1990 by McGraw-Hill, served as an early example of the genre among pentecostals and charismatics. Though the majority of the book relied on data culled from a variety of contemporary sources, in the introduction she informed the reader that specific Bible verses provided the "acorn" out of which the material in each of the chapters grew. Quoting the Living Bible, Salaman discerned support for her condemnation of junk food in the words of the biblical prophet Isaiah: "Why spend money on foodstuffs that don't give you strength? Why pay for groceries that don't do you any good?" Turning to the King James Version, she noticed a psalm condemning wicked individuals "enclosed in their own fat." "Discovering and using these pertinent verses again," Salaman wrote, "illustrates to me that the Bible covers every human situation. . . . It comes as no surprise that the Word of God deals with all aspects of human nutrition and even supplies guideposts for stabilizing and losing weight."[70]

Whereas Salaman at times portrayed the Bible as the ultimate vindication of her crusade against the medical establishment, asserting that "the Bible goes against the weight of scientific and medical opinion," the abundant references to medical and scientific authorities in her books suggested a much more ambivalent relationship with traditional medicine.[71] Regardless, the majority of Salaman's successors in the pentecostal-charismatic movement certainly took a much less adversarial position; whenever possible, they seemed more inclined to highlight the correspondence between naturopathic-style assumptions and the best scientific and medical studies.

For instance, Cherry's claims closely mirrored Salaman's perspective insofar as he insisted that the nature-based healing principles he advocated derived from "deciphering the ancient Hebrew dietary laws, understanding how Jesus anointed natural substances to heal, and how we can pray specifically for healing and overcoming the mountain of our illness." These insights, he taught, led to cures for everything from cancer to fatigue, genetic defects, and "even the annoyances of allergies."[72] Quite unlike Salaman's statement above, however, Cherry consistently stressed the close correspondence between the biblical record and medical and scientific research.

Exemplary of Cherry's approach, he attempted to correlate modern-day research on fat with biblical dietary restrictions. In his 1998 book *The Bible Cure*, Cherry quoted the Amplified Bible's rendering of Leviticus 3:17: "Say to the Israelites, You shall eat no kind of fat, of ox, or sheep, or goat. The fat of the beast that dies of itself, and the fat of one that is torn with beasts, may be put to any other use, but under no circumstances are you to eat of it." According to Cherry's interpretation of the text, he concluded that verses such as these not only warned against the dangers of eating too much fat but also anticipated modern science by restricting foods with high levels of saturated fats. Other verses, he claimed, in turn promoted foods high in monounsaturated fats that boost high-density lipoprotein (HDL or "good cholesterol") levels. Cherry's conclusion? "Thousands of years before we had any knowledge of LDL and HDL cholesterol, the Bible cure indicated that certain foods, including meats, could be eaten, giving specific health benefits to our bodies and lifestyles."[73]

Colbert's writings similarly brimmed with simultaneous appeals to science and the Bible. A glance at the table of contents for his 2002 book *What Would Jesus Eat?*, which attracted national attention, illuminates his basic approach: "The Food That Jesus Ate Most Often"; "A Staple in Jesus's Diet"; "The Meats That Jesus Ate"; "The Vegetables That Jesus Ate"; "Did Jesus Exercise?" (Apparently,

Jesus even identified with Americans' chronic struggle with weight. In chapter 11, the reader learned how to use the "Foods Jesus Ate to Lose Weight.") In an effort to determine what in fact Jesus ate, Colbert drew on specific references Jesus made to food, on prescriptions in the Jewish law that Jesus likely abided by, and on current knowledge regarding the typical "Mediterranean diet" prevalent during Jesus's lifetime. As the reader continued into the heart of the book, it also quickly became evident that according to Colbert, Jesus's diet had been validated by recent science. "The medical and scientific facts confirm it," he wrote. "If we eat as Jesus ate, we will be healthier."[74] The message throughout was clear: the modern diet and lifestyle drove humans away from the natural, life-giving patterns of diet and exercise prescribed by God and modeled by Jesus. Subtract Jesus from the equation, and a naturopath could not have said it better.

Colbert's books also sought to establish biblical precedent for the naturopathic stress on "detoxifying" the body—a theme implicit in *What Would Jesus Eat?* but addressed more directly in Colbert's other works. Here, Colbert tacked back and forth between the language of physical detoxification stressed by naturopaths and the more traditional Christian focus on a spiritual "detoxification" achieved through fasting. Regarding fasting, Colbert dedicated a third of his book *Toxic Relief* to specific types of fasts for "detoxing your whole person" modeled by various biblical figures such as Daniel and Esther. Most of the book, however, offered up standard naturopathic fare, stressing the power of diet and fasting to "cleanse your body from years of accumulated toxins and their effects" and to "support your body's own elaborate system of detoxification." In juxtaposing biblical fasting with nutritional research in this manner, Colbert promoted "detoxification" as a route to physical and spiritual purity backed by the twin authorities of science and the Bible.[75]

Like Colbert and Cherry, Rubin insisted that his claims carried scientific and biblical guarantees. In his *New York Times* best seller he offered readers the "Maker's Diet" as revealed in scripture. At the same time, Rubin stressed the fact that "much of the information you are about to read has been confirmed by numerous double-blind, placebo-controlled, scientific studies conducted over many years as well as by thousands of years of history." Rubin highlighted "healing foods" mentioned in the Bible, including fish, barley, wheat, olive oil, figs, grapes, berries, soups, and honey, among others. He also identified twenty-one healing herbs and fourteen healing oils—all of which were mentioned in scripture. (Unlike Cherry, Rubin never detected biblical evidence for restrictions on saturated fat. "Contrary to the myth, perpetuated since the late 1950s, supposedly linking saturated fat and dietary cholesterol with coronary heart diease," he wrote, "many saturated fats are actually good for you!") Like alternative healers more generally, Rubin pinpointed numerous strategies beyond diet that offered God-ordained means for health. He linked hydrotherapy and music therapy to various biblical examples and emphasized the importance of managing stress by controlling negative thoughts and of taking enough time to rest and exercise. In addition to the multitudinous biblical references, Rubin interspersed throughout references to research studies that reinforced insights he found in the biblical text. Sometimes these references were drawn from sources associated with traditional medicine, such as the *New England Journal of Medicine* and the *Journal of the American Medical Association*, and at other times they were drawn from sources written for alternative physicians and their patients, for example the *Townsend Letter for Doctors and Patients* and the *Encyclopedia of Natural Medicine.*[76]

Others joined Salaman, Cherry, Colbert, and Rubin in stressing biblical affirmations of alternative methodologies. According to VerHulst, the Bible represented "absolutely the most current, most accurate text on every subject—including physiology and all the sciences." Believers could rest assured that "every divine principle Scripture has stated about physical health and healing is steadfastly accurate." Conversely, in the "academic arena . . . the exact opposite is the case," considering the fact that "medical advice changes all the time."[77] The promotional materials for Ted Broer, who was endorsed by charismatic ministers such as Benny Hinn and Rod Parsley, proclaimed that individuals who listened to his teachings would "find out what the Bible really teaches about optimal health and the secrets of scriptural nutrition."[78]

Judging from the popularity of charismatic healers influenced by naturopathic philosophies and convinced of nature's healing power, their approach to healing struck a responsive chord among the faithful. Due in no small part to these health evangelists' ability to connect alternative forms of healing with the Bible, numerous believers bought into the message of God-ordained forms of natural healing. Figures such as Cherry, Colbert, and Rubin appeared frequently in the pages of *Charisma* and on popular Christian television ranging from Kenneth Copeland's *Believer's Voice of Victory* to Benny Hinn's *This Is Your Day!* and *The Jim Bakker Show*. High-profile charismatic leaders, including Joyce Meyer and John Hagee, similarly promoted some of these authors in their ministry magazines and periodicals. This is not to mention the television programs hosted by these healers. In addition to those hosted by Salaman and Whitaker, TBN also eventually broadcast Cherry's *Doctor and the Word* and Rubin's *Great Physician's Rx for Health and Wellness*.

In the end, by seeking out a divine stamp of approval for more natural approaches to healing, innovative healers in the pentecostal-charismatic movement did not entirely abandon distinctions between supernatural and natural healing. Colbert, for example, speaking of his relationship with Benny Hinn, whose healing crusades featured more traditional forms of divine healing and built on the legacy of the midcentury deliverance evangelists, distinguished between the overt supernatural cures offered by Hinn and more mundane prescriptions. Colbert insisted that many of the individuals who waited "in line for five hours" at Hinn's meetings could avoid that wait if they simply "would take 10 minutes a day and walk around their block." A profile of Colbert in *Charisma* summarized his understanding of divine healing: "not as many Christians would need God's supernatural healing touch if they would learn to live according to His principles for divine health."[79]

If the inclination to distinguish natural and supernatural pathways to healing did not disappear entirely in the writings of healers promoting naturopathic-style forms of healing in the pentecostal-charismatic movement, in other ways the wall separating the two approaches proved quite permeable. In their efforts to connect natural healing methodologies to divine sources of authority, prominent healers discovered more than just divine approval for their healing programs. By promoting the "Diet Bible," "Bible cures," and the "Maker's Diet," figures such as Salaman, Cherry, Colbert, and Rubin cultivated—even as they capitalized on it—a metaphysical-like confidence in all things natural that circulated widely throughout U.S. culture in the later decades of the twentieth century, and that animated other alternative healers as well.

The Commodification of Pentecostal and Charismatic Healing

Pentecostal and charismatic healers' embrace of nature-based forms of healing as God's form of healing represented a logical next step building on Roberts's vision to merge natural and supernatural healing. (Not coincidentally, Salaman received an honorary doctorate from ORU.) At the same time, the promotion of natural healing methods also opened the door for significant commodification of healing in the pentecostal-charismatic movement, as pentecostals' and charismatics' willingness to combine divine healing with medical and especially dietary regimens made the healing process more predictable and therefore more marketable.

Pentecostals, to be sure, evidenced an entrepreneurial spirit from the pentecostal movement's inception. Early believers hawked everything from Christian Hero books to Precious Promise Boxes and "The Leak-Proof Wigglesworth Anointing Bottle." The flamboyant pentecostal evangelist Aimee Semple McPherson even attempted to sell burial plots next to her own using the advertising slogan "Go Up with Aimee!"[80] Observers also have highlighted the parallel between the saints' emphasis on divine healing and a U.S. therapeutic culture increasingly drawn to a "plethora of products for enhancing bodily presentation."[81]

A key distinction separating early pentecostals' entrepreneurial ways from that of their successors lay in later pentecostals' and charismatics' new-found ability to explicitly commodify divine healing. Unlike their predecessors, pentecostals and charismatics in the later decades of the twentieth century developed their own tangible healing products that directly competed for the billions of dollars Americans spent each year on health and fitness. Previous pentecostal and charismatic healers certainly implied (and in some cases even explicitly stated) at times that financial gifts would lead to healing. Leaders in the Word of Faith wing of the pentecostal-charismatic movement in particular frequently emphasized the importance of "seed-faith" (which was frequently associated with monetary donations and tithing), which resulted in every sort of blessing for the giver, including healing.[82] It also can be argued that healing throughout the movement's entire history reflected a consumer mentality and at least some semblance of an economic transaction: in exchange for their faith, adherents confidently expected to receive healing in return. Never before, though, had an economic model taken such a concrete form. The traditional emphasis on faith healing by no means disappeared in the movement, yet increasingly, a healthy dose of money was needed to supplement one's faith.

In large part, Salaman, Whitaker, Cherry, Colbert, and Rubin served as some of the most prominent healers spearheading the commodification of healing in the pentecostal-charismatic movement. These healers' promotion of natural healing substances in conjunction with divine healing paved the way for entire lines of natural supplements that dovetailed with the insights that they gleaned from scripture. Beginning in the early 1990s Salaman joined with the osteopathic physician Ross Gordon to develop the supplement MineralRich, while Whitaker promoted "Dr. Whitaker's Vitamins."[83] In the next decade, Cherry, Colbert, and Rubin discovered that they, too, could cash in on their message regarding divinely ordained natural healing pathways. Assuring his customers of his dedication to help them "stay healthy so they can go forth and tell others about Jesus," in 2006 Cherry offered products ranging from $15.95 for a one-month supply of "Digestion Support" tablets to $49.95 for a one-month supply of "Basic Nutrient Support." (Men in need of "Potency Support" could obtain a month's supply for $39.95.)[84] Likewise, the incorporation of predictable, science-based remedies alongside spiritual healing allowed Don Colbert to sell not only a lot of books but also a lot of his "Divine Health Nutritional Products." According to his website, his company received over 5.2 million online requests for his products in a little over a year and a half beginning in 2007.[85] Jordan Rubin's combination of biblical and scientific prescriptions similarly created predictable pathways to healing based on the use of natural substances, and he, too, parlayed these pathways into his own nutritional supplement company, Garden of Life, Inc., based out of West Palm Beach, Florida. Popular supplements such as "Primal Defense," "Virgin Coconut Oil," and "FYI (For Your Inflammation)" fueled the rapid expansion of the business. As an indication of Rubin's success, sales in 2003 alone reached $43.2 million, and in 2004 a mainstream financial publication listed Garden of Life as the fifth fastest growing company in the United States.[86]

Other prominent leaders also profited from the late-twentieth-century changes in pentecostal and charismatic healing, though with less concern for linking the use of their products to biblical precedents. Lee Haney, who hosted a fitness program on TBN, combined his message of health and well-being with a line of nutritional products dubbed "Lee Haney's Nutritional Support Systems." Sold at GNC stores around the nation, Haney's products ranged from the more typical multivitamins to "Competitive Nitro," designed to "enhance the muscles ability to retain Nitrogen for muscle growth" and protein blends geared toward building muscle. "It has been said, 'knowledge is power,'" he wrote on his website. "If you believe that statement, then 'We've Got The Power to Empower You.' (II Samuel 22:33)."[87] Along the same lines, the Southern Baptist charismatic Pat Robertson, often better known for his forays into politics, as opposed to his involvement in health and healing in the pentecostal-charismatic movement, created a diet shake that was eventually marketed by GNC.[88] Randy and Paula White, the nationally recognized charismatic pastors of the 26,000-member Without Walls International Church in Tampa, Florida, promoted the dietary supplement Omega XL prior to their divorce in 2007. A combination of "marine sterols and lipid fractions," Omega XL was billed by its producers as the "the most effective delivery system that assists in treating inflammatory disorders by inhibiting the 5-lipoxygenase pathway." A thirty-minute infomercial for this product aired in approximately 150 markets via stations that typically carried religious programming.[89] Not to be outdone, the charismatic televangelist James Robison promoted vitamins on behalf of Tri-Vita, Inc.[90]

Despite their prominence, pentecostals and charismatics were not the only conservative Christians profiting from the sale of nutritional supplements by the turn of the twenty-first century, nor was this the first instance of evangelicals peddling healing products whose efficacy was premised on a metaphysical-like confidence in the healing power of nature. Dating back to the early 1700s, German Pietists based out of Halle developed a thriving pharmaceutical trade network that extended all the way to North America. Indicative of the metaphysical inclinations that helped underwrite this eighteenth-century business, the most popular medication, a tincture of gold labeled "essentia dulcis," sold briskly even as its use attracted criticism from the medical and religious establishment due to its "alchemical genealogy" and connections to Paracelsian mysticism.[91] To a significant degree, the commodification of healing by pentecostals and fellow evangelicals, as well as their stress on God-ordained natural pathways to health, represented a revival of these earlier Pietist practices. One key difference remained, however: the dramatic before-and-after photos and the frequent discussions of weight loss, not to mention the beautiful, fit, toned bodies of the healers themselves, confirmed the fact that late-twentieth and early-twenty-first-century healers offered their customers much more than just dietary treatment for specific ailments. Building on the efforts of weight-loss gurus in the pentecostal-charismatic movement beginning in the 1970s, professionally trained healers who stressed the importance of diet also frequently promised their customers levels of physical beauty and perfection that far exceeded the kind of promises made by evangelical healers of previous generations.

The Evangelicalization of Pentecostal and Charismatic Healing?

While it became harder and harder for individuals to avoid exposure to the metaphysically friendly forms of dietary healing circulating in the pentecostal-charismatic movement by the turn of the twenty-first century, certainly not all pentecostals or charismatics bought into nature-based forms of healing or were thrilled with the stress on physical perfection that frequently accompanied their fellow believers' focus on dietary healing. Lisa Bevere's 1998 book on the subject of diet and weight loss, for instance, stood apart for its strong criticism of the unrealistic body type portrayed in the U.S. diet and fitness culture that "is never what we are and is always just beyond our reach." Instead, when the Spirit spoke to Bevere, she heard a voice say: "If you'll repent, I will heal your metabolism. Do not diet, and do not weigh yourself. . . . I will teach you how to eat again. Write down the weight you should be, and put it in your Bible."[92] Linda Mintle, a popular speaker and author with strong ties to the pentecostal-charismatic movement who disseminated her views well beyond just pentecostal and charismatic audiences, similarly combated unrealistic body expectations in her books, including *Breaking Free from a Negative Self-Image* and *Making Peace with Your Thighs: Get Off the Scales and Get On with Your Life*.[93] Criticisms such as Bevere and Mintle's notwithstanding, by the end of the twentieth century, numerous pentecostals and charismatics had embarked on the quest for the perfect, spirit-empowered body.

The explicit "naturalization" and commodification of healing in the pentecostal-charismatic movement in the late twentieth and early twenty-first centuries raises important questions regarding pentecostals' evolving relationship with fellow evangelicals. To what extent should the various adaptations of the U.S. diet culture among pentecostals and charismatics be read as an example of "evangelicalization," wherein adherents shed their distinctive stress on spiritual warfare in the broader evangelical world and in U.S. society more generally? Had pentecostals and charismatics struck a Faustian bargain of sorts, sacrificing the soul of pentecostal healing at the altar of mainstream Christian success?

For several late-twentieth-century ministers who discussed the power of dietary healing and weight loss, acculturation proved a far too simplistic explanation of pentecostals' and charismatics' attraction to modified notions of healing;

many perpetuated the inclination evident among earlier proponents of God-ordained weight loss in the 1970s and 1980s to juxtapose more traditional language regarding the activities of supernatural powers right alongside more naturalized notions of dietary healing. Marty Copeland, the daughter-in-law of Word of Faith leader Kenneth Copeland, for instance, transposed the language of spiritual warfare into a new key while retaining discussion of direct spiritual conflict. In a description of her renewed battle with unhealthy habits following one of her pregnancies, she recounted her initial fitness breakthrough using the terminology of spiritual warfare. "Did God set me free seven years ago [when she initially gained control of her weight and fitness problems]?" she asked her readers. "Yes. Did I receive deliverance from overeating? Yes. Have I enjoyed freedom from the bondage of weight, and kept my weight at a very healthy weight? Yes. Was I experiencing complete control over my eating, and in the best shape of my life? Yes, for all these years." Significantly, Satan by no means had disappeared from the scene. "When you let your shield of faith down," she warned, "Satan comes immediately to steal the Word. Whatever areas you were weak in, that's where he'll try to tempt you." "We must be mindful of the devil's tactics," she continued, "and keep our spirits and our mouths full of His words—even when we don't feel like it. . . . All I had to do was repent, get back in prayer, back in the Word, and sow to the spirit with my eating and exercise, and I was on my way!" For Copeland, Satan still lurked in the shadows as a menacing presence, even though her utilization of the language of spiritual warfare at times looked very different from its more traditional antecedents among pentecostals and charismatics.[94]

Explicit references to the highly spiritualized framework so familiar to pentecostal and charismatic audiences also continued unabated in references to dietary healing and weight loss made by high-profile figures such as T. D. Jakes and Joyce Meyer—individuals whose ministries flourished as the pentecostal-charismatic movement headed into the twenty-first century. As with previous pentecostal leaders, Jakes explicitly cast his struggle for health as a war against satanic forces. He detailed his father's losing battle with weight and its devastating consequences for his father's health. "Twenty-two years later, I found myself at a similar age fighting a similar challenge," he wrote. "It was as if Satan had left our family for a season and then returned for the next generation. The devil thought he was going to get a fresh harvest of Jakes' blood." Drawing on a familiar discourse among pentecostal and charismatic adherents regarding generational curses and generational spirits that afflict entire families, Jakes concluded that Satan took aim at his family utilizing the weapon of food and weight. "Satan could have at least used a new demon," Jakes explained. "But no, he used that same demon that attacked my dad. It was then that I realized every man has got to fight his father's enemy—in one form or another. We all must fight the spirits that have been assigned to our families."[95]

Similarly, though much of Joyce Meyer's advice drew on recurring themes in mainstream weight-loss programs—including the importance of recognizing how one can turn to food to satisfy emotional deprivations, and of choosing a balanced diet coupled with exercise—she also taught her readers the importance of listening directly to God's voice for guidance pertaining to their unique dieting situation. "Seek God to discover the particular course of action He wants *you* to take," she instructed. "The Lord may tell one person to fast, as He did with me at one point for a particular reason, but He may not want *you* to fast when you begin changing your eating habits. The Lord will guide you in the way most effective for you." This personalized guidance extended to the smallest details regarding a person's choices. "If [the Holy Spirit] leads you one day to eat a bowl of cereal for breakfast instead of half a grapefruit and toast, or an occasional small piece of pie after a satisfying dinner," she added, "do it." By listening to the Holy Spirit and "spending time with God before each meal and listening to Him before we start eating," Christians could bring their habits under control.[96]

LaVita Weaver provided very similar advice to her readers in 2004. "When you sit down and eat," she instructed, "bless your food, pray, and ask the Holy Spirit of God to lead you in your eating." If believers listened carefully enough, they would recognize when the Spirit indicated "'You know you have had enough,' or 'That's too much.'"[97]

Copeland, Jakes, Meyer, and Weaver's comments corresponded neatly with other developments in the pentecostal-charismatic movement that also pointed to spiritual warfare's staying power. The popular novels by the Assemblies of God minister-turned-author Frank Peretti, for instance, first published in the mid-1980s, revolved around spiritual warfare.[98] Shortly thereafter, Peter Wagner, a professor at Fuller Theological Seminary, wrote a series of books distributed widely among pentecostals and charismatics teaching believers how to map out the domains of specific types of demons over specific regions of the world, which in turn would enhance the effectiveness of their prayers.[99] As the writings of Wagner and Peretti suggest, fascination with demons was still alive and well for many adherents during the late twentieth and early twenty-first centuries.

Despite these trends, for at least some figures connected to healing in the pentecostal-charismatic movement, dramatic encounters with spiritual powers moved decidedly into the background as they learned to apply the traditional pentecostal language of spiritual warfare to weight and toxic chemicals without mentioning angels, demons, or the like. In fact, by the turn of the twenty-first century, more and more space in the healing manuals published by various pentecostal and charismatic diet gurus was dedicated simply to disseminating the basic insights garnered from modern nutritional science.

Pamela Smith's columns written for *Charisma* during the 1990s illustrate the growing tendency among at least some pentecostals and charismatics to omit the language of spiritual warfare or explicitly supernatural references in their discourse. For Smith, who worked with NBA athletes and with Hyatt Hotels and Resorts, deliverance equaled a release "from the dieting mind-set and embarking on a lifestyle of health." In one typical article on diet, she pointed to studies highlighting the role of vegetables in reducing the risk of diseases, particularly cancer. She then recommended that her readers buy locally grown, colorful produce that was "as fresh as possible" and directed them to steam, microwave, stir-fry, or pressure cook them in order to preserve their nutritional content. The only religious reference in the column occurred in the last sentence, when she encouraged readers to "read Daniel 1 for inspiration." As in much of her writing for *Charisma*, no references were made to demonic powers or spiritual warfare.[100]

Kara Davis sounded identical themes in her book *Spiritual Secrets to Weight Loss*. Like Smith, Davis incorporated the language of deliverance to describe believers' battle with unhealthy foods. "Instead of cutting calories and restricting or eliminating those foods that contribute to poor health," she instructed, "a food addict craves them, never associating them with bondage to illness, medications and hospitalizations." "The solution to any addiction," she concluded, "is deliverance."[101] That Davis was intent on downplaying the more traditional notions of spiritual warfare in the pentecostal-charismatic movement became apparent in her discussion of the importance of fasting. Insisting that "any Christian who is trying to lose weight must make fasting and prayer regular practices for life," she related the story of Jesus's healing of a demon-possessed boy recounted in Mark. When Jesus's disciples asked him why they were unable to cast the spirit out of the boy, he responded: "This kind cannot be driven out by anything but prayer and fasting." In her rendition of the story, however, Davis specifically elided the demonic aspects of the biblical account. In the biblical text, the boy's father told Jesus and his disciples that his son had "a spirit that makes him unable to speak; and whenever it seizes him, it dashes him down; and he foams and grinds his teeth and becomes rigid." The father specifically requested that Jesus cast the demon out of the boy. Davis simply indicated that that the father "knelt before Christ and asked that He heal his son." "The man described the illness and added that Jesus's other disciples had tried," Davis continued, "but they were unable to heal the boy. Jesus then healed the child in the presence of His disciples."[102]

Davis's careful substitution of the language of healing for the more specific language of exorcism freed her to apply Jesus's words regarding the power of fasting to weight loss and not simply to demonic possession, yet it also signaled the growing tendency among some pentecostal and charismatic writers to moderate the traditional emphasis in the pentecostal-charismatic movement on spiritual warfare. When figures such as Colbert and Rubin described a world full of dangerous chemicals and touted the importance of detoxification, they transposed early believers' vision of a world contaminated by evil spirits into a naturopathic key, describing a world contaminated instead by toxins. More than just exorcism, the world was in desperate need of natural cleansing. A similar trend could be seen among proponents of inner healing who frequently psychologized human behavior that previous generations labeled as sinful and demonic. Along these lines, David Hazard informed *Charisma* readers that ministers in the past would have "cast a 'demon of irresponsibility'" out of a husband who was not fulfilling his role as a spouse. "In 1986, we pray him through a series of images."[103]

One of the main consequences of various adherents' willingness to downplay the role of the demonic and the like in the healing process was to draw believers much closer to fellow evangelicals. While several figures stressed spiritual warfare more than their nonpentecostal, noncharismatic counterparts, overall much of the advice doled out regarding dietary healing differed little from the advice found in materials produced by other successful Christian conservatives promoting dietary healing, for example Gwen Shamblin, and George Malkmus.[104] One clear sign of the close relationship between the broader evangelical diet culture and pentecostals' and charismatics' similar participation in these themes could be seen in a *Charisma* article that provided a largely positive overview of the various Christian weight-loss programs prominent during the 1990s. Though authors such as the charismatic pastor T. D. Jakes were highlighted, many nonpentecostals and noncharismatics, including Shamblin, were discussed as well.[105] Along similar lines, Malkmus, a former Southern Baptist minister, found significant success marketing his vegan-based "Hallelujah Diet" among charismatics; he established a relationship with the Oasis of Hope Cancer Hospital in Tijuana, Mexico, for instance, which was directed by Ernesto and Francisco Contreras, who had strong ties to the charismatic movement.[106]

The parallels between the pentecostal and charismatic diet culture and other evangelicals' appropriation of similar trends was so strong, in fact, that it sometimes proved difficult to discern which particular group healers belonged to. Jordan Rubin serves as a case in point. Rubin appeared to fit squarely in the pentecostal and charismatic camp. His *New York Times* best seller *The Maker's Diet* was published by the charismatic press Siloam, an imprint of Charisma Media, and TBN aired his television program. An article in *Charisma* confirmed the fact that his diet had been "promoted heavily among charismatics," listing several ministers who endorsed his work, including Paula White, Richard and Lindsey Roberts, Paul Morton, Ted Haggard, Kenneth Copeland, and Jentezen Franklin. "There is so much excitement among charismatics about this message," Rubin indicated. "They are so open to healing." But Rubin's use of the third person hinted that he did not fully identify with the pentecostal-charismatic movement, despite the close ties, and the article simply noted his Messianic Jewish upbringing and previous participation in a Baptist youth group. He certainly did not restrict his message to pentecostal and charismatic audiences. The well-known Southern Baptist pastor Charles Stanley, for example, invited Rubin to serve as his personal nutritionist and discuss the diet with his 200-plus staff in Atlanta. Stanley also wrote the introduction to *The Maker's Diet*.[107]

The varying degrees of emphasis that pentecostals and charismatics placed on the continued importance of overt supernatural intervention relative to natural forms of healing and weight loss highlights the dangers of any one-size-fits-all explanation of the development of late-twentieth-century dietary healing in the pentecostal-charismatic movement, or its relationship to the wider evangelical world. At least a few figures in the pentecostal-charismatic movement from the 1990s seemed more comfortable battling metaphorical inner demons, as opposed to the vivid supernatural powers their forebears confronted. For others, the decided deemphasis on spiritual warfare likely reflected a pragmatic distinction between a "public transcript" revealed to outsiders and a more supernaturalized "hidden transcript" that challenged naturalistic assumptions prevalent in U.S. society and was primarily employed only in the company of fellow believers. In this regard, pentecostals' and charismatics' desire to expand their potential market would have provided significant motivation to shy away from explicit references to supernatural beings and powers when presenting their message to the broader public.[108] A final, third group never wavered in their commitment to a distinctly pentecostal and charismatic niche market. For these individuals, while the language of spiritual warfare was broadened to encompass the war against toxins, calories, untoned bodies, and even psychological hangups, spiritual forces still emerged as powerful players in the healing process.

For all the differences separating the major exemplars of the pentecostal and charismatic diet culture at the turn of the twenty-first century, significant commonalities remained. Even those healers who evidenced the most thorough substitution of nutritional science for dramatic divine healing and moved believers closest to the evangelical mainstream nevertheless built on deeply ingrained holiness proclivities that had always linked pentecostals with their evangelical brethren. All of the participants in the pentecostal and charismatic diet culture reinforced the pentecostal movement's ascetic roots and could affirm Kara Davis's admonishment to adherents who assumed that God was "Jehovah Rapha" (The Lord My Healer) yet missed the conditional nature of God's promise to keep his people in health. "When God identified Himself as Jehovah Rapha and assured us of protection from disease," she wrote, "it was under the conditions that His children separate themselves from worldliness. The promise made at Marah was a conditional agreement, with protection from disease contingent upon steadfast obedience to God. My point is this: If we expect God to respond to our infirmities as Jehovah Rapha, the least we should do is keep our part of the agreement."[109] By emphasizing the importance of disciplining the flesh, all of the participants in the pentecostal and charismatic diet culture harkened back to themes long resonant in the early pentecostal movement.

All of the participants in the pentecostal and charismatic diet culture also built on pentecostals' long-standing embrace of a Wesleyan theology regarding the Spirit's direct interaction with and transformation of the body. Early pentecostals—and indeed Wesley himself—would not have approved of believers' growing preoccupation with their physical appearance (much less the ostentatious lifestyles or the conspicuous consumption advocated by Word of Faith ministers), yet the avid pursuit of beautiful, fit bodies functioned as a radicalized form of Wesley's teachings regarding the material manifestations of the Spirit's activity. Indicative of the strengthening metaphysical impulse in the pentecostal-charismatic movement that blurred distinctions between material and supernatural realms, believers' bodies functioned as never before as an index of the operation of the Spirit, making spiritual perfection visible in the natural realm.

Perhaps the most obvious common denominator linking the various participants in the pentecostal and charismatic diet culture involved the way each recast healing to a significant degree as a predictable, commodifiable process. Those looking for divine sanction as they purchased nutritional supplements, organic foods, or the latest dietary guides learned that they could find that sanction in abundant supply in the Bible itself (though it helped to have one of the healer's guidebooks nearby).

The commodification of healing in the pentecostal-charismatic movement did more than just place a spiritual stamp of approval on U.S. consumer culture, however.[110] Modern advertisers have long understood the power of products to signify to the buyer concepts, emotions, and status in ways that go well beyond the merchandise's stated functions and contents.[111] Specifically for individuals with pentecostal backgrounds, those who bought into the ubiquitous U.S. diet culture—whether through the actual purchase of supplements and the like or through a more general pursuit of the perfect body—also discovered a fruitful medium for affirming their new-found socioeconomic status in a manner that nevertheless recalled the familiar cadences of the movement's past.

In many respects, the trajectory of pentecostal healing in the late twentieth and early twenty-first centuries mirrored the history of modern U.S. holidays such as Christmas. A historian has noted how simplistic narratives that are fixated on the steady encroachment of rationalizing, secularizing forces associated with consumer capitalism miss the various ways the marketplace simultaneously became a "realm of religious enchantment."[112] In much the same way, as a significant number of pentecostals and charismatics adopted healing methodologies steeped in metaphysical assumptions regarding the healing power of nature, they accommodated U.S. consumer culture to a very significant degree, but they also insisted on a spiritually infused form of materialism that affirmed their identity as people of the Spirit. The repackaged forms of divine healing allowed believers to take on a dual identity of sorts: the faithful were free to consume healing practices in tune with materialist, scientific currents in the United States while maintaining their sense of connection to a readily accessible spiritual reality. Purists undoubtedly lamented the compromise at work, as the traditional healing emphasis on faith often took a backseat to more mundane choices. At the same time, those willing to reconfigure the healing formula passed down from generations past carved out a place in mainstream U.S. culture that hardly could have been more secure.

Conclusion

*Pentecostal Healing in the Late Twentieth and Early
Twenty-First Centuries*

In an early chapter of his 1986 supernatural thriller *This Present Darkness*, Frank Peretti described an encounter between the reigning evil spirits of the fictional town of Ashton and a much more powerful demon who arrived to take command. The scene unfolded with a demon of complacency descending into the basement of a building where other evil spirits in Ashton were meeting to plot their infiltration of the city. The building itself proved a fitting meeting place for its occupants, a "dismal nether world" with a "low and oppressive" ceiling and "water pipes and heat ducts that seemed like so many huge snakes waiting to drop." Conveniently enough, the demons met in a conference room at the end of a hall, which Peretti described as a veritable "cauldron of living evil." "The room was dark," he wrote, "but the darkness seemed more of a presence than a physical condition. . . . Out of that darkness glared many pairs of dull yellow cat-eyes belonging to a horrible gallery of grotesque [demonic] faces."[1]

This demonic brainstorming session did not occur in just any building or in just any conference room in the fictional town of Ashton. It took place in a building on the local university campus "set aside for administration and the private offices of the Psychology Department."[2] In case Peretti's readers missed the point, a psychology professor in the department worked to promote "Eastern religions" and New Age teachings in her classes and therapy sessions even as she served as the main ringleader of a demonically inspired group of elite power brokers in the city.

By linking psychotherapy and the New Age to purely evil spiritual forces, Peretti reflected the deeply ingrained wariness toward mental forms of healing and toward the metaphysical underpinnings of New Age spirituality that persisted among pentecostals and charismatics as the pentecostal-charismatic movement headed toward the twenty-first century. Sales of Peretti's book eventually reached over 2.5 million copies, serving as a stark reminder that not all pentecostals and charismatics were comfortable with the changing landscape of pentecostal and charismatic healing over the course of the twentieth century. (Doubtless, numerous others simply lacked the motivation or the inclination to implement the type of wholesale lifestyle changes promoted by some of the most prominent healers.) Though "psychologized" forms of divine healing provoked the most opposition, resistance flared up at times as adherents questioned the metaphysical assumptions shaping other popular healing practices in the United States that were embraced by various pentecostal and charismatic leaders. One charismatic mother, for instance, discussed her research into the importance of diet for health in 1979 after she and her husband "felt that the Lord wanted us to explore nutrition more seriously." As they moved forward, they were uneasy about the non-Christian influences shaping some of the literature on diet and health. The "occult overtones often associated with health foods" and the health "authorities'" connections to "yoga, astrology, TM, or other occult practices" dismayed her. The realization then hit her that "a Christian's perspective about health food had to be different from the world's."[3]

Similar anxieties continued to appear into the early twenty-first century. A January 2003 article in *Charisma* highlighted the spiritual darkness associated with New Age religions, specifically mentioning their promotion of "holistic medicine." Though the article keyed in on the use of crystals and spirit guides, it also drew attention to mainstream physicians in Australia who worried about the appeal of unorthodox methodologies more generally. In one case, a young boy died after his parents "denied him palliative care because they believed an alternative treatment would cure him," while another boy died of cancer when his parents stopped chemotherapy "in favor of a natural remedy."[4] At the turn of the twenty-first century, many saints remained leery of any affirmations of the New Age movement or anything remotely related to it.

The Metaphysical Turn in Pentecostal Healing

For all the religious boundary-maintenance evidenced by pentecostals' and charismatics' vigilant attacks on their New Age rivals, however, such efforts did little to prevent believers' cultivation of their own versions of metaphysical-style healing—albeit versions baptized in biblical waters and premised on the ubiquitous power of the Holy Spirit. Attentive readers of the January 2003 issue of *Charisma* that disparaged "natural remedies" may have picked up on this deep-seated ambivalence: shortly after reading the condemnations of holistic medicine, they encountered a column written by Francisco Contreras, a regular contributor to the periodical, highlighting his cancer care facility in Tijuana, "widely known for alternative-treatment methods."[5] The medical clinic, dubbed the "Oasis of Hope," was begun by Contreras's father, Ernesto Contreras, and attracted a significant U.S. clientele beginning in the 1960s due in large part to this physician's willingness to administer laetrile and other alternative cancer treatments just as the state of California and the FDA cracked down on distribution of laetrile. (Not surprisingly, Maureen Salaman developed a close friendship with the Contreras family.)[6] While open to the potential value of chemotherapy, Contreras targeted individuals who "express a preference for integrative cancer treatment approaches," including natural, diet-based regimens, or whose cancer proved "inherently resistant to conventional cancer treatments."[7] As Contreras's formal relationship with *Charisma* indicated, numerous indicators in the pentecostal-charismatic movement at the turn of the twentieth century suggested increasing acceptance, not rejection, of holistic methodologies.

Jordan Rubin's comments to the *New York Times* in 2005 likewise signaled the warm reception he and other naturopathic healers in the pentecostal-charismatic movement increasingly enjoyed. Describing the opposition to alternative healing methodologies that he had initially discovered throughout the entire evangelical world, Rubin referred to that resistance as thing of the past. "When I started nine years ago, coming to the natural products industry with a message that had to do with the Bible wasn't accepted in the least," he explained. "At that point the evangelical community would not go into a health food store because they thought it was New Age." Rubin may have been unaware of the significant precursors, particularly in pentecostal and charismatic circles, that arose well before the mid-1990s and set the stage for his success, yet it is easy to see why he was optimistic about the future: in 2004 his company hauled in more than $60 million in sales.[8]

Rubin's ability to appeal simultaneously to pentecostals and charismatics, as well as other conservative Christians, illuminates the way pentecostals' interactions with fellow evangelicals contributed to the faithful's eventual attraction to natural, metaphysical-friendly forms of healing. From the start, some of the earliest saints drew on emphases in the late-nineteenth-century divine healing movement and acknowledged the importance of taking practical, common-sense actions to aid nature in protecting against disease. The significance of these lines of influence only increased with time, as pentecostalism moved closer and closer to the evangelical mainstream over the course of the twentieth century.

More than any other factor, however, pentecostals' very tangible conceptions of the Holy Spirit set them apart from most other evangelicals and highlighted the inadequacy of an evangelicalization thesis in explaining many believers' turn to spiritualized forms of natural healing. Like their counterparts in the alternative healing world who espoused metaphysical conceptions of the universe, pentecostals had long evidenced a penchant for metaphysical-style descriptions of the Holy Spirit's work that treated the divine as an impersonal force thoroughly connected to the physical, natural world.

The real genius behind much of the late-twentieth- and early-twenty-first-century popularity of pentecostal and charismatic healers' appropriation of holistic medicine involved their ability to repackage prominent trends in the U.S. healing marketplace and sell them as authentic forms of biblical healing backed by the latest research. At the same time that many alternative healers improved their public image by aligning more closely with science, figures such as Maureen Salaman, Don Colbert, Reginald Cherry, and Jordan Rubin stripped the New Age label from metaphysical healing practices, declaring natural healing God's kind of healing.

Mary Colbert's reactions to her husband's explorations of alternative therapies exemplified the kind of selective appropriation involved in adherents' engagement with other alternative healers. "Some of the avenues in which he was headed scared the dickens out of me," she admitted. "The people he was learning from were New Agers, some were Hindus, some were involved in Chinese medicines, all these different areas." "Coming from a charismatic background," she added, "I'm thinking, Oh no, something's going to get in him or on him." After praying over the matter, however, she believed that God revealed to her the fact that "He had been revealing truths related to health and healing to people around the world, regardless of their religion, and that the truths were separate from the religious aspect. He assured her it was possible to have one without the other."[9]

Ironically, Mary Colbert's comments revealed the degree to which various pentecostals and charismatics borrowed a page out of the playbook of the New Age movement as they reconceptualized pentecostal and charismatic healing. One historian has described the "politics of appropriation" at work in Americans' appropriation of Eastern healing traditions ranging from Reiki to acupuncture and yoga. Operating on the assumption that "all traditions were fundamentally identical, all expressing the same reality," New Age practitioners epitomized a "core sense of entitlement on the part of European Americans to appropriate whatever appealed to them." Pentecostals and charismatics stopped well short of the assertion that all religions were equal, yet at least in the realm of healing, a similar dynamic was at work as prominent figures laid claim to rival methodologies on God's behalf.[10]

Ultimately, pentecostals' and charismatics' open engagement with metaphysical healing traditions at the turn of the twenty-first century pointed to more than believers' skill at selective appropriation or, for that matter, the efforts of both groups to associate more closely with scientific, research-based medicine. While pentecostals and many metaphysical practitioners' simultaneous movement toward the medical mainstream played an important role in opening up room for dialogue, the convergence of pentecostal and metaphysical healing also represented the culmination of a century-long process wherein the shared features linking pentecostalism and metaphysical spirituality increasingly moved from the background to the foreground. From the start, the bright, sharp line pentecostals attempted to draw separating their healing methods from metaphysical healers' vision of a divinized natural world proved quite permeable, as early believers evidenced an incipient confidence in the healing power of the mind and of all things natural. The saints believed physical objects could transmit divine power. Their call for an unflinching confidence in God's promises mirrored emphases among proponents of mind-cure and New Thought stressing the power of positive thinking. Most important, early pentecostal conceptions of the Holy Spirit often approximated alternative physicians' metaphysical notions of the universe that treated the supernatural as an impersonal force governed by spiritual laws that were just as discernible as the laws governing the natural realm.

In the end, the metaphysical inclinations that united the fresh faces on the pentecostal and charismatic healing scene in the second half of the twentieth century did not represent as radical or as sharp of a departure from the early pentecostal movement as might appear at first glance. When Oral Roberts fought to bring the Holy Spirit into the doctor's office, he expanded the list of potential physical objects and tools that could serve as carriers of divine power—scalpels and stethoscopes certainly required more technical skill to wield than did prayer cloths and praying hands—yet the same Spirit's power coursed through medical instruments as through handkerchiefs. The success of Word of Faith healers who prioritized the mind's role in the healing process brought to the fore early metaphysical precursors in the pentecostal movement, including E. W. Kenyon's early advocacy of New Thought–inflected theology, as well as notions of faith predicated on the existence of an absolutely reliable God who responded like clockwork to faith-filled prayers. Late-twentieth-century pentecostal and charismatic healers' identification of natural pathways for divine healing also built in important respects on early adherents' tendency to describe the Holy Spirit's activity utilizing imagery drawn from nature and from the material, physical world.

All of this is not to deny the fact that much of pentecostal healing at the turn of the twenty-first century looked very different than it had a century earlier. Nor is it to claim that any self-respecting pentecostal or charismatic would deny the Holy Spirit's role as the third person in the Trinity or would simplistically equate the Holy Spirit with nature. It is to suggest that pentecostalism always provided the faithful with a very tangible, experiential form of spirituality that frequently treated the Holy Spirit as an impersonal entity intimately tied to the natural, physical world. Innovative late-twentieth-century healers in the pentecostal-charismatic movement built on and accentuated this inclination. In the process, they brought their healing practices into alignment with broader trends in the U.S. healing marketplace to a degree not seen in the movement's history.

Healing and the Off-Modern in the United States

In addition to the specific healing practices linking believers to their metaphysi-cal rivals, at the turn of the twenty-first century a shared "off-modern" sensibil-ity also played a pivotal role in both groups' growing appeal throughout U.S. culture. Like a wide variety of alternative healers, prominent pentecostal and charismatic figures sought to promote their practices as timeless pathways to healing rooted in nature and available to all throughout history yet simultane-ously validated by modern science and recent research studies. Neither a full-fledged embrace of a teleology of progress nor a pure backward-looking attempt to restore a lost, Edenic past, the off-modern impulse instead combined a "fasci-nation for the present with longing for another time."[11]

Among healers operating in an explicitly metaphysical context, an off-modern inclination had long been apparent, given their tendency to juxtapose overt su-pernatural claims and scientific—or at least scientific-like—jargon. Not all of these individuals stressed the scientific nature of their practices to the same degree, yet as one scholar notes, metaphysical *healers* in particular, due to their proximity to the medical establishment, tended to stress the "rule-bound nature of energetic, vital forces."[12] Such an explicit combination of scientific-like claims with overt supernaturalism allowed practitioners to tap into the cultural author-ity of scientific knowledge while simultaneously critiquing the thoroughgoing naturalistic and rationalistic assumptions espoused by mainstream physicians.

Over the course of the twentieth century, some alternative healers backed away from the off-modern dynamic in their traditions in response to orthodox medicine's rising power, downplaying the metaphysical origins of chiropractic medicine, homeopathy, and the like. While purists in the various branches of alternative medicine decried these changes as an abdication of the original mis-sions of their particular healing systems, these pragmatists responded by point-ing to the genuine successes of medical orthodoxy, arguing that compromise was the only workable route if their alternative approaches to healing were to remain a reputable option.[13] Other metaphysically inclined healers, of course, including many associated with the New Age movement, resisted the allure of "profession-alization," magnifying the spiritual frameworks in their traditions while still borrowing liberally from scientific studies deemed supportive of their cause. Pentecostal and charismatic healers of the late twentieth century belonged somewhere in between these two trajectories.

On the one hand, pentecostal and charismatic healers' abdication of early believers' staunch repudiation of the medical profession mirrored the more pragmatic alternative healers who sought out workable areas of compromise acknowledging the benefits of mainstream medicine. For a variety of reasons, including changing class dynamics in the pentecostal movement, the appear-ance of charismatic renewal, and especially the rising prestige of the medical establishment, adherents became increasingly unsatisfied with early pentecostals' long-standing resistance to medical and other natural approaches to healing. This dissatisfaction led many pentecostal and charismatic healers to renegotiate their stance toward the medical profession and mimic more pragmatic alternative healers who achieved a significant degree of mainstream respectability through strategic compromise.

Instead of simply imbibing the scientific and natural healing practices prevalent in U.S. society, however, a number of high-profile pentecostals and charismatics simultaneously reworked the same practices into new hybrid approaches that specifically Christianized traditional medicine, alternative medicine, and psychology. Comment after comment made by pentecostal and charismatic healers revealed their intentions to transform the healing landscape—and by extension U.S. culture—by merging supernatural healing with natural, scientifically based approaches. The paradigmatic figure in the pentecostal-charismatic movement in this regard was Oral Roberts. When Roberts described his vision for the City of Faith, he pictured there "some of the greatest medical scientists of the world seeking a breakthrough for cancer, and heart disease, and studying the problems of aging, and researching in other problem areas in an atmosphere that's filled with prayer and faith."[14] All in all, Roberts envisioned a "new concept in medical science,"[15] a "coming together for the first time, at least in my lifetime of the great healing systems of God" (i.e., medical and divine healing).[16]

William Standish Reed, a friend of Roberts and early proponent of pentecostal and charismatic doctors, likewise advocated for a deliberate merger of scientific and religious healing. "Medicine and nursing," he insisted, "must be seen as holy ministries utilizing believing prayer as their greatest therapeutic instrument of compassion." Reed concluded that the medical establishment in the United States and the "entire Western world" had "failed in only one major respect. We have ignored Jesus Christ, his holy word and his holiness in our professions." The lone solution he saw for the difficulties faced by the medical profession was "to make medicine spiritual" by combining traditional medicine with prayer.[17]

The deliberate and conscious nature of prominent leaders' efforts to harmonize divine healing and natural forms of healing extended to the attempts by dietary healers to simultaneously appeal to both biblical and scientific sources of authority to validate their approach to healing. In a section of his book simply entitled "The Scientific Bible," Don VerHulst affirmed: "The more scientists and medical experts discover about our 'earth suits,' these bodies we have while we're on this planet, the more amazed they are at how the Bible's physiological statements keep proving true."[18] "Are you looking for a health plan that is biblically based and scientifically proven?" Jordan Rubin asked on the dust jacket of his bestselling book. "*The Maker's Diet* is just that."[19]

Similar impulses to explicitly merge secular and spiritual forms of healing animated the ministers of inner healing who offered the faithful a form of

psychotherapy not only condoned by God but also predicated on God's willingness to participate in the therapeutic process. Ruth Carter Stapleton described
the "revolutionary discovery," initially identified by Jesus himself, that "nothing
is secular, that every day, every person, every principle rooted in truth and life is
sacred, therefore spiritual." "Dedicated Christians have 'discovered' the corol-
lary truth," she continued, "that even psychology is filled with insights and concepts that are spiritual—though they are found in a 'secular' context." On the
basis of these observations, Stapleton concluded that "to be led through secular
psychological disciplines by the Holy Spirit is to be led into the experience of
emotional healing. And this means that one is reconstructed by the Holy Spirit
of God."[20] In the words of Martin Lynch, a Catholic charismatic commenting in
Charisma on the growing influence of psychology among pentecostals and charismatics, "The inner healing movement has paved the way for an authentic
Christian psychology." "We feel driven by the wind of the Holy Spirit to undo
these deceptions [of secular psychology]," he continued, "replacing them with a
new, sacred psychology."[21] By the early 1990s, Richard Dobbins sought to expand
his ministry's reach, formally partnering with a hospital in Ohio to provide
"Christian psychiatric treatment that includes spiritual warfare, prayer and
Bible reading in a hospital ward." According to an article describing the move,
Dobbins indicated that it was not "fair to the Christians" that his ministry had
been "limited to outpatient care and hospitalizing patients in secular facilities
that use secular program."[22]

Individuals in the Word of Faith branch of pentecostalism proved much more
reticent in acknowledging any debt to secular psychology and therefore never
claimed to sanctify the discipline. Even here, however, figures who promoted
themes closely linked to the Word of Faith movement, for example Joyce Meyer
and T. D. Jakes, repeatedly incorporated popular psychological jargon into their
books, and their emphasis on emotional healing can be read as an attempt to
sacralize psychology and claim it as part of their own spiritual repertoire. In
sum, at the turn of the twenty-first century, a wide variety of believers increasingly refused to acknowledge the fields of psychology and psychiatry—or any
form of science-based healing, for that matter—as outside the realm of authentic Christian healing.

Transforming Evangelicalism, Transforming U.S. Culture

While pentecostals' and charismatics' appropriation of rival healing techniques
illuminated believers' ability to compromise and adapt their message to coincide with off-modern sensibilities in U.S. culture, it also revealed their increasingly creative and transformational relationship with key aspects of modern
U.S. culture. As a growing number of pentecostals and charismatics engaged

with orthodox medicine and metaphysical groups in the United States, they crafted their own particular brand of spiritually infused materialism—a brand they marketed with remarkable success. The net effect of adherents' retooled healing practices was broad influence and exposure in the broader evangelical world and in U.S. society more generally.

Among evangelicals, charismatics in particular were key players in the emergence of hybrid psychological-spiritual forms of healing associated with inner healing. Ruth Carter Stapleton, for instance, participated in the charismatic renewal and helped spread charismatic forms of inner healing in evangelical circles.[23] Inner healing practitioners were especially influential in shaping evangelicals' response to homosexuality in the later decades of the twentieth century. As one former Methodist noted in 1997, he "had to be dragged 'kicking and screaming' into the charismatic movement." He changed his mind, however, "when he learned of the charismatic ties of most ex-gay organizations."[24] Along these very lines, works written by the Episcopal laywoman Leanne Payne frequently zeroed in on gender issues and sexuality. Significantly, her books found an audience not simply among pentecostals and charismatics but also in the broader evangelical world. Her 1996 book *Restoring the Christian Soul* addressed the interconnections between Christian theology, psychology, and the healing of the emotions and received *Christianity Today*'s "Critics' Choice" award.[25]

The ability of healers such as Payne to straddle the boundaries separating pentecostals and charismatics from other conservative Christians suggests that for all of the evidence of an "evangelicalization" of pentecostal and charismatic healing, taken as a whole, the term "convergence" does a better job of capturing the adherents' relationship to the wider evangelical world. As one historian has written of pentecostal culture more broadly, by the late twentieth century, "Pentecostal acculturation . . . was matched by the Pentecostalization of both the Black Church and white evangelicalism, so that the mainstream currents Pentecostals now joined more closely resembled the revised ethos and assumptions of their own movement."[26] The new healing identities espoused by many pentecostals and charismatics reinforced these trends, further destabilizing rigid religious boundaries that separated adherents from fellow evangelicals, and at times Catholics as well.

Pentecostals' and charismatics' willingness to transform their approach to healing and health also led to much greater exposure for Bible-based forms of alternative therapy outside conservative Christian circles. Don Colbert's *Seven Pillars of Health* was a *New York Times* best seller, and his *What Would Jesus Eat* also garnered national attention. Building on his success among pentecostals and charismatics as well as other evangelicals, Jordan Rubin disseminated his ideas via mainstream media outlets ranging from ABC's *Good Morning America* to *Newsweek*, while his dietary supplements were available through nonreligious health-food distributors such as Whole Foods Market and the Vitamin Shoppe.

Lee Haney gained additional visibility as personal trainer for the comedian Steve Harvey.[27] Meanwhile, Joyce Meyer, Joel Osteen, and T. D. Jakes proclaimed the healing power of positive thinking utilizing mainstream retailers such as Wal-Mart, while Jakes also parlayed his success into several appearances on the nationally syndicated *Dr. Phil* show.

It is impossible to tell just how many nonevangelical or non-Christian outsiders were influenced by pentecostal and charismatic healers. It seems very safe to say that by opening themselves up to such unprecedented changes in one of the core anchors of pentecostal and charismatic identity—divine healing—pentecostals and charismatic gained significant influence in the broader culture as they spread explicitly Christian forms of divine healing that dovetailed neatly with broader trends in the U.S. healing marketplace.

Pentecostal and Charismatic Healing at the Turn of the Twenty-First Century

Despite all of the changes in pentecostal healing from the early 1900s, pentecostals and charismatics at the turn of the twenty-first century did not give up on the possibility of God's direct and dramatic transformation of their bodies. As the popularity of the Canadian-born evangelist Todd Bentley during a 2008 healing revival in Lakeland, Florida, attested, natural and psychological forms of divine healing coexisted with but did not displace overt supernaturalism or more traditional methods of healing. A heavily tattooed thirty-two-year-old known for his unconventional (and on occasion physically aggressive) style, Bentley claimed to be aided by the midcentury healing evangelist William Branham's angel, and his meetings—which consistently attracted crowds upward of 10,000 over a period of four months—featured frequent claims to dramatic, instantaneous healings, including claims of the dead being raised.[28] This healing evangelist proved controversial even in pentecostal and charismatic circles; he abruptly halted his participation in the meetings in August 2008 due to marital problems and revelations regarding an "unhealthy relationship on an emotional level with a female member of his staff." Even so, the attention garnered by his ministry pointed to believers' desire for vivid displays of God's healing power.[29]

The ministry of Benny Hinn, one of the most prominent U.S. healers of the 1990s and the early twenty-first century, likewise offered compelling evidence of the continued appetite for more traditional forms of divine healing in pentecostal and charismatic circles. Hinn's crusades featured testimony after testimony of instantaneous healings and deliverance from demonic powers, attracting thousands of individuals hungry to experience God's healing touch. In one typical meeting, he called forward a woman who testified regarding a lump that disappeared from her chest. With a choir worshiping in the background, Hinn asked the woman to pray with him for those watching the service on television. "Jesus heal the people in their homes," he prayed. "We command the sickness to leave. . . . We the saints of God command the very devils of hell that afflict the people of God, Come Out! Leave God's people. Oh, people of God be made whole. Jesus Christ makes you whole." Following this prayer, Hinn instructed the woman to return to her doctor, promising her that the doctor would be transformed by her testimony.[30]

Figure 6.1 Indicative of the continued presence of dramatic claims to divine healing among pentecostals and charismatics during the late twentieth and early twenty-first centuries, this 1977 cover of *Charisma* highlights a believer's healing from multiple sclerosis and diabetes. Reprinted with permission from "Charisma," January/February 1977. Copyright Charisma Media, USA. All rights reserved. www.charismamag.com.

Both Bentley's and Hinn's healing crusades may seem to provide a caution-
ary tale about the impact of increasingly naturalized forms of healing in the
pentecostal-charismatic movement, yet even here metaphysical-style emphases prove readily detectable. At the revival meetings led by Bentley, the pastor
of the local pentecostal church where the revival began was careful to affirm the
value of the medical profession, explicitly citing Oral Roberts's vision of the
merger of supernatural and natural methodologies.[31] Bentley's testimonies and
preaching also brimmed with the same type of impersonal, metaphysical-like
descriptions of the Holy Spirit's power that had saturated pentecostal discourse
throughout the pentecostal movement's history. He spoke of a special angel
whose presence magnified the healing power at a meeting. When present,
Bentley explained, "there is just a whole new thickness of the healing anointing" and a "definite increase [sic] awareness of atmosphere."[32] He described another healing service where a "pillar of smoke and pillar of fire appeared, and
energy filled the room." The presence was so tangible, he continued, that "I
stuck my hand out to touch it and it felt as if my hand was going into an electric
force field." God then instructed him to "climb in, climb in. Just soak."[33]

Hinn went beyond Bentley's metaphysical language by stocking his ministry
website with advertisements for numerous books written by Maureen Salaman,
Don Colbert, Jordan Rubin, and other authors steeped in naturopathic assumptions. The site also offered tips on nutrition, exercise plans, and dietary supplements, frequently posting articles with medical information drawn from sources
such as the National Diabetes Information Clearinghouse and healthandage.
com.[34] Even more telling, Hinn was instrumental in introducing the charismatic
healer Don Colbert to the world of natural healing. Colbert attended Hinn's
church and traveled with Hinn to verify healings. "In travelling all over the earth
Benny got to meet many different people in natural medicines from chiropractors to naturopaths to whatever," Colbert recalled, "and he used to come to me
and say, 'Dr. Colbert, what about this?'" On the basis of these interactions, Colbert credited Hinn with showing him that "there are other paths to healing besides traditional medicine."[35]

In large part, Colbert's leap into the pentecostal and charismatic spotlight can
be traced back to Hinn's promotion of Colbert on his television program in the
mid-1990s. Around the same time, Hinn prophesied regarding Colbert indicating that the physician would impact millions with his message of health and healing. Judging by Colbert's subsequent visibility in the pentecostal-charismatic
movement, Hinn's words were in fact prophetic.[36] Colbert's success—and Hinn's
role in that success—illuminated the pervasive impact of metaphysical themes
among believers by the later decades of the twentieth century.

An article published on page 5 of the *New York Times* in the fall of 1907 undoubtedly caught the attention of more than a few readers. Entitled "Mobbed 'Healer'

Asks Court's Aid," the piece chronicled a chaotic series of events that unfolded when a "Pentecostal preacher" plied his new-found healing trade in Greenwich, Connecticut. Identified as a "mulatto 'divine healer'" who had graduated from Berkeley University, the Reverend Albert Derosa sparked more than a little outrage in that New England town with his unorthodox healing methods. One individual threw a homemade bomb into the home where Derosa was holding a Sunday night service, and later in the week farmers in the area burned down his tent and chased him to a nearby barn with cries of "Lynch him! Burn him!" Derosa charged his attackers with "bomb throwing and arson," only to be accused of "improper conduct, mesmerism, and hypnotism or pretending to heal the sick and of obtaining money under false pretenses." Residents of the town, not to mention the reporter covering the events, clearly did not know what to make of Derosa and his message. The byline referred to the "Weird Religious Services in House" and the townspeople's objections to "Incantations." After the prosecuting attorney and the arsonist's lawyer questioned Derosa regarding the "occurrences of the last few days, and on the nature of his faith and teachings," they reportedly "had little clearer conception of the man's ideas than they had before." In his defense, Derosa stated that he was "simply preaching the truth," denying any connections to traditions such as mesmerism, which had strong metaphysical ties. Instead, he "believed in the healing of the sick by prayer, as the Bible teaches."[37]

Derosa and his fellow pentecostals stood much closer to their metaphysical rivals than they would have liked to admit. A few short decades after Derosa ran for his life, the metaphysical leanings already present in early pentecostalism burst into full view, spawning numerous innovative healing practices as believers embraced a number of the alternative pathways to healing that circulated in U.S. culture. Like metaphysical groups throughout U.S. history, later healers in the pentecostal-charismatic movement assumed an inherent correspondence between the natural world and intangible realities in the cosmos. Oral Roberts not only accepted the prescriptions dispensed by medical doctors, he built a hospital and medical school dedicated to the merger of medical healing and divine healing. Word of Faith ministers and advocates of inner healing not only acknowledged the benefits of positive thinking, they stressed the mind as the key point of mediation controlling the influx of divine power into an individual. Other pentecostal and charismatic healers discovered more than just biblical precedent for eating healthy; they marketed a whole range of very tangible— and often expensive—products as crucial natural pathways to divine health and healing.

Clearly, much changed in pentecostal healing after the early twentieth century. Few would dispute the statement of the charismatic Catholic Francis MacNutt in his widely popular book on healing, first published in 1974, that "sometimes God works through nature and the skill of doctors; sometimes he works directly through prayer and sometimes through both, but always there should be cooperation, mutual respect and an admiration for the variety of ways in which God manifests his glory."[38] Believers may not have acknowledged the connection, but several of the most popular healing practices endorsed by the faithful in the late twentieth century bore the distinct imprint of metaphysical mind-cure movements and nature-based forms of alternative medicine with their roots in the nineteenth-century United States. For most adherents, explicit endorsements of New Age and similar metaphysical movements remained unthinkable, and important differences continued to separate the faithful from individuals in more thoroughly metaphysical traditions. At the same time, metaphysical-like conceptions of divine healing centered on the mind or on the healing power of natural substances peacefully coexisted with dramatic claims of divine intervention. The Holy Spirit, it turns out, proved more tangible than ever.

Epilogue

Healing the Wounds of the Modern World

Observers of the global spread of pentecostalism over the course of the twentieth century frequently zero in on pentecostal healing as a key catalyst—if not *the* key catalyst—fueling the pentecostal movement's rapid growth. In Africa, pentecostal healing has been described as the "heartbeat of the liturgy and the entire religious life."[1] A scholar assessing pentecostalism in Brazil suggests that "in some churches, faith-healing so dominates the liturgy that the sanctuary resembles a hospital."[2] In another overview of worldwide pentecostalism, the historian Allan Anderson makes it clear that "in many cultures of the world, where the religious specialist or 'person of God' has the power to heal the sick and ward off evil spirits and sorcery, the offer of healing by pentecostalism has been one of its major attractions." The pentecostal stress on "freedom in the Spirit" only strengthened this appeal, as pentecostalism across the globe demonstrated a remarkable flexibility and "innate ability to make itself at home in almost any context."[3]

In many respects, the development of pentecostal healing in the United States mirrored key features of pentecostal healing on the global stage. Considering the ubiquity of the pentecostal and charismatic healers who dot the religious and not-so-religious landscape of the United States, it is clear that the various forms of pentecostal healing that took shape in the U.S. context played a crucial role in pentecostals' and charismatics' rapid growth and unmistakable cultural influence over the course of the twentieth century. Believers and unbelievers alike encountered pentecostal and charismatic discourses regarding healing via broadcasts on a variety of television outlets, in the literature that appeared on the shelves of religious and secular retailers, and on the Internet.

In addition, just as pentecostal healing outside North America benefited from a pragmatic adaptability, incorporating elements of Hindu demonology in India, for example, or beliefs regarding the spirits of dead relatives that were prevalent in places like South Korea, very similar dynamics fueled the "contextualization" of pentecostal healing in the United States.[4] The history of divine healing among

U.S. pentecostals and their charismatic successors provides a fascinating window into the saints' ever-increasing attunement to the rising prestige of the medical establishment, to the ubiquitous presence of New Thought emphases and psychological paradigms, to the explosion of holistic methodologies rooted in metaphysical assumptions, and to a burgeoning diet and fitness culture. Pentecostals and charismatics reconfigured their healing practices to coincide with each of these developments, bringing them into closer alignment with the broader culture than ever before.

Believers' sensitivity to the surrounding milieu, of course, was present throughout the pentecostal movement's history in the United States. From the beginning, pentecostal spirituality radiated a pragmatic malleability that freed participants to utilize and assimilate key features of modern U.S. culture.[5] Pentecostals' long-standing predilection for more experiential as opposed to theoretical approaches to the third person of the Trinity in particular made it relatively easy for believers to recast the Holy Spirit's role in the healing process and merge divine healing with a variety of currents circulating throughout U.S. society.

As U.S. believers' educational and economic standing steadily improved over the course of the twentieth century, however, adherents introduced a new element into the equation that had profound implications for the trajectory of pentecostal healing. Never before had the faithful evinced such a keen desire to explicitly minimize the dissonance between their own practices and the conclusions of modern science. Early pentecostals never hesitated to draw on the testimony of physicians or other trained professionals who could testify to the reality of pentecostals' claims, but when the methodological materialism associated with the growing prestige of science and technology butted heads with their religious convictions, the latter won the battle handily. The saints lambasted psychologists and psychiatrists for relativizing the causes and consequences of behaviors that believers deemed sinful, and they mocked liberal theologians, physicians, and others whom they believed denied the reality of God's miraculous intervention in the world. Similar tensions persisted over the course of the twentieth century in numerous manifestations of pentecostalism outside North America, and especially in the global South, due in no small part to the lack of "serious competition from modern scientific medicine, since this is so far beyond the reach of most of the poorest."[6]

In sharp contrast to early pentecostals and many participants in the worldwide movement, several prominent pentecostal and charismatic healers in the United States during the later decades of the twentieth century modified their approach to healing in order to obtain a scientific stamp of approval for their practices. Early pentecostals would never have dreamed that someone from their ranks, for example Oral Roberts, not only would condone the use of medicines but actually depict divine healing as a marriage of medicine and spirituality. Even those who endorsed the use of natural substances to sustain health would have balked at the idea of promoting those natural substances under the banner of divine healing. Combining supernatural healing with "Godless" psychology and psychoanalysis would have made about as much sense to early pentecostals as offering their pulpits to unrepentant atheists. In short, the degree to which later pentecostal and charismatic adherents in the United States accepted the authority of experts associated with the fields of medicine, psychology, and alternative healing would have shocked their forebears. In a culture increasingly beholden to scientific models of healing, metaphysical-like understandings of the close similarities between the operation of the supernatural and the natural world provided a workable medium in which many pentecostal and charismatic adherents could "naturalize" their practices while simultaneously preserving and promoting God's role in the restoration of their bodies.

Pentecostals' and charismatics' frequent attraction to alternative forms of medicine as they negotiated their place in the U.S. healing marketplace suggested that many had not fully relinquished early pentecostals' antiestablishment streak, despite the overtures to mainstream medicine. In carving out an identity betwixt and between scientific medicine and more spiritual alternatives, and in working to heal the breach between religious and scientific perspectives, believers highlighted not only the unparalleled success of scientific, allopathic medicine in U.S. culture over the course of the twentieth century, but the limits of the medical establishment's power as well. Like most Americans, the vast majority of pentecostals and charismatics at the turn of the twenty-first century did not think twice about consulting a traditional doctor for treatment of everything from the common cold to more serious ailments. Also like numerous other Americans, a healthy proportion of pentecostals and charismatics felt quite comfortable combining traditional medicine with extrascientific—and at times antiscientific—methodologies in their quest for bodily restoration.

The newly minted forms of pentecostal healing facilitated the dramatic transition of pentecostals and their successors from a despised minority to major players in mainstream U.S. culture. Whether through television, radio, or print, whether in churches, big box retail stores, or local health food co-ops, religious and nonreligious Americans alike increasingly encountered messages of healing, reconfigured by pentecostals and charismatics, that dovetailed neatly with the therapeutic and consumerist dictates of U.S. culture. Judging by the success of healers who championed the transformation of pentecostal healing, many Americans liked what they found.

In the end, healing in the pentecostal-charismatic movement was about much more than just healing the body. Skeptics may have questioned whether divinized forms of medicine, psychotherapy, and dietary healing produced tangible benefits any different from the purely secular applications of similar methodologies, yet there is no doubt that pentecostals' and charismatics' willingness to modify their healing practices spoke to adherents' keen awareness of their location in a rapidly modernizing society. Their pushes to merge divine healing and medicine, to find parallels between biblical dietary guidelines and modern research in nutrition, and to spiritualize psychology each indicate a very deliberate effort to heal the rifts between their faith and the expectations of the surrounding culture and to mitigate apparent conflicts between religion and science. Unwilling either to discard their supernatural worldview or to ignore the firmly established authority of medical science, numerous believers instead cultivated preexisting metaphysical inclinations already present in the early pentecostal movement. The subsequent transformation of pentecostal healing allowed the faithful to define medicine in their own terms and to compete with the numerous other voices in U.S. culture that likewise promised access to the secret of unparalleled health, happiness, and beauty. In the process, the faithful reworked key aspects of traditional and alternative medicine, New Thought spirituality, and psychology, tailoring them to their own agenda. They openly embraced the modern world as never before—that is, as long it was baptized in the Holy Spirit.

NOTES

Introduction

1. Mrs. T. Mathews Izor, "I Am the Lord That Healeth Thee," *Pentecostal Evangel*, no. 678 (1927): 8. Throughout this book I set aside larger questions regarding the efficacy of pentecostals' healing practices. Instead, I focus on changes in pentecostals' approaches to healing over the course of the twentieth and early twenty-first centuries and what that history reveals regarding the internal dynamics of pentecostal culture, as well as its evolving relationship with various aspects of the broader U.S. society. For examples of scholarship addressing the efficacy of religious healing practices, including those of pentecostals and charismatics, see Candy Gunther Brown, *Testing Prayer: Science and Healing* (Cambridge, Mass.: Harvard University Press, 2012); Amanda Porterfield, *Healing in the History of Christianity* (New York: Oxford University Press, 2005), 3–19.

2. Grant Wacker, "The Pentecostal Tradition," in *Caring and Curing*, ed. Ronald L. Numbers and Darrel W. Amundsen (New York: Macmillan, 1986), 520–521.

3. In articulating various functions of divine healing that went beyond the obvious attempt to cure illness and mitigate suffering, I am not suggesting that pentecostals themselves necessarily would have recognized each of these functions. As Catherine Bell notes, religious rituals often reflect a form of "misrecognition" whereby ritual activity such as healing "does not see how its own actions reorder and reinterpret the circumstances so as to afford the sense of fit among the main spheres of experience—body, community, and cosmos." Catherine M. Bell, *Ritual Theory, Ritual Practice* (New York: Oxford University Press, 1992), 108–110.

4. Throughout I use a variety of terms to contrast the forms of medicine practiced by M.D.s with their competitors. As an indication of M.D.s' greater numbers and their claims to purely scientific forms of healing, I use terms such as "conventional," "mainstream," and "orthodox" medicine to distinguish their methods from rival healing models on the American healing scene, which I label "alternative," "holistic," and "unorthodox," and so on.

5. For discussion of Calvinism's declining power during the nineteenth century and its import for the emergence of the divine healing movement, see Heather D. Curtis, *Faith in the Great Physician: Suffering and Divine Healing in American Culture, 1860–1900* (Baltimore, Md.: Johns Hopkins University Press, 2007), esp. 15; Jonathan R. Baer, "Perfectly Empowered Bodies: Divine Healing in Modernizing America" (Ph.D. diss., Yale University, 2002), esp. 14–15. Robert Mullin also discusses the decreasing influence of Calvinism in the intellectual debates over miracles by the end of the nineteenth century in *Miracles and the Modern Religious Imagination* (New Haven, Conn.: Yale University Press, 1996).

6. A. B. Simpson, *The Gospel of Healing* (1888), rev. ed. (Harrisburg, Pa.: Christian Alliance, 1915), 59–60, 25. Despite the strong similarities between Simpson's message and pentecostal themes, Simpson never accepted pentecostals' teachings regarding speaking in tongues as the "initial evidence" of the baptism in the Holy Spirit, and at times he criticized various excesses he associated with pentecostal groups. For more on Simpson, see

Daniel J. Evearitt, *Body and Soul: Evangelism and the Social Concern of A. B. Simpson* (Camp Hill, Pa.: Christian Publications, 1994); Charles Nienkirchen, *A. B. Simpson and the Pentecostal Movement: A Study in Continuity, Crisis, and Change* (Peabody, Mass.: Hendrickson, 1992); Nancy Hardesty, *Faith Cure: Divine Healing in the Holiness and Pentecostal Movements* (Peabody, Mass.: Hendrickson, 2003), 41–44.

7. Heather Curtis provides a helpful overview of these developments in *Faith in the Great Physician*, esp. 1–25. Regarding the changing notions of masculinity in U.S. culture that helped spur the emergence of "muscular Christianity," see for example Gail Bederman, *Manliness and Civilization: A Cultural History of Gender and Race in the United States, 1880–1917* (Chicago: University of Chicago Press, 1996); Clifford Putney, *Muscular Christianity: Manhood and Sports in Protestant America, 1880–1920* (Cambridge, Mass.: Harvard University Press, 2001).

8. Isaiah 53:5 and 1 Peter 2:24 (King James Version).

9. Gordon referred to Mark 16:17–18, A. J. Gordon, *The Ministry of Healing* (London: Hodder and Stoughton, 1882), 26. For more on Gordon and his significance, see Scott M. Gibson, *A. J. Gordon: American Premillennialist* (Lanham, Md.: University Press of America, 2001); Edith Waldvogel Blumhofer, *Restoring the Faith: The Assemblies of God, Pentecostalism, and American Culture* (Urbana: University of Illinois Press, 1993), 20–21.

10. As the historian Heather Curtis explains, for nineteenth-century proponents, faith "meant believing that God had banished sickness from the body, despite any sensory evidence to the contrary, and acting accordingly. Trusting the Great Physician, therefore, involved training the senses to ignore lingering pain or symptoms of sickness and disciplining the body to 'act faith' by getting out of bed and serving God through energetic engagement with others." Curtis, *Faith in the Great Physician*, 12.

11. Simpson, *Gospel of Healing*, 163.

12. See especially John Wesley, *A Plain Account of Christian Perfection* (1767; reprint, London: Epworth Press, 1952). As David Bebbington clarifies, "Experience taught [Wesley] . . . that believers may progress to a state in which they are free from all known sin. No aspect of Methodist teaching gave more openings for ridicule. There was much glee when a 'perfect' sister was detected stealing coal from a 'sanctified' brother. Wesley sorrowfully noted such cases, concluding that the state could readily be lost, but he nevertheless insisted on its reality," D. W. Bebbington, *Evangelicalism in Modern Britain: A History from the 1730s to the 1980s* (London: Routledge, 1993), 60.

13. Due to their Calvinistic understanding regarding human nature, individuals in the Reformed Higher Life movement (sometimes referred to as the Keswick tradition) often rejected the language of perfectionism that circulated among holiness advocates, pointing instead to the pervasive presence of sin in individuals' lives. Even in these circles, however, influential leaders such as the Presbyterian William E. Boardman eventually adapted holiness themes for Reformed audiences as can be seen in Boardman's *The Higher Christian Life* (1858). For further discussion of the development of the holiness movement, see Melvin Easterday Dieter, *The Holiness Revival of the Nineteenth Century*, 2nd ed. (Lanham, Md.: Scarecrow Press, 1996); Charles Edwin Jones, *Perfectionist Persuasion: The Holiness Movement and American Methodism, 1867–1936* (Lanham, Md.: Scarecrow Press, 2002). For discussion of the relationship between the Wesleyan-holiness tradition and the Reformed Higher Life movement, see David D. Bundy, "Keswick and the Experience of Evangelical Piety," in *Modern Christian Revivals*, ed. Edith Waldvogel Blumhofer and Randall Balmer (Urbana, IL: University of Illinois Press, 1993), 118–144; Donald W. Dayton, *Theological Roots of Pentecostalism* (Grand Rapids, Mich.: Francis Asbury, 1987), 87–113. For further discussion of the connections between divine healing and these movements, see Jonathan R. Baer, "Redeemed Bodies: The Functions of Divine Healing in Incipient Pentecostalism," *Church History* 70 (2001): 735–737; Blumhofer, *Restoring the Faith*, 11–42; Curtis, *Faith in the Great Physician*, 6–11; Wacker, "Pentecostal Tradition," 516–520.

14. See Dayton, *Theological Roots*, esp. 115–141.

15. Phoebe Palmer, *Present to My Christian Friend on Entire Devotion to God*, rev. ed. (London: Alexander Heylin, 1857), 101.

16. Phoebe Palmer, *The Life and Letters of Mrs. Phoebe Palmer*, ed. Richard Wheatley (1881; reprint, New York: Garland, 1984), 101. Wesley fasted one and sometimes two days a week throughout his lifetime, and many who followed in his footsteps tried to emulate his spiritual discipline. See for example the following sermon by Wesley on fasting, "Upon Our Lord's Sermon on the Mount, VII," in *The Works of John Wesley*, ed. Albert Cook Outler (Nashville: Abingdon Press, 1984), 1:592–611.

17. Ida M. Garlock, "Joy for Mourning," *Triumphs of Faith* 2, no. 1 (1882): 12. For further discussion of the role of fasting among late-nineteenth-century proponents of divine healing, see Curtis, *Faith in the Great Physician*, 116–117.

18. Andrew Murray, *With Christ in the School of Prayer* (London: James Nisbet, 1887), 98–99. Walter Hollenweger discusses Murray's impact on early pentecostalism in South Africa in *The Pentecostals: The Charismatic Movement in the Churches* (Minneapolis: Augsburg, 1972), 111–116.

19. John Wesley, *Primitive Physick; or, an Easy and Natural Method of Curing Most Diseases* (Philadelphia: Andrew Steuart, 1764), xii–xvi. The majority of *Primitive Physick* listed a host of maladies and their attendant cures, and it can best be categorized as an early form of alternative medicine. For further discussion regarding *Primitive Physick* and Wesley's approach to health and healing, see E. Brooks Holifield, *Health and Medicine in the Methodist Tradition: Journey toward Wholeness* (New York: Crossroad, 1986), esp. 29–38; R. Marie Griffith, *Born Again Bodies: Flesh and Spirit in American Christianity* (Berkeley: University of California Press, 2004), 41–43.

20. As a theological position, Arminianism stressed individuals' ability to take responsibility for their salvation by choosing to respond to God's grace, and Wesley staunchly supported this view. I borrow the term "physical Arminianism" from James Whorton, who describes nineteenth- and early-twentieth-century American health reformers' widely held assumption that "bodily happiness is intended by nature (God), but each person must assume responsibility for his physical salvation and earn it by physiological rectitude"; *Crusaders for Fitness: The History of American Health Reformers* (Princeton, N.J.: Princeton University Press, 1982), 5.

21. Sarah Hill, "Zion Literature Mission," *Leaves of Healing* 5, no. 29 (1899): 553.

22. R. L. Stanton, "Health for Body and Soul—Two Experiences," *Triumphs of Faith* 3, no. 3 (1883): 61. Also see Curtis, *Faith in the Great Physician*, 65–66.

23. Mark 16:18 (King James Version), James 5:14–15.

24. See Curtis, *Faith in the Great Physician*, 118–122.

25. See for example Dayton, *Theological Roots*, 115–141; Wacker, "Pentecostal Tradition," 516–525. Two studies that focus on the divine healing movement more broadly reinforce the same conclusions. See Baer, "Perfectly Empowered Bodies"; Hardesty, *Faith Cure*.

26. Regarding pentecostals' indebtedness to Wesley and the holiness tradition that developed among his followers, see for example Vinson Synan, *The Holiness-Pentecostal Tradition: Charismatic Movements in the Twentieth Century* (Grand Rapids, Mich.: Eerdmans, 1997), esp. 105–106. Despite Synan's articulation of a direct lineage from Wesley to the holiness movement to pentecostalism, other historians stress pentecostalism's indebtedness to Reformed emphases as well. See Blumhofer, *Restoring the Faith*, esp. 11–42; Edith Lydia Waldvogel, "The 'Overcoming Life': A Study in the Reformed Evangelical Origins of Pentecostalism" (Ph.D. diss., Harvard University, 1977).

27. Blumhofer, *Restoring the Faith*, 254–260, quotation 256.

28. For discussion of the centrality of the baptism in the Holy Spirit and speaking in tongues in pentecostalism, see Grant Wacker, *Heaven Below: Early Pentecostals and American Culture* (Cambridge, Mass.: Harvard University Press, 2001), 35–57; Allan Anderson, *An Introduction to Pentecostalism: Global Charismatic Christianity* (Cambridge: Cambridge University Press, 2004), 197–198. Though pentecostals' insistence that tongues accompany the baptism in the Holy Spirit was unique, the language of the baptism in the Holy Spirit circulated widely among evangelicals during the latter decades of the nineteenth century. See especially Dayton, *Theological Roots*, 87–113.

29. While important signs of charismatic renewal began to appear before the 1960s, Dennis Bennett's declaration to his Episcopal congregation in Van Nuys, California, on April 3, 1960, that he experienced the baptism in the Holy Spirit and spoke "in other tongues," is often highlighted as a useful historical marker signifying the clear emergence of the charismatic movement. News of Bennett's controversial announcement spread rapidly via articles in *Newsweek* and *Time*. For useful overviews of the charismatic movement, see Peter Hocken, "Charismatic Movement," in *The New International Dictionary of Pentecostal and Charismatic Movements*, ed. Stanley M. Burgess and Ed M. Van der Maas (Grand Rapids, Mich.: Zondervan, 2002), 477–519; Stanley M. Burgess, "Charismatic Revival and Renewal," in *Encyclopedia of Religious Revivals in America*, ed. Michael James McClymond (Westport, Conn.: Greenwood Press, 2007), 1:99–102; Margaret M. Poloma, *The Charismatic Movement: Is There a New Pentecost?* (Boston: Twayne, 1982); Richard Quebedeaux, *The New Charismatics II*, rev. ed. (San Francisco: Harper and Row, 1983).

30. For further discussion of the antagonism that existed between some pentecostals and charismatics, see Blumhofer, *Restoring the Faith*, 232–238; David Edwin Harrell, Jr., *All Things Are Possible: The Healing and Charismatic Revivals in Modern America* (Bloomington: Indiana University Press, 1975), esp. 231–233; Quebedeaux, *New Charismatics II*, 208–210. Another important distinction separating classical pentecostals from charismatics bears mentioning: while charismatics shared pentecostals' stress on the empowerment of the Holy Spirit in a believer's life and similarly practiced the spiritual gifts mentioned in 1 Corinthians 12, not all charismatics agreed with pentecostals' clear prioritization of tongues as *the* necessary mark of the baptism in the Holy Spirit. Instead, many formulated their understanding of the baptism in the Holy Spirit in relation to preexisting theological frameworks in their particular tradition.

31. Virginia H. Hine, "Pentecostal Glossolalia: Toward a Functional Interpretation," *Journal for the Scientific Study of Religion* 8, no. 2 (1969): 224.

32. Quebedeaux, *New Charismatics II*, 175–192. Despite the fact that many observers initially identified the charismatic renewal as a largely white, middle-class phenomenon, as Scott Billingsley notes, African Americans also figured prominently in the charismatic movement, beginning especially in the 1980s. See Scott Billingsley, *It's a New Day: Race and Gender in the Modern Charismatic Movement* (Tuscaloosa: University of Alabama Press, 2008).

33. Harrell discusses Lindsay's, Cerullo's, and Roberts's appeal to charismatics in *All Things Are Possible*, 165–168, 206–208, 150–159.

34. Regarding the socioeconomic status of early believers, according to the historian Grant Wacker, even in the early pentecostal movement a "conspicuous minority" of pentecostal leaders "plainly enjoyed upper-middle-class standing," or "at least a solidly middle-class position." Though a much smaller percentage of "rank-and-file" believers achieved a high level of wealth, education, or profession, Wacker stresses that even here the "typical convert paralleled the demographic and biographical profile of the typical American in most though not quite all respects," Wacker, *Heaven Below*, 197–216, quotations 203, 205. Subsequent research by R. G. Robins and Randall Stephens corroborates Wacker's claims. See for example R. G. Robins, *A. J. Tomlinson: Plainfolk Modernist* (New York: Oxford University Press, 2004), 31; Randall J. Stephens, *The Fire Spreads: Holiness and Pentecostalism in the American South* (Cambridge, Mass.: Harvard University Press, 2008), 206–207. Prominent individuals with pentecostal backgrounds who helped facilitate charismatic renewal include David du Plessis and Demos Shakarian, not to mention several of the midcentury healing evangelists and others whose emphasis on healing attracted a signficant charismatic audience. While I highlight pentecostals' contributions to the charismatic renewal, it is important to recognize the way the charismatic movement also built on antecedents in a variety of Christian denominations and traditions. For discussion of both pentecostal and nonpentecostal factors that contributed to the emergence of the charismatic movement, see Blumhofer, *Restoring the Faith*, 222–241; Harrell, *All Things are Possible*, esp. 138–193; Peter Hocken, "Charismatic Movement," 477–519; Peter Hocken, *Streams of Renewal*, rev. ed. (Carlisle, England: Paternoster Press, 1997), esp. 1–4, 50–55, 189–192;

Vinson Synan, *The Twentieth-Century Pentecostal Explosion* (Altamonte, Fl.: Creation House, 1987); Synan, *Holiness-Pentecostal Tradition*, esp. 220–52.

35. Due to the growing rapprochement between unorthodox healers and the medical establishment by the late twentieth century, as well as the growing number of patients who explore unorthodox options while still consulting their medical doctors, observers increasingly dub orthodox medicine's rivals as "complementary medicine" as opposed to "alternative medicine." Given the fact that the relationship between nontraditional physicians and their mainstream counterparts was not nearly so cordial throughout most of the twentieth century, throughout this book I typically use "alternative medicine" in place of its more recent substitute.

36. Useful discussions of nontraditional healing practices in the colonies and early republic can be found in Catherine L. Albanese, *A Republic of Mind and Spirit: A Cultural History of American Metaphysical Religion* (New Haven, Conn.: Yale University Press, 2007), esp. 21–118; Jon Butler, *Awash in a Sea of Faith: Christianizing the American People* (Cambridge, Mass.: Harvard University Press, 1990), 67–97. For discussion of more traditional medicine in the colonies, see Eric H. Christianson, "Medicine in New England," in *Medicine in the New World: New Spain, New France, and New England*, ed. Ronald L. Numbers (Knoxville: University of Tennessee Press, 1987), 101–153.

37. On the appearance of full-fledged alternative healing systems, see James C. Whorton, *Nature Cures: The History of Alternative Medicine in America* (New York: Oxford University Press, 2002).

38. For statistics on the growing number of medical schools and societies during the early nineteenth century, see William G. Rothstein, *American Physicians in the Nineteenth Century: From Sects to Science* (Baltimore: Johns Hopkins University Press, 1992), esp. 71, 92, 93.

39. In the words of a historian of U.S. medical history, "the physician's most potent weapon was his ability to 'regulate the secretions'—to extract blood, to promote the perspiration, or the urination, or defecation which attested to his having helped the body to regain its customary equilibrium"; Charles Rosenberg, "The Therapeutic Revolution: Medicine, Meaning, and Social Change in Nineteenth-Century America," in *The Therapeutic Revolution*, ed. Morris J. Vogel (Philadelphia: University of Pennsylvania Press, 1979), 6. Some medical historians are careful to point out that the "heroic procedures" were not followed as aggressively by many in the profession even during the early nineteenth century. See for example Whorton, *Nature Cures*, 6–7.

40. James Whorton stresses alternative practitioners' faith in nature as *the* common denominator joining a widely diverse set of beliefs and practices and setting them apart from orthodox medicine. See Whorton, *Nature Cures*, esp. 4–7. Useful overviews of alternative medicine in the United States include Whorton, *Nature Cures*; Norman Gevitz, ed., *Other Healers: Unorthodox Medicine in America* (Baltimore: Johns Hopkins University Press, 1988). For discussion of the relationship between alternative medicine and religion, see esp. Robert C. Fuller, *Alternative Medicine and American Religious Life* (New York: Oxford University Press, 1989).

41. James C. Whorton, "Patient, Heal Thyself: Popular Health Reform Movements as Unorthodox Medicine," in Gevitz, *Other Healers*, 80.

42. For discussion of physicians' greater willingness during the second half of the nineteenth century to countenance the role of nature to produce healing, see Rosenberg, "Therapeutic Revolution," esp. 14–21.

43. For further discussion of Thomsonianism, see Fuller, *Alternative Medicine*, 17–22; William G. Rothstein, "The Botanical Movements and Orthodox Medicine," in Gevitz, *Other Healers*, esp. 42–46; Whorton, *Nature Cures*, 25–48.

44. For further discussion of homeopathy, see Fuller, *Alternative Medicine*, 22–26; Martin Kaufman, "Homeopathy in America: The Rise and Fall and Persistence of a Medical Heresy," in Gevitz, *Other Healers*, 99–123; Whorton, *Nature Cures*, 49–75; Naomi Rogers, *An Alternative Path: The Making and Remaking of Hahnemann Medical College and Hospital of Philadelphia* (New Brunswick, N.J.: Rutgers University Press, 1998).

45. See Rothstein, *American Physicians*, 345; Paul Starr, *The Social Transformation of American Medicine* (New York: Basic Books, 1982), 126–127.

46. This list does not include other alternative systems (such as mesmerism, hydropathy, and the like) that reached their apex in the nineteenth century—and helped shaped the assumptions and practices of later groups—but lacked a coherent following in the early 1900s. I also group osteopathic and chiropractic medicine together here due to their similar procedures, despite the fact that the underlying theories motivating those actions proved very different (and often led to bitter recriminations between the two groups). For an overview of the history of osteopathy, see Norman Gevitz, *The DOs: Osteopathic Medicine in America*, 2nd ed. (Baltimore: Johns Hopkins University Press, 2004). For surveys of the history of chiropractic medicine, see Walter I. Wardwell, "Chiropractors: Evolution to Acceptance," in Gevitz, *Other Healers*, 157–191; J. Stuart Moore, *Chiropractic in America: The History of a Medical Alternative* (Baltimore: Johns Hopkins University Press, 1993).

47. Sylvester Graham, *Lectures on the Science of Human Life* (London: Horsell, 1849), 258.

48. For more on Graham, see Stephen Nissenbaum, *Sex, Diet, and Debility in Jacksonian America: Sylvester Graham and Health Reform* (Westport, Conn.: Greenwood Press, 1980); Whorton, *Crusaders for Fitness*, esp. 38–91; Karen Iacobbo and Michael Iacobbo, *Vegetarian America: A History* (Westport, Conn.: Praeger, 2004), 15–70. For further discussion of Ellen G. White and John H. Kellogg's impact on health reform, see esp. Ronald L. Numbers, *Prophetess of Health: Ellen G. White and the Origins of Seventh-Day Adventist Health Reform* (Knoxville: University of Tennessee Press, 1992); Ronald L. Numbers, "Sex, Science and Salvation: The Sexual Advice of Ellen G. White and John Harvey Kellogg," in *Right Living: An Anglo-American Tradition of Self-Help Medicine and Hygiene*, ed. Charles E. Rosenberg (Baltimore: Johns Hopkins University Press, 2003), 206–226; Iacobbo and Iacobbo, *Vegetarian America*, esp. 97–100, 126–130.

49. Mary Baker Eddy, *Science and Health, with Key to the Scriptures* rev. ed. (Boston: A. V. Stewart, 1905), 109. For more on Eddy, see Gillian Gill, *Mary Baker Eddy* (Reading, Mass.: Perseus Books, 1998); Robert Peel, *Mary Baker Eddy* (New York: Holt, Rinehart and Winston, 1966). For discussion of Christian Scientists' struggles with the medical establishment, see Rennie B. Schoepflin, *Christian Science on Trial: Religious Healing in America* (Baltimore: Johns Hopkins University Press, 2003).

50. For helpful discussions of New Thought spirituality that place the tradition in the broader context of American religious history, see Ann Taves, *Fits, Trances, and Visions: Experiencing Religion and Explaining Experience from Wesley to James* (Princeton, N.J.: Princeton University Press, 1999), 213–215, 222–225; Albanese, *Republic of Mind and Spirit*, esp. 300–329; Amanda Porterfield, *The Transformation of American Religion: The Story of a Late-Twentieth-Century Awakening* (New York: Oxford University Press, 2001), 196–198. For a useful diagram illustrating some of the complex sources of New Thought emphases—ranging from Swedenborgianism to Universalism and to nineteenth-century mesmerism, among others—see Catherine L. Albanese, *America, Religions and Religion*, 4th ed. (Belmont, Calif.: Thomson Wadsworth, 2007), 192.

51. Ralph Waldo Trine, *In Tune with the Infinite; or, Fullness of Peace, Power, and Plenty* (London: G. Bell, 1905), 179–181.

52. For surveys of American religion that incorporate significant discussion of the history of metaphysical religion in the United States, see esp. Albanese, *Republic of Mind and Spirit*; Fuller, *Alternative Medicine*; Taves, *Fits, Trances, and Visions*. In her own definition, Albanese identifies the American metaphysical tradition with the following four traits: (1) a preoccupation with the mind—broadly defined—and its powers; (2) a confidence in the theory of correspondence wherein the visible world proves a microcosm of powers and essences in the universe; (3) a focus on movement and energy; and (4) a "yearning for salvation understood as solace, comfort, therapy, and healing." Albanese, *Republic of Mind and Spirit*, 13–16, 399–412. Despite the overlap between my definition of "metaphysical" and Albanese's, my own use of the term places less stress on mind-oriented metaphysical groups (though it certainly encompasses those groups), and highlights the deemphasis on

personal notions of the divine that often accompanied metaphysical practitioners' focus on movement and energy.

53. Sydney E. Ahlstrom, *A Religious History of the American People*, 2nd ed. (New Haven, Conn.: Yale University Press, 2004), 1019. Ahlstrom characterized metaphysical groups as examples of "harmonial religion." Also see Albanese, *Republic of Mind and Spirit*, 13–14.

54. For further discussion of Swedenborg and his influence, see John S. Haller, Jr., *Swedenborg, Mesmer, and the Mind/Body Connection: The Roots of Complementary Medicine* (West Chester, Pa.: Swedenborg Foundation, 2010); Albanese, *Republic of Mind and Spirit*, esp. 140–144, 175–176, 303–311.

55. Albanese, *Republic of Mind and Spirit*, 14.

56. See Robert C. Fuller, *Mesmerism and the American Cure of Souls* (Philadelphia: University of Pennsylvania Press, 1982).

57. Quoted in Fuller, *Alternative Medicine*, 72.

58. Andrew Still quoted in Fuller, *Alternative Medicine*, 84.

59. See Eddy, *Science and Health, with Key to the Scriptures*.

60. For an overview of the history of naturopathic medicine and philosophy, see Whorton, *Nature Cures*, 191–217.

61. See for example John Harley Warner, "From Specificity to Universalism in Medical Therapeutics: Transformation in the Nineteenth-Century United States," in *Sickness and Health in America: Readings in the History of Medicine and Public Health*, ed. Judith Walzer Leavitt and Ronald L. Numbers, 3rd ed. (Madison: University of Wisconsin Press, 1997), esp. 93–99, quotation 94. Whorton addresses the historical connections between holistic-type approaches to well-being and traditional medicine in Whorton, *Nature Cures*, esp. 15.

62. Throughout this book I define materialism simply as a focus on the tangible, visible world in contrast to a focus on an otherworldly supernatural realm. I am not using the term in the stronger, philosophical sense, which indicates a belief that only the physical world actually exists, nor am I using it to suggest a preoccupation with worldly possessions, though interest in the material world obviously can reinforce consumerist tendencies.

63. Though not focused on healing, in his work on pentecostalism in the United States, R. G. Robins highlights "zones of convergence where Pentecostalism, evangelicalism, and the charismatic movement meet and overlap." In many respects, the core narrative in this book reinforces this type of paradigm, even as it expands the story to include the convergence of pentecostalism with key aspects of medical science, natural healing, and metaphysical religion. For Robins's discussion of these "zones of convergence," see *Pentecostalism in America* (Santa Barbara, Calif.: Praeger, 2010), esp. xii–iii, 95–99, 106, 120–126, quotation xiii. Also see Blumhofer, *Restoring the Faith*, esp. 180–202.

64. Griffith, *Born Again Bodies*, esp. 69–159, quotation 108–109.

65. Trine, *In Tune with the Infinite*, 181–182. Emma Curtis Hopkins represented one of the earliest New Thought practitioners to stress prosperity. See Albanese, *Republic of Mind and Spirit*, esp. 320–321.

66. For a classic discussion of the emergence of American therapeutic culture see T. J. Jackson Lears, "From Salvation to Self-Realization: Advertising and the Therapeutic Roots of the Consumer Culture, 1880–1930," in *The Culture of Consumption: Critical Essays in American History, 1880–1980*, ed. Richard Wightman Fox and T. J. Jackson Lears (New York: Pantheon, 1983), 1–38. While Lears's analysis has helped shaped my own thinking regarding key aspects of American therapeutic culture, in this book I also build on more recent scholarship that is critical of Lears's and others' arguments regarding the relationship between religion and the therapeutic. Whereas Lears suggests that the therapeutic largely replaced previously dominant religious discourses, recent scholarship highlights religious traditions' ability to coexist with and reinforce therapeutic and consumerist emphases. Representative examples include Eva Moskowitz, *In Therapy We Trust: America's Obsession with Self-Fulfillment* (Baltimore: Johns Hopkins University Press, 2001), esp. 10–29; Bethany Moreton, *To Serve God and Wal-Mart: The Making of Christian Free Enterprise* (Cambridge, Mass.: Harvard University Press, 2009), esp. 86–99. For discussion of charismatic women's participation in American therapeutic culture, specifically through the Woman's

Aglow Fellowship, see R. Marie Griffith, *God's Daughters: Evangelical Women and the Power of Submission* (Berkeley: University of California Press, 1997), esp. 33–39, 80–109.

67. Representative critiques of American therapeutic culture include Christopher Lasch, *The Culture of Narcissism: American Life in an Age of Diminishing Expectations* (New York: Norton, 1978); Robert N. Bellah et al., *Habits of the Heart: Individualism and Commitment in American Life* (Berkeley: University of California Press, 1985).

68. For discussion of the diverse applications of "holism" and holistic sensibilities in a variety of arenas in U.S. culture following World War II, see Linda Sargent Wood, *A More Perfect Union: Holistic Worldviews and the Transformation of American Culture after World War II* (New York: Oxford University Press, 2010).

69. For discussion of different models for understanding the relationship between holistic thinking and healing, see Charles Rosenberg, "Holism in Twentieth-Century Medicine," in *Greater Than the Parts: Holism in Biomedicine, 1920–50,* ed. Christopher Lawrence and George Weisz (New York: Oxford University Press, 1998), 335–355.

70. See for example the various chapters included in Lawrence and Weisz, *Greater Than the Parts.*

71. In many respects, the instability of the categories "natural" and "supernatural" in relation to religious healing rituals highlights the value of histories focusing on religious practice in addition to analyses of religious traditions' more formal statements of belief. Not only do such histories illuminate the potential disconnect between official statements of belief and adherents' actual practices, they also capture the capacity of rituals—and not just the more formal teachings in a movement—to construct the religious worlds that individuals inhabit. For examples of the growing interest among scholars of religion regarding the significance of religious ritual and practice, several of which deal directly with the history of American religion, see Bell, *Ritual Theory, Ritual Practice*; Catherine M. Bell, "Performance," in *Critical Terms for Religious Studies,* ed. Mark C. Taylor (Chicago: University of Chicago Press, 1998), 205–224; Laurie F. Maffly-Kipp, Leigh Eric Schmidt, and Mark R. Valeri, eds., *Practicing Protestants: Histories of Christian Life in America, 1630–1965* (Baltimore: Johns Hopkins University Press, 2006); David D. Hall, ed., *Lived Religion in America: Toward a History of Practice* (Princeton, N.J.: Princeton University Press, 1997). In the latter volume, see esp. Robert Orsi, "Everyday Miracles: The Study of Lived Religion," 3–21.

72. As a testament to the influence of *Charisma* both in pentecostal and charismatic circles as well as the broader evangelical world, the magazine's founder, Stephen Strang, was listed as one of the twenty-five most influential evangelicals by *Time* in 2005. The Trinity Broadcast Network, which bills itself as the largest religious network in the world, was founded by Paul and Jan Crouch.

73. See Dave Hunt and T. A. McMahon, *The Seduction of Christianity: Spiritual Discernment in the Last Days* (Eugene, Ore.: Harvest House, 1985); D. R. McConnell, *A Different Gospel: Historical and Biblical Analysis of the Modern Faith Movement* (Peabody, Mass.: Hendrickson, 1988). In an attempt to refute the type of criticisms articulated by Hunt, McMahon, and McConnell, William L. DeArteaga published *Quenching the Spirit* (Lake Mary, Fl.: Charisma House, 1996).

74. Like the more theologically minded works mentioned in note 73, to date, most of the scholarship assessing the relationship between pentecostalism and metaphysical groups has focused on the influence of New Thought on proponents of the "prosperity gospel" who were closely associated with the Word of Faith and inner healing branches of the pentecostal-charismatic movement. See for example Dale H. Simmons *E. W. Kenyon and the Postbellum Pursuit of Peace, Power, and Plenty* (Lanham, Md.: Scarecrow Press, 1997); Milmon F. Harrison, *Righteous Riches: The Word of Faith Movement in Contemporary African American Religion* (New York: Oxford University Press, 2005); Jonathan L. Walton, *Watch This! The Ethics and Aesthetics of Black Televangelism* (New York: New York University Press, 2009); Catherine Bowler, "Blessed Bodies: Healing in the African-American Faith Movement," in *Global Pentecostal and Charismatic Healing,* ed. Candy Gunther Brown (New York: Oxford University Press, 2011), 81–105. Other notable works that also have influenced

my thinking regarding the relationship between the pentecostal-charismatic movement and metaphysical traditions include Candy Gunther Brown's assessment of charismatics and other evangelicals' appropriation of chiropractic medicine, and William L. De Arteaga's discussion of Agnes Sanford's importance in the charismatic movement. See Candy Gunther Brown, "Chiropractic and Christianity: The Power of Pain to Adjust Cultural Alignments," *Church History* 79, no. 1 (2010): 144–181; William L. DeArteaga, "Agnes Sanford: Apostle of Healing, and First Theologian of the Charismatic Renewal," pt. 1, *Pneuma Review* 9, no. 2 (2006): 6–17; William L. DeArteaga, "Agnes Sanford: Apostle of Healing, and First Theologian of the Charismatic Renewal," pt. 2 *Pneuma Review* 9, no. 3 (2006): 4–17; DeArteaga, *Quenching the Spirit*. Finally, though neither focuses specifically on the pentecostal-charismatic movement, Heather Curtis's discussion of the late-nineteenth-century divine healing movement and R. Marie Griffith's study of evangelical diet culture have significant import for the history of pentecostalism as well. Both analyze the relationship between evangelicalism and groups closely associated with the metaphysical tradition. See Curtis, *Faith in the Great Physician*, esp. 60–68; Griffith, *Born Again Bodies*, esp. 160–238.

Chapter One

1. "Dr. Straton Defies Departing Critics," *New York Times*, November 2, 1927, 11; "Son Inspired by God, Straton Declares," *New York Times*, June 25, 1927, 15; "Straton Defends Healing Services," *New York Times*, June 24, 1927, 4. Also see J. Terry Todd, "New York, the New Babylon? Fundamentalism and the Modern City in Reverend Straton's Jazz Age Crusade," in *Faith in the Market: Religion and the Rise of Urban Commercial Culture*, ed. John Michael Giggie and Diane H. Winston (New Brunswick, N.J.: Rutgers University Press, 2002), 74–87.

2. A. J. Tomlinson, *The Last Great Conflict*, ed. Donald W. Dayton (1913; reprint, New York: Garland, 1985), 17.

3. J. Roswell Flower, "An Important Warning," *Pentecost* 2, no. 5 (April 1910): 6.

4. F. M. Britton, "What We Believe," *Pentecostal Holiness Advocate* 7, no. 2 (1923): 3.

5. A. E. L., "Pictures of Pentecost in the Old Testament," *Weekly Evangel*, no. 200 (1917): 7.

6. B. C. Miller, "The Fundamentalist and Divine Healing," *Golden Grain* 1, no. 5 (1926): 7–8.

7. Quoted from a section entitled "Invocation in Part, Sunday, December 7, 1919," in C. H. Mason, *The History and Life Work of Elder C. H. Mason, Chief Apostle, and His Co-Laborers*, ed. Mary Mason (1924; reprint, Memphis: Church of God in Christ, 1987), 47–50.

8. "Threw Away His Crutches," *Apostolic Faith* 1, no. 5 (January 1907): 4. The periodical *Apostolic Faith* was published out of the Azusa Mission in Los Angeles. Printed from 1906 through 1908, the periodical reached a circulation of 40,000. For more regarding its origins and publishing history, see Edith L. Blumhofer and Grant Wacker, "Who Edited the Azusa Apostolic Faith Papers?," *Assemblies of God Heritage* 21 (2001): 15–21.

9. See "At Azusa Mission," *Apostolic Faith* 1, no. 8 (May 1907): 2; Anthea Butler, "Observing the Lives of the Saints: Sanctification as Practice in the Church of God in Christ," in *Practicing Protestants: Histories of Christian Life in America, 1630–1965*, ed. Laurie F. Maffly-Kipp, Leigh Eric Schmidt, and Mark R. Valeri (Baltimore: Johns Hopkins University Press, 2006), 162–163.

10. In the same article, McPherson went on to describe the entire crowd attending her healing crusade in similar terms: "They declared that they had been fasting and praying, and KNEW they had faith to be healed"; Aimee Semple McPherson, "Glimpses of the Great San Diego Revival," *Bridal Call* 4, no. 10 (1921): 11, 13, 17.

11. My understanding of the distinctions setting early pentecostal healing apart from its late-nineteenth-century forebears has been shaped especially by Jonathan R. Baer, "Perfectly Empowered Bodies: Divine Healing in Modernizing America" (Ph.D. diss., Yale University, 2002), 200–326; Heather D. Curtis, *Faith in the Great Physician: Suffering and Divine Healing in American Culture, 1860–1900* (Baltimore: Johns Hopkins University Press, 2007), esp. 196–202; James William Opp, *The Lord for the Body: Religion, Medicine and Protestant*

Faith Healing in Canada, 1880–1930 (Montreal: Ithaca, 2005), 121–175; Grant Wacker, *Heaven Below: Early Pentecostals and American Culture* (Cambridge, Mass.: Harvard University Press, 2001), esp. 26–28.

12. Quoted in Vinson Synan, *The Holiness-Pentecostal Tradition: Charismatic Movements in the Twentieth Century* (Grand Rapids, Mich.: Eerdmans, 1997), 57.

13. For discussion of the role of divine healing in these separatist Methodist groups, see Baer, "Perfectly Empowered Bodies," 173–175; Curtis, *Faith in the Great Physician*, 196–202.

14. Dowie died in 1907, shortly after the outbreak of the pentecostal revivals. Despite his influence on numerous early believers, he never identified with the pentecostal movement. For further discussion of Dowie and his significance, see Jonathan R. Baer, "Redeemed Bodies: The Functions of Divine Healing in Incipient Pentecostalism," *Church History* 70 (2001): 784–754; Paul G. Chappell, "The Divine Healing Movement in America" (Ph.D. diss., Drew University, 1983), 284–340; Curtis, *Faith in the Great Physician*, esp. 197–198; Grant Wacker, "Marching to Zion: Religion in a Modern Utopian Community," *Church History* 54 (1985): 496–511; Edith L. Blumhofer, "The Christian Catholic Apostolic Church and the Apostolic Faith: A Study in the 1906 Pentecostal Revival," in *Charismatic Experiences in History*, ed. Cecil M. Robeck (Peabody, Mass.: Hendrickson, 1985), 126–146. Sandford established his Holy Ghost and Us Bible School in the mid-1890s. Like Dowie, Sandford never identified with pentecostalism, though he did influence early pentecostal leaders such as Charles Parham and A. J. Tomlinson. See Wacker, *Heaven Below*, 155–156; Baer, "Perfectly Empowered Bodies," 219–232.

15. John Alexander Dowie, "Do You Know God's Way of Healing?," *Leaves of Healing* 3, no. 35 (1897): 547.

16. Holman F. Day, "The Saints of Shiloh," *Leslie's Monthly Magazine* 59, no. 6 (April 1905): 689–690.

17. "Healing," *Apostolic Faith* 1, no. 10 (September 1910): 2.

18. "Demoniac Possession," *Pentecost* 2, nos. 9–10 (1910): 10.

19. F. J. Lee, "Insanity—Demonology," *Church of God Evangel* 11, no. 47 (1920): 3. For further discussion of the role of demons in early pentecostal healing, see Robert Mapes Anderson, *Vision of the Disinherited: The Making of American Pentecostalism* (New York: Oxford University Press, 1979), 93–97; Baer, "Perfectly Empowered Bodies," 254–288; Grant Wacker, "The Pentecostal Tradition," in *Caring and Curing*, ed. Ronald L. Numbers and Darrel W. Amundsen (New York: Macmillan, 1986), 523–524.

20. C. H. Mason, *Whole Truth* 4, no. 4 (October 1911): 2.

21. Mason, *History and Life Work of Elder C. H. Mason*, 31.

22. Maria B. Woodworth-Etter, *Questions and Answers on Divine Healing* (Indianapolis: author, n.d.), 37.

23. Margaret Gill, *Apostolic Faith*, 1, no. 6 (February–March 1907): 6.

24. For examples of pentecostals' discussion of factors other than demons and deliverance in the healing process, see P. C. Nelson, *Does Christ Heal Today? Messages of Faith, Hope and Cheer for the Afflicted* (Dallas: Herald of Healing, n.d.), 28–30; Woodworth-Etter, *Questions and Answers*, 18–19.

25. For further discussion of late-nineteenth-century evangelical healers' attitudes toward physicians, see Curtis, *Faith in the Great Physician*, esp. 159–160.

26. Charles Cullis, *Faith Cures; or, Answers to Prayer in the Healing of the Sick* (Boston: Willard Tract Repository, 1879), 6. For more on Cullis's attitudes toward the medical profession, see esp. Baer, "Perfectly Empowered Bodies," 67–68. Also see Curtis, *Faith in the Great Physician*, 59–63.

27. In highlighting Simpson's acknowledgment of the usefulness of the medical profession, I do not mean to deny the fact that he typically depicted reliance on medicine as a sign of weak faith. Contrasting the use of means with the prayer of faith, Simpson added, "But for the trusting and obedient child of God, there is the more excellent way which His Word has clearly prescribed, and by which His name will be ever glorified afresh, and our spiritual life continually renewed." A. B. Simpson, *The Gospel of Healing* (1888), rev. ed. (Harrisburg, Pa.: Christian Alliance, 1915), 70.

28. "Questions Answered," *Apostolic Faith* 1, no. 11 (January 1908): 2.

29. Frank Bartleman, *From Plow to Pulpit: From Maine to California*, in *Witness to Pentecost: The Life of Frank Bartleman* (1924; reprint, New York: Garland, 1985), 23.

30. Tomlinson, *Last Great Conflict*, 15–16.

31. C. W. Conn, "Lee, Flavius Josephus," in *The New International Dictionary of Pentecostal and Charismatic Movements*, ed. Stanley M. Burgess and Ed M. Van der Maas (Grand Rapids, Mich.: Zondervan, 2002), 837.

32. Wacker continues, "Indeed, one of the constant problems for responsible denominational officials was 'extremism,' which they defined as refusal to cooperate with nature by washing a wound, wearing eyeglasses, or seeing a dentist"; "Pentecostal Tradition," 516–525, quotation 524. For other works assessing early pentecostals' relationship with the medical establishment see Baer, "Perfectly Empowered Bodies," esp. 200–326; Wacker, *Heaven Below*, esp. 191–192; R. G. Robins, *A .J. Tomlinson: Plainfolk Modernist* (New York: Oxford University Press, 2004), esp. 40–46; Nancy Hardesty, *Faith Cure: Divine Healing in the Holiness and Pentecostal Movements* (Peabody, Mass.: Hendrickson, 2003), 72–86.

33. Lilian B. Yeomans, "Divine Healing," *Pentecostal Evangel*, nos. 484–485 (1923): 5. For brief discussions of Yeomans's life and significance in the divine healing movement, see Edith Waldvogel Blumhofer, *Aimee Semple McPherson: Everybody's Sister* (Grand Rapids, Mich.: Eerdmans, 1993), 255–256; Baer, "Perfectly Empowered Bodies," 300–301.

34. "Healing and Health," *Church of God Evangel* 9, no. 2 (1918): 1.

35. F. J. Lee, "Reality of Demons," *Church of God Evangel* 11, no. 23 (1920): 3.

36. F. B., "Hints Regarding Divine Healing," *Golden Grain* 3, no. 10 (1928): 28.

37. Charles Parham, *A Voice Crying in the Wilderness*, in *The Sermons of Charles F. Parham*, ed. Donald W. Dayton (1944; reprint, New York: Garland, 1985), 41.

38. Charles Parham, *The Everlasting Gospel*, in Dayton, *Sermons of Charles F. Parham*, 64, 39.

39. Robins, *A. J. Tomlinson*, 31, 20.

40. "Sickness and Health," *Church of God Evangel* 5, no. 28 (1914): 2.

41. Tomlinson, *Last Great Conflict*, 81.

42. Lilian B. Yeomans, "Bible Studies in Divine Healing: Dietetics," *Pentecostal Evangel*, no. 497 (1923): 7.

43. Sarah E. Mitchel, "Testimonies," *Pentecostal Holiness Advocate* 4, no. 25 (1920): 16.

44. Lilian B. Yeomans, *Healing from Heaven* (1926; reprint, Springfield, Mo.: Gospel Publishing House, 1973), 68.

45. Mrs. George Martin, "Healed When Doctor Was Dismissed," *Church of God Evangel* 13, no. 32 (1922): 3.

46. John Harley Warner, "From Specificity to Universalism in Medical Therapeutics: Transformation in the Nineteenth-Century United States," in *Sickness and Health in America: Readings in the History of Medicine and Public Health*, ed. Judith Walzer Leavitt and Ronald L. Numbers, 3rd ed. (Madison: University of Wisconsin Press, 1997), 87–101.

47. Paul Starr, *The Social Transformation of American Medicine* (New York: Basic Books, 1982), 119. Also see Ronald L. Numbers, "The Fall and Rise of the American Medical Profession," in Leavitt and Numbers, *Sickness and Health in America*, esp. 231.

48. John Alexander Dowie, "A Voice to Zion and God's People in Every Land," *Leaves of Healing* 7, no. 23 (1900): 717.

49. Quoted in W. A. Redding, "Doctors and Medicine," *Latter Rain Evangel* 11, no. 8 (1919): 20.

50. John G. Lake, *The John G. Lake Sermons on Dominion over Demons, Disease and Death*, ed. Gordon Lindsay (Shreveport, La.: Christ for the Nations, 1949), 134–135.

51. L. Howard Juillerat, "Many Shall Run to and Fro," *Church of God Evangel* 9, no. 34 (1918): 1.

52. George F. Taylor, editorial, *Pentecostal Holiness Advocate* 4, no. 23 (1920): 9.

53. Tomlinson, *Last Great Conflict*, 37–38.

54. "Healing and Health," 1.

55. Parham, *Voice Crying in the Wilderness*, 41.

56. Woodworth-Etter, *Questions and Answers*, 15.

57. Quoted in Redding, "Doctors and Medicine," 20–22.

58. S. R. Mitchell, "Divine Healing," *Church of God Evangel* 12, no. 28 (1921): 2.

59. Gordon Lindsay, "Demon Oppression and Sickness," *Voice of Healing* 2, no. 12 (1950): 12.

60. E. N. Bell, "Questions and Answers," *Pentecostal Evangel*, nos. 452–453 (1922): 8. For further discussion of Bell as a moderating figure, see Baer, "Perfectly Empowered Bodies," 287–288.

61. Jonathan Baer provides a helpful overview of the debates over divine healing that erupted in pentecostal denominations during the late 1910s and the 1920s. While the Assemblies of God stands out for its moderation, the more conservative factions won out in both the Pentecostal Holiness Church and the Church of God (Cleveland, Tennessee). See Baer, "Perfectly Empowered Bodies," 273–288.

62. Hugh Bowling, "My Position on Divine Healing," *Pentecostal Holiness Advocate* 3, no. 53 (1920): 5. Following Bowling and Sorrow's expulsion, they and their followers established the Congregational Holiness Church. For more on Bowling and the subsequent denomination he formed, see Baer, "Perfectly Empowered Bodies," 277–279; Synan, *Holiness-Pentecostal Tradition*, 196–197.

63. George F. Taylor, editorial, *Pentecostal Holiness Advocate* 3, no. 51 (1920): 9; George F. Taylor, "A Statement," *Pentecostal Holiness Advocate* 3, no. 53 (1920): 3. For a helpful overview of these debates in the church, see Baer, "Perfectly Empowered Bodies," 274–279.

64. Lilian B. Yeomans, *The Great Physician* (1933; reprint, Springfield, Mo.: Gospel Publishing House, 1961), 50.

65. Yeomans, *Healing from Heaven*, 3–4, 42–43.

66. Fred Knutson, "From Dark Despair to Sunlit Service," *Bridal Call Foursquare* 12, no. 7 (1928): 29.

67. J. M. Perkins and Jessie Arms Perkins, "Two Veterans Return from the Field," *Christ's Ambassadors Monthly* 4, no. 10 (1929): 8.

68. John Alexander Dowie, "God Afflicted in His People's Affliction," *Leaves of Healing* 5, no. 17 (1899): 316.

69. See for example Yeomans, *Healing from Heaven*, 68; Bell, "Questions and Answers," *Pentecostal Evangel*, nos. 452–453 (1922): 8.

70. John Alexander Dowie, "A Voice from Zion to God's People in Every Land," *Leaves of Healing* 3, no. 6 (1896): 83. For similar examples of this tripartite notion of human nature, body, mind, and spirit, see D. Wesley Myland, *The Latter Rain Covenant and Pentecostal Power*, in *Three Early Pentecostal Tracts*, ed. Donald W. Dayton (1910; repr., New York: Garland, 1985), esp. 12–16; "Question Box," *Pentecostal Holiness Advocate* 5, no. 35 (1921): 5. For an exception, see the following editorial wherein the author collapses the notion of soul and spirit, George F. Taylor, "Editorial," *Pentecostal Holiness Advocate* 15, no. 12 (1931): 1, 8.

71. T. Smart, "Not Sons of God but Children of Wrath," *Pentecostal Holiness Advocate* 4, no. 21 (1920): 11.

72. "Faith and Works," *Pentecostal Evangel*, no. 358–359 (1920): 9.

73. Ernest S. Williams, "Questions and Answers," *Pentecostal Evangel*, no. 1091 (1935): 5.

74. George F. Taylor, "Basis of Union," *Pentecostal Holiness Advocate* 1, no. 51 (1918): 4.

75. Parham, *Everlasting Gospel*, 17. As the historian Ann Taves notes regarding Parham's comments, "Here, in an exclusivist tradition where we would least expect it, we find the appropriation of a rich mix of concepts borrowed from psychical research (the subconscious) and New Thought (mind, wisdom) to explain the means whereby the 'spiritual man' enters into 'direct communication with the mind of God,'" Ann Taves, *Fits, Trances, and Visions: Experiencing Religion and Explaining Experience from Wesley to James* (Princeton, N.J.: Princeton University Press, 1999), 331.

76. Yeomans, *Healing from Heaven*, 89.

77. William D. Gentry, *The Problem of Life, or the Royal Road to Health* (Chicago: author, 1916), 390–416, 231–257, quotations 243, 12. I thank Darrin Rodgers, director of the Flower Pentecostal Heritage Center, for bringing Gentry to my attention.

78. For an overview of alternative healers' typical perspectives on the use of medicines and drugs, see James C. Whorton, *Nature Cures: The History of Alternative Medicine in America* (New York: Oxford University Press, 2002), 4–16. Heather Curtis also discusses the

overlap between alternative medicine and the divine healing movement during the late nineteenth century, focusing in particular on the two groups' shared focus on personal responsibility for health as well as their shared resistance to medicines; Curtis, *Faith in the Great Physician*, esp. 59–68.

79. Parham, *Voice Crying in the Wilderness*, 41.

80. John Alexander Dowie, "New York Visitation of Elijah the Restorer and Zion Restoration Host," *Leaves of Healing* 16, no. 17 (1905): 541.

81. *Apostolic Faith*, 1, no. 8 (May 1907): 2.

82. Charles S. Price, "Is Healing in the Atonement?," *Golden Grain* 5, no. 8 (1930): 22–23.

83. For discussion of physicians' appreciation of the cultural authority provided by linking medical therapeutics to experimental science around the turn of the twentieth century, see Gerald L. Geison, "Divided We Stand: Physiologists and Clinicians in the American Context," in Leavitt and Numbers, *Sickness and Health in America*, esp. 125–127.

84. Advertisement for Drs. Clyde and Margaret Crow, Chiropractors, *Duluth News Tribune*, November 25, 1917, 6.

85. Elbert Hubbard, "The Success of Osteopathy," *El Paso Herald*, October 26, 1912, 24.

86. Far from being relegated to a few intellectual elites, Common Sense assumptions filtered down to the average evangelical parishioner during the nineteenth century. See Mark A. Noll, "Common Sense Traditions and American Evangelical Thought," *American Quarterly* 37 (1985): 222–223; George M. Marsden, "Everyone One's Own Interpreter: The Bible, Science, and Authority in Mid-nineteenth-century America," in *The Bible in America: Essays in Cultural History*, ed. Nathan O. Hatch and Mark A. Noll (New York: Oxford University Press, 1982), 79–100. For discussion of these trends in relation to pentecostals, and in particular in relation to their reading of scripture, see Wacker, *Heaven Below*, 75.

87. For further discussion of pentecostals' use of their experiences as proof of the Spirit's reality, see Joseph Williams, "Modernity Baptized in the Spirit," in *Agency in the Margins: Stories of Outsider Rhetoric*, ed. Anne Meade Stockdell-Giesler (Madison, N.J.: Fairleigh Dickinson University Press, 2009), 241–260.

88. McPherson, "Glimpses of the Great San Diego Revival," 10.

89. Robins, *A. J. Tomlinson*, 38–39.

90. In *Heaven Below*, Wacker is careful to highlight the sense of impending doom that often accompanied pentecostals' eschatological emphases, yet he simultaneously points to the "exhilarating sense of hope" that these beliefs also engendered and the way they contributed to pentecostals' "invincible confidence in their own prospects for religious and perhaps even cultural victory in this present world." *Heaven Below*, 250–265, quotation 251–252.

91. For further discussion of the overlap linking mind-cure proponents' stress on "positive confession" and trends in the nineteenth-century divine healing movement, see Dale H. Simmons, *E. W. Kenyon and the Postbellum Pursuit of Peace, Power, and Plenty* (Lanham, Md.: Scarecrow Press, 1997), esp. 159–160, 171–173, 207–232.

92. Carrie Judd [Montgomery], *The Prayer of Faith*, in *The Life and Teachings of Carrie Judd Montgomery*, ed. Donald W. Dayton (1880; reprint, New York: Garland, 1985), 93. For more on Montgomery's attitude toward faith and healing, see Curtis, *Faith in the Great Physician*, 91–94.

93. F. B., "Hints Regarding Divine Healing," 28.

94. Fannie F. Rowe, "The House Top Healing," *Bridal Call Foursquare* 8, no. 1 (1924): 29.

95. George F. Taylor, "Question Box," *Pentecostal Holiness Advocate* 3, no. 51 (1920): 10.

96. J. R. Miller, "How to Keep in Health," *Pentecostal Evangel*, nos. 402–403 (1921): 5.

97. Alice E. Luce, "The Great Physician and His Medicines," *Pentecostal Evangel*, no. 864 (September 1930): 6.

98. Yeomans, "Bible Studies in Divine Healing," 6–7.

99. George F. Taylor, "Sunday School Lesson," *Pentecostal Holiness Advocate* 2, no. 26 (1918): 1–2.

100. William H. Piper, "Be Not Deceived; God Is Not Mocked," *Latter Rain Evangel* 3, no. 4 (1911): 16.

101. Gentry, *Problem of Life*, esp. 106–126, 138–211.
102. "Health of Body," *Whole Truth* 10, no. 1 (1934): 9. Also see Butler, "Observing the Lives of the Saints," 163.
103. "Prayer Requests," *Pentecostal Evangel*, no. 478–479 (1923): 14.
104. S. S. Times, "Appreciating Salvation," *Pentecostal Holiness Advocate* 9, no. 43 (1926): 11.
105. E. N. Bell, "Questions and Answers," *Weekly Evangel*, no. 131 (1916): 8.
106. Bell, "Questions and Answers," *Pentecostal Evangel*, nos. 452–453 (1922): 8.
107. Fannie Reif quoted in "One Who Walked and Talked with God," *Latter Rain Evangel* 23, no. 12 (1931): 19. It is also worth highlighting the fact that Reif's testimony occurred in the context of a parent seeking divine healing for a child, a very controversial subject that led states to pass laws forcing parents to seek medical care for minors regardless of the parents' religious beliefs.
108. F. B., "Hints Regarding Divine Healing," 28–29.
109. Taylor, "Basis of Union," 4.
110. Yeomans, *Healing from Heaven*, 92.
111. John 4:8 (King James Version).
112. Acts 2:2–3 (King James Version).
113. "The Baptism with the Holy Ghost Foreshadowed," *Apostolic Faith* 1, no. 4 (December 1906): 2; William J. Seymour, "The Baptism of the Holy Ghost," *Apostolic Faith* 2, no. 13 (May 1908): 3. For a more detailed discussion of early pentecostals' conceptions of "Shekina glory," see Taves, Fits, Trances, and Visions, 337–341.
114. Alan Trachtenberg and Eric Foner, *The Incorporation of America: Culture and Society in the Gilded Age* (New York: Hill and Wang, 1982), 38–69. Also see David E. Nye, *Electrifying America: Social Meanings of a New Technology, 1880–1940* (Cambridge, Mass.: MIT Press, 1990).
115. Martin Wells Knapp, *Out of Egypt into Canaan; or, Lessons in Spiritual Geography*, 2nd ed. (Cincinnati: Cranston & Stowe, 1888), 193.
116. Martin Wells Knapp, *Revival Tornadoes; or, Life and Labors of Rev. Joseph H. Weber: Evangelist, the Converted Roman Catholic*, 3rd ed. (Boston: McDonald, Gill & Co., 1890), 81. For more on the life and ministry of Martin Wells Knapp, see William Kostlevy, *Holy Jumpers: Evangelicals and Radicals in Progressive Era America* (New York: Oxford University Press, 2010), esp. 17–36.
117. Lake, *John G. Lake Sermons*, 47, 56. In a manner very similar to Lake's description of the Holy Spirit, William Gentry described faith as an "invisible substance as much as gas, electricity, or air are substances." *Problem of Life*, 258.
118. *Apostolic Faith* 1, no. 8 (May 1907): 4.
119. George E. Berg, "Baptized with the Holy Ghost," *Apostolic Faith* 1, no. 4 (December 1906): 3.
120. T. Hezmalhalch, "Pentecost in Pueblo, Colo.," *Apostolic Faith* 1, no. 5 (January 1907): 4.
121. For numerous examples of the ways early pentecostals used the human body or other physical objects to transmit God's power, see Kimberly Ervin Alexander's detailed description of healing practices in the various denominations in *Pentecostal Healing: Models in Theology and Practice* (Dorset, England: Deo, 2006), 64–194.
122. References in the New Testament to laying hands on the sick, anointing with oil, and the use of handkerchiefs can be found in Mark 16:18, James 5:14, and Acts 19:11–12.
123. W. R. Ward, *Early Evangelicalism: A Global Intellectual History, 1670–1789* (Cambridge: Cambridge University Press, 2006), esp. 6–23, quotations 4, 11. Also see Mark A. Noll and Bruce Hindmarsh, "Rewriting the History of Evangelicalism," *Books and Culture* 17, no. 2 (2011): 8.
124. For a classic discussion of the "experiential strain" in Puritan spirituality, see Sydney E. Ahlstrom, *A Religious History of the American People*, 2nd ed. (New Haven, Conn.: Yale University Press, 2004), esp. 126–128. Also see Amanda Porterfield, *The Transformation of American Religion: The Story of a Late-Twentieth-Century Awakening* (New York: Oxford University Press, 2001), esp. 12–20.

125. Ann Taves details the differences separating Edwards and Wesley's views of the Spirit's interaction with the body, drawing interesting parallels to the differences separating the views of the early pentecostal leaders Charles Parham and William Seymour on the same subject. Nevertheless, all pentecostals stood closer to Wesley than to Edwards on the matter. For pentecostals, she writes, "possession swept away all barriers between the believer and God and allowed the Spirit to take control of the person." Taves, *Fits, Trances, and Visions*, esp. 20–75, 328–341, quotation 334.

126. See Curtis, *Faith in the Great Physician*, esp. 118–120. For examples of similar explanations of the symbolic functions of oil in early pentecostal literature see Maria Beulah Woodworth-Etter, *Signs and Wonders God Wrought in the Ministry for Forty Years* (Indianapolis: author, 1916), 502; B. R. Dean, "Divine Healing as in the Atonement," *Pentecostal Holiness Advocate* 4 no. 11 (July 1920): 2.

127. E. N. Bell, "Remarkable Revival in London," *Pentecostal Evangel*, nos. 426–427 (1922): 10. Elsewhere, Bell responded affirmatively to the question whether or not the Holy Spirit could "be imparted by the laying on of hands." As long as the person praying was "authorized by God to do so," then "it can be done." E. N. Bell, *Questions and Answers* (Springfield, Mo.: Gospel Publishing House, 1923), 27.

128. N. Lecomte, "I Am the Lord that Healeth Thee," *Pentecostal Evangel*, no. 534 (1924): 8.

129. Lillian Hardister, "The Woodworth-Etter Revival," *Christian Evangel*, nos. 308–309 (1919): 13.

130. Woodworth-Etter, *Questions and Answers*, 39.

131. Yeomans, *Healing from Heaven*, 13.

132. Maria Beulah Woodworth-Etter, *Life and Experience Including Sermons and Visions of Mrs. M. B. Woodworth-Etter*, rev. ed. (St. Louis, Mo.: Commercial Printing, 1904), 270.

133. William D. Gentry, "God's Provision for the Healing of the Body," in *Health and Healing: The Key to Holiness, Happiness, Health and Long Life*, ed. M. B. Case (Greeley, Colo.: M. B. Case, 1909), 200. As Grant Wacker notes, "where most Christians and a majority of radical evangelicals had considered prayer for healing a petition for God's favor, Pentecostals effectively considered it a causal agent in itself. God had promised to respond positively to all genuine prayers, therefore He would." Wacker, *Heaven Below*, 26.

134. Lake, *John G. Lake Sermons*, 47.

135. During the same message, Dowie explained that the root word for science "means accurate and positive knowledge." John Alexander Dowie, "Elijah's Restoration: Messages of Purity, Peace and Power," *Leaves of Healing* 10, no. 18 (1902): 817, 821. R. G. Robins notes similar examples related to Dowie's ministry, see Robins, *A. J. Tomlinson*, 46.

136. F. F. Bosworth, *Christ the Healer*, rev. ed. (1948; reprint, Old Tappan, N.J.: Fleming H. Revell, 1973), 125–126. Also see Wacker, *Heaven Below*, 26.

Chapter Two

1. Cecil Bridges, "Divine Healing," *Church of God Evangel* 44, no. 4 (1953): 11.

2. David Burris, "Making the Pentecostal Sunday School Go," *Pentecostal Evangel*, no. 942 (1932): 6.

3. J. Bashford Bishop, "The Sunday School Lesson," *Pentecostal Evangel*, no. 1373 (1940): 10.

4. Vance Byars, "A Doctor Calls upon the Great Physician," *Full Gospel Business Men's Voice* 12, no. 9 (1964): 14.

5. For discussion of the impact of World War I on pentecostals, and discussion of institution-building in the pentecostal movement as seen in the Assemblies of God, see R. G. Robins, *Pentecostalism in America* (Santa Barbara, Calif.: Praeger, 2010), 51–56; Edith Waldvogel Blumhofer, *Restoring the Faith: The Assemblies of God, Pentecostalism, and American Culture* (Urbana: University of Illinois Press, 1993), 142–163. R. Laurence Moore also discusses pentecostals' movement away from their early apolitical stance and toward full-fledged patriotism and engagement with the wider culture in *Religious Outsiders and the Making of Americans* (New York: Oxford University Press, 1986), 128–149. Other historians

highlight the role of healing evangelists in bringing pentecostal spirituality closer to the mainstream beginning in the 1920s, frequently highlighting the role of Aimee Semple McPherson. See Jonathan R. Baer, "Perfectly Empowered Bodies: Divine Healing in Modernizing America" (Ph.D. diss., Yale University, 2002), 289–326; James William Opp, *The Lord for the Body: Religion, Medicine and Protestant Faith Healing in Canada, 1880–1930* (Montreal: Ithaca, 2005), 146–175; Matthew Avery Sutton, *Aimee Semple McPherson and the Resurrection of Christian America* (Cambridge, Mass.: Harvard University Press, 2007).

6. See Blumhofer, *Restoring the Faith*, esp. 180–202. R. G. Robins also addresses the evangelicalization of pentecostalism at several points throughout *Pentecostalism in America*.

7. Christian Smith, *American Evangelicalism: Embattled and Thriving* (Chicago: University of Chicago Press, 1998), esp. 1–15. On evangelicals' changing relationship with the broader culture, also see Joel A. Carpenter, *Revive Us Again: The Reawakening of American Fundamentalism* (New York: Oxford University Press, 1997); George M. Marsden, *Reforming Fundamentalism: Fuller Seminary and the New Evangelicalism* (Grand Rapids, Mich.: Eerdmans, 1987).

8. As one historian notes, by the late 1940s and 1950s, pentecostals "began to show up in places where they had not been seen before. . . . For the first time, there were Pentecostal lawyers, medical doctors, and university professors." Vinson Synan, *The Holiness-Pentecostal Tradition: Charismatic Movements in the Twentieth Century* (Grand Rapids, Mich.: Eerdmans, 1997), 222. For further discussion of the impact of post–World War II demographic changes in the pentecostal movement on pentecostal healing and on pentecostals' relationship with the medical profession, see Grant Wacker, "The Pentecostal Tradition," in *Caring and Curing*, ed. Ronald L. Numbers and Darrel W. Amundsen (New York: Macmillan, 1986), esp. 525–532. For more on the FGBMFI see Blumhofer, *Restoring the Faith*, 225–226; David Edwin Harrell, Jr., *All Things Are Possible: The Healing and Charismatic Revivals in Modern America* (Bloomington: Indiana University Press, 1975), 146–149; Synan, *Holiness-Pentecostal Tradition*, 223–224; J. R. Ziegler, "Full Gospel Business Men's Fellowship International," in *The New International Dictionary of Pentecostal and Charismatic Movements*, ed. Stanley M. Burgess and Ed M. Van der Maas (Grand Rapids, Mich.: Zondervan, 2002), 653–654.

9. For discussion of these changes, see Paul Starr, *The Social Transformation of American Medicine* (New York: Basic Books, 1982), 134–144.

10. For discussion of twentieth-century improvements in American health care, such as physicians' use of antibiotics, the "wonder drugs," see John Parascandola, "The Introduction of Antibiotics into Therapeutics," in *Sickness and Health in America: Readings in the History of Medicine and Public Health*, ed. Judith Walzer Leavitt and Ronald L. Numbers (Madison: University of Wisconsin Press, 1997), 102–112; John Duffy, *From Humors to Medical Science: A History of American Medicine* (Urbana, Ill.: University of Illinois Press, 1993), esp. 240–241, 251–252, 257–274; Richard Hollingham, *Blood and Guts: A History of Surgery* (New York: Macmillan, 2009), 299–301.

11. Ronald L. Numbers, "The Fall and Rise of the American Medical Profession," in Leavitt and Numbers, *Sickness and Health in America*, 225.

12. Starr, *Social Transformation of American Medicine*, 134–144, 262.

13. "Socialized Medicine Viewed by Angell," *New York Times*, October 17, 1931, 8.

14. Margaret M. Poloma, *The Assemblies of God at the Crossroads: Charisma and Institutional Dilemmas* (Knoxville: University of Tennessee Press, 1989), 58–60.

15. For further discussions of the healing revivalists' relationship with pentecostal denominations see Harrell, *All Things Are Possible*, 107–116.

16. R. G. Robins provides helpful discussion of developments during this period in *Pentecostalism in America*, esp. 75–91. In addition, in his work on divine healing among early pentecostals, Jonathan Baer notes the frequent correlation between major wars and healing revivals, suggesting that "Cold War fears may have helped lay the groundwork for [the mid–century healing revivals]," "Perfectly Empowered Bodies," 53n76.

17. For more on the New Order of the Latter Rain, see Robins, *Pentecostalism in America*, 79–80; Blumhofer, *Restoring the Faith*, 203–211; L. Thomas Holdcroft, "The New Order of

the Latter Rain," *Pneuma* 2 (1980): 46–60; R. M. Riss, "Latter Rain Movement," in Burgess and Van der Maas, *New International Dictionary of Pentecostal and Charismatic Movements*, 830–833; Wacker, "Pentecostal Tradition," 525.

18. For helpful profiles of a number of the deliverance evangelists of the 1940s, 1950s, and 1960s, see Blumhofer, *Restoring the Faith*, 211–221; David R. Kinsley, *Health, Healing, and Religion: A Cross-cultural Perspective* (Upper Saddle River, N.J.: Prentice Hall, 1996), 119–138; Harrell, *All Things Are Possible*; Stephen Jackson Pullum, *"Foul Demons, Come Out!" The Rhetoric of Twentieth-Century American Faith Healing* (Westport, Conn.: Praeger, 1999), 25–86; C. Douglas Weaver, *The Healer-Prophet, William Marrion Branham: A Study of the Prophetic in American Pentecostalism* (Macon, Ga.: Mercer University Press, 1987); Wacker, "Pentecostal Tradition," 526–527.

19. A. A. Allen, "My Statement on Healing," *Miracle Magazine* 4, no. 3 (1958): 2.

20. Gordon Lindsay, "The Casting Out of Demon Spirits," *Voice of Healing* 1, no. 5 (1948): 11.

21. William Branham, *Demonology* (Jeffersonville, Ind.: Spoken Word, 1976), 31–32. Oneness pentecostals, who emerged as a distinctive branch in American pentecostalism in the early years of the pentecostal movement, denied the traditional Trinitarian conceptions of God in Christianity, emphasizing instead the "oneness" of God and his full manifestation in the person of Jesus. See David Reed, *In Jesus Name: The History and Beliefs of Oneness Pentecostals* (Blandford Forum, England: Deo, 2008); Robins, *Pentecostalism in America*, 40–41, 45–46.

22. T. L. Osborn, *Healing the Sick* (Tulsa: T. L. Osborn Evangelistic Association, 1959), 127.

23. Harrell, *All Things Are Possible*, 28, 37.

24. Roberts indicated that he eventually backed off claims that all diseases reflected demonic influence after being confronted by a group of pentecostal ministers; David Edwin Harrell, Jr., *Oral Roberts: An American Life* (Bloomington: Indiana University Press, 1985), 89–90. Also see Oral Roberts, *If You Need Healing Do These Things*, 2nd ed. (Tulsa Okla.: Oral Roberts Evangelistic Association, 1957), 30–33.

25. Gordon Lindsay, "Nature of the Gifts of Healing," *Voice of Healing* 1, no. 4 (1948): 11.

26. Jack Coe, *Curing the Incurable* (Dallas: Herald of Healing, n.d.), 42. For more on Jack Coe's career, see Blumhofer, *Restoring the Faith*, 214–215; Harrell, *All Things Are Possible*, esp. 58–63.

27. O. L. Jaggers, *Everlasting Spiritual and Physical Health* (Dexter, Mo.: author, 1949), 157.

28. See Harrell, *All Things Are Possible*, 59, 101.

29. Osborn, *Healing the Sick*, 192–193.

30. A. A. Allen, "Does God Heal thru Medicine?," pt. 2, *Miracle Magazine* 6, no. 6 (1961): 2–3.

31. Oral Roberts, "The Healing of Cancer," *Healing Waters* 2, no. 3 (1949): 2, 14.

32. Roberts, *If You Need Healing Do These Things*, 80–81.

33. Oral Roberts, "The Science of Faith," *Abundant Life* 11, no. 2 (1957): 4. While Roberts was not the first pentecostal to express such a clear endorsement of the medical profession, considering his influence, Roberts undoubtedly spurred the growing approval of mainstream medicine in pentecostal circles.

34. This was not the only instance when Branham and his family accepted medical treatment. On the whole, however, Branham's biographer concludes that Branham's attitude toward medicine was "more akin to the earliest Pentecostals [for whom medicine was suspect]," Weaver, *Healer-Prophet*, 66–68, quotation 67.

35. "Questions and Answers on Divine Healing," *Voice of Healing* 1, no. 9 (1948): 13, 15. The response was likely written by the editor of *Voice of Healing*, Gordon Lindsay.

36. Quoted in Harrell, *All Things Are Possible*, 101.

37. Branham, *Demonology*, 33; Weaver, *Healer-Prophet*, 66.

38. Osborn, *Healing the Sick*, 131.

39. Allen, "Does God Heal thru Medicine?," pt. 2, 3.

40. "When the Enemy Comes in Like a Flood," *Pentecostal Evangel*, no. 563 (1924): 1.

41. A. G. Ward, "Where Are the Weeping Prophets Today?" *Latter Rain Evangel* 20, no. 12 (1928): 6.

42. In the words of James Whorton, historian of alternative medicine, for naturopaths, "impos-
ing self–control and returning to nature's intended mode of life (hygeiotherapy, in other
words) was a necessary first step but was not always sufficient. Then active measures to rid
the body of impurities had to be brought into play—but only measures that were friendly to
nature by offering support or stimulation." *Nature Cures: The History of Alternative Medicine
in America* (New York: Oxford University Press, 2002), 191–217. For further discussion of
naturopaths' commitment to vitalism and to conceptions of a "life force," see ibid., 224–225.

43. E. B. Noel, "Fasting," *Church of God Evangel* 19, no. 6 (1928): 2.

44. E. N. Bell, "Questions and Answers," *Weekly Evangel*, no. 181 (1917): 9.

45. For a brief but useful overview of Hall and his influence, see Harrell, *All Things Are Possible*,
80–82, 212–214, quotation 81. Hall contributed an article on fasting in the early years of
the revival in the *Voice of Healing*, one of the earliest and most prominent periodicals dedicated to broadcasting the activities of the healing evangelists such as William Branham;
see Franklin Hall, "The Power of Healing," *Voice of Healing* 2, no. 7 (1949): 11. His books
also were advertised in the periodicals of other evangelists, including A. A. Allen's *Miracle
Magazine*. See for example *Miracle Magazine* 2, no. 6 (1957): 22.

46. Franklin Hall, *Glorified Fasting: The Abc of Fasting* (San Diego, Calif.: Franklin Hall, 1948),
15.

47. Franklin Hall, *The Fasting Prayer* (San Diego, Calif.: Franklin Hall, 1947), 196.

48. Hall, "Power of Healing," 11.

49. Hall, *Glorified Fasting*, 39.

50. Hall, *Fasting Prayer*, 97, 116–119, 194.

51. Hall, *Glorified Fasting*, 15.

52. Hall, *Fasting Prayer*, 194.

53. Quoted in Hall, *Glorified Fasting*, 22–25.

54. Gordon Lindsay, for example, the editor of the *Voice of Healing*, eventually told Hall he
would not publish advertisements for his books or meetings due to resistance from pentecostal denominations. See Harrell, *All Things Are Possible*, 81.

55. Hall, *Fasting Prayer*, 120.

56. To the contrary, Gee wanted to "clear away the rubbish," arguing instead that "our souls
should be extremely active in all that pertains to divine worship." "Music and the Spirit–
Filled Life," *Pentecostal Evangel*, no. 1150 (1936): 6.

57. Donald Gee, "Mental Illness and Pentecostal Religion," *Pentecost*, no. 39 (1957): 17.

58. For a helpful overview of evangelicals' initial rejection of psychology (as well as their growing affinities to American therapeutic culture), see David Harrington Watt, *A Transforming
Faith: Explorations of Twentieth-Century American Evangelicalism* (New Brunswick, N.J.:
Rutgers University Press, 1991), esp. 137–154. Despite distinctive trends among pentecostals and charismatics, the overall trajectory of pentecostals and charismatics' changing
relationship with psychology and psychiatry over the course of the twentieth century cor-
responds with Watt's discussion.

59. Robert C. McQuilkin, "The Problem of Purity," *Pentecostal Evangel*, no. 755 (1928): 5.

60. G. H. Montgomery, "The Face of the Future," *Pentecostal Holiness Advocate* 29, no. 10
(1945): 2.

61. Jonathan E. Perkins, "Higher Education and Lower Infidelity," *Pentecostal Evangel*, no. 575
(1924): 3.

62. Lilian B. Yeomans, "The Lame Man of Lystra," *Pentecostal Evangel*, no. 637 (1926): 7.

63. Charles S. Price, "The Gospel According to Jonah," *Golden Grain* 4, no. 4 (1929): 17.

64. Charles S. Price, "Healing from Heaven," *Golden Grain* 7, no. 6 (1932): 9.

65. E. N. Bell, "Questions and Answers," *Pentecostal Evangel*, nos. 392–393 (1921): 10.

66. George F. Taylor, editorial, *Pentecostal Holiness Advocate* 13, no. 12 (1929): 1. It also is interesting to note that educational institutions associated with the Pentecostal Holiness
Church offered courses on psychology to high schoolers and to individuals training for
ministry both at home and abroad. See for example Nina C. Holmes, "Sketch of the Holmes
Bible and Missionary Institute," *Pentecostal Holiness Advocate* 15, no. 30 (1931): 2; "Franklin Springs Institute," *Pentecostal Holiness Advocate* 6, no. 3 (1922): 10–11.

67. M. L. Bradbury, "Biodivinity: The Encounter of Religion and Medicine," in *Transforming Faith: The Sacred and Secular in Modern American History*, ed. James Burkhart Gilbert (New York: Greenwood Press, 1989), 161–182. For further discussion of evangelicals' initial reticence to accept psychology and the eventual formation of evangelical counseling and training centers, see R. Marie Griffith, *God's Daughters: Evangelical Women and the Power of Submission* (Berkeley: University of California Press, 1997), 35–36; Watt, *Transforming Faith*, esp. 137–154.

68. Watt, *Transforming Faith*, 143.

69. Quoted in Ann Taves, *Fits, Trances, and Visions: Experiencing Religion and Explaining Experience from Wesley to James* (Princeton, N.J.: Princeton University Press, 1999), 314. For more on the Emmanuel Movement see ibid., 314–325. Also see Raymond J. Cunningham, "The Emmanuel Movement: A Variety of American Religious Experience," *American Quarterly* 14, no. 1 (1962): 48–63; Bradbury, "Biodivinity."

70. For further discussion of Peale see Catherine L. Albanese, *A Republic of Mind and Spirit: A Cultural History of American Metaphysical Religion* (New Haven, Conn.: Yale University Press, 2007), 442–447; Roy M. Anker, *Self-Help and Popular Religion in Early American Culture: An Interpretive Guide* (Westport, Conn.: Greenwood Press, 1999), 101–146. For discussion of Liebman and his significance, see Andrew R. Heinze, *Jews and the American Soul: Human Nature in the Twentieth Century* (Princeton, N.J.: Princeton University Press, 2004), 195–239.

71. Oral Roberts, "The Ministry of Casting Out Demons," *Healing Waters* (August 1948): 2.

72. Roberts, "Healing of Cancer," 2, 14.

73. Roberts, "Ministry of Casting Out Demons," 2.

74. Oral Roberts, "Christ's Command Is Not Merely to Heal Sickness . . . But to Heal the Sick Person," *Abundant Life* 18, no. 8 (1964): 3.

75. Lester Frank Sumrall, "Conquest of the Mind," *World Harvest* 4, no. 2 (1965): 4.

76. As one *Time* article indicated in 1945, "the vogue of psychosomatic (mind and body) medicine is so new that the word is in only the newest medical dictionaries. But good doctors have always known that the mind can cause aches & pains, can even be a major factor in diseases, including infections." "All in Your Mind," *Time*, November 26, 1945.

77. Lester Frank Sumrall, "Emotions and Divine Healing," *World Harvest* 3, no. 6 (1964): 4.

78. Gordon Lindsay, "Divine Health or Divine Healing, Which?," *Voice of Healing* 17, no. 2 (May 1964): 12–13.

79. R. C. Logefeil, "Hidden Hunger," *Pentecostal Evangel*, no. 2386 (1960): 32.

80. Charles W. Conn, "Heritage of Healing," *Church of God Evangel* 51, no. 36 (1961): 4.

81. Donald Gee, "The Value of the Supernatural," *Pentecost*, no. 62 (December 1962–February 1963): 17. For further discussion of the ministry of Donald Gee, see Harrell, *All Things Are Possible*, esp. 139–140.

82. A. A. Allen, "The Curse of Madness," *Miracle Magazine* 4, no. 5 (1959): 5.

83. In an advertisement for his books Allen quoted chaplain George Christian Anderson, who carved out a place for nondemonic forms of mental illness. Anderson wrote, "Man is often a slave to demonic forces but a fruitful and worthy inquiry would be to determine what unconscious forces are demonic and what are the results of disease." The ad included an additional assertion that "most mental illness is caused by demon oppression or possession," yet even here it is instructive that Allen utilized the term "most" as opposed to "all." "1 out of Every 10 Today Is Mentally or Emotionally Ill!," *Miracle Magazine* 3, no. 5 (1958): 25.

84. Allen, "Curse of Madness," 13–14.

85. Norman Vincent Peale, *The Power of Positive Thinking* (1952; reprint, New York: Prentice Hall Press, 1987), 32, xiv.

86. Albanese, *Republic of Mind and Spirit*, 442–447, quotation 445.

87. Norman Vincent Peale, "Christ's Healing Power," *Healing Waters* 3, no. 1 (1949): 6; Norman Vincent Peale, "How Faith Shapes Events," *Voice of Healing* 14, no. 4 (1961): 13.

88. Quoted in Albanese, *Republic of Mind and Spirit*, 306.

89. Ibid.

90. Essek William Kenyon, *Jesus the Healer* (Seattle: Kenyon Gospel Publishing Society, 1968), 90, 14, 66.

91. Ibid., 24.

92. Dale H. Simmons, *E. W. Kenyon and the Postbellum Pursuit of Peace, Power, and Plenty* (Lanham, Md.: Scarecrow Press, 1997), 4–14.

93. Ibid., 159, 304–305, 172–173. While I quote the historian Dale Simmons's nuanced study of Kenyon's teachings here to support my claims regarding Kenyon's connections to New Thought, the main thrust of Simmons's argument is to refute those who see Kenyon's theology simply as an extension of New Thought positions. Simmons highlights the preexisting parallels between New Thought teachings and the faith-cure movement, and he also underscores Kenyon's consistent condemnations of New Thought throughout his lifetime.

94. F. F. Bosworth, *Christ the Healer*, rev. ed. (1948; reprint, Old Tappan, N.J.: Fleming H. Revell, 1973), 148.

95. Jaggers, *Everlasting Spiritual and Physical Health*, 129–130.

96. Simmons, *E. W. Kenyon*, 296–298.

97. Osborn, *Healing the Sick*, 83–85. In addition to Bosworth and Osborn, other leaders whose ministries were shaped in part by Kenyon included David Nunn and Ern Baxter. See R. M. Riss, "Kenyon, Essek William," in Burgess and Van der Maas, *New International Dictionary of Pentecostal and Charismatic Movements*, 819–820.

98. Hagin's ministry actually began in the 1930s, though he did not rise to a position of prominence until he began publishing books in the mid-1960s. See Simmons, *E. W. Kenyon*, 298–304.

99. "Rev. A. A. Allen, Evangelist, Dies," *New York Times*, June 14, 1970, 93.

Chapter Three

1. Jaggers quoted in David Edwin Harrell, Jr., *All Things Are Possible: The Healing and Charismatic Revivals in Modern America* (Bloomington: Indiana University Press, 1975), 78–79, quotation 79.

2. "Alligator Scales Disappear," *Miracle Magazine* 5, no. 12 (1960): 6, 14; Alvester Williams, "I Lost over 200 Pounds When I Used God's Reducing Plan," *Miracle Magazine* 6, no. 12 (1961): 3.

3. "The Mark Rawls Story: I Lived 21 Years a Girl Now I Am a Man!" *Miracle Magazine* 5, no. 11 (1960): 7.

4. See Harrell, *All Things Are Possible*, 199.

5. I rely here on David Harrell's summation of Montgomery's critiques. See ibid., 140–144, figures on 142.

6. Robins discusses the new "cultural mood" and its impact on pentecostalism in *Pentecostalism in America* (Santa Barbara, Calif.: Praeger, 2010), esp. 74, 88.

7. Agnes Sanford, *The Healing Light*, rev. ed. (Plainfield, N.J.: Logos International, 1972), 64. I quote a revised edition of *Healing Light* published by a charismatic press, though the first edition of *Healing Light* appeared in 1947.

8. For more on charismatics' ties to Glenn Clark's Camps Farthest Out, as well as brief commentary on the Order of St. Luke, see William L. De Arteaga, "Glenn Clark's Camps Furthest Out: The Schoolhouse of Charismatic Renewal," *Pneuma* 25, no. 2 (2003): 265–288. Though focused on pentecostal and charismatic developments in the United Kingdom, Peter Hocken also briefly discusses adherents' interactions with the Order of St. Luke and the Camps Farthest Out in *Streams of Renewal*, rev. ed. (Carlisle, England: Paternoster Press, 1997), esp. 50–55, 189–192.

9. William Standish Reed, *Surgery of the Soul* (Old Tappan, N.J.: Fleming H. Revell, 1969), 54. By 1984, the Christian Medical Foundation International had a mailing list of over 20,000, including over 4,000 physicians. See Janet Shaffer, "A Christian Alternative to Traditional Medicine," *Charisma* 10, no. 2 (1984): 38. For an archived copy of the "Who

We Are" section of the Christian Medical Foundation's website, see http://web.archive.
org/web/20060323121237/http://www.wwmedical.com/cmf/.

10. Kuhlman's reference to pentecostalism here derives from an undated radio broadcast included in a volume compiled by Jaime Buckingham after Kuhlman's death; Kathryn Kuhlman, *A Glimpse into Glory* (Plainfield, N.J.: Logos International, 1979), 111–112.

11. On Kuhlman's relationship with pentecostals and charismatics, see for example Wayne E.
Warner, *Kathryn Kuhlman: The Woman Behind the Miracles* (Ann Arbor, Mich.: Servant, 1993),
75–76, 161–162. Also see D. J. Wilson, "Kuhlman, Kathryn," in *The New International Dic-
tionary of Pentecostal and Charismatic Movements*, ed. Stanley M. Burgess and Ed M. Van der
Maas (Grand Rapids, Mich.: Zondervan, 2002), 826–827; Jamie Buckingham, *Daughter of
Destiny: Kathryn Kuhlman, Her Story* (Plainfield, N.J.: Logos International, 1976).

12. Stephen Strang, "A Gift of Healing," *Charisma* 1, no. 2 (1975): 9.

13. See William A. Nolen, *Healing: A Doctor in Search of a Miracle* (1974; reprint, Greenwich,
Conn.: Fawcett, 1976), 39–94.

14. Warner, *Kathryn Kuhlman*, 178.

15. As R. G. Robins suggests, the significance of sites of "syncretistic interface" in the
pentecostal-charismatic movement only increased with time. "Denominations provided the motive force of Pentecostalism during most of its first century," he writes,
"but by the end of the 20th century the center of dynamism had begun to shift to the
zones where denominational Pentecostalism, independent Pentecostalism, and the
charismatic movement converged and overlapped." *Pentecostalism in America*, esp.
90–99, 120–126, quotations 91, 120. For further discussion of the various connections and relationships between pentecostals and charismatics, see Edith Waldvogel
Blumhofer, *Restoring the Faith: The Assemblies of God, Pentecostalism, and American
Culture* (Urbana: University of Illinois Press, 1993), 222–241; Peter Hocken, "Charismatic Movement," in Burgess and Van der Maas, *The New International Dictionary of
Pentecostal and Charismatic Movements*, 477–519; Hocken, *Streams of Renewal*, esp.
1–4. Hocken's *Streams of Renewal* focuses primarily on pentecostals and charismatics
in Britain, yet his history frequently incorporates related developments in the United
States and elsewhere.

16. Everett A. Wilson, *Strategy of the Spirit: J. Philip Hogan and the Growth of the Assemblies of
God Worldwide, 1960–1990* (Carlisle, England: Paternoster Press, 1997), 142–146.

17. Melilli quoted in ibid., 144.

18. Quoted in Wilson, *Strategy of the Spirit*, 142–143.

19. "Dirty Hospitals?," *Time* 69, no. 13 (April 1957): 54. Also see John C. Burnham, "American
Medicine's Golden Age: What Happened to It?," in *Sickness and Health in America: Reading
in the History of Medicine and Public Health*, ed. Judith Walzer Leavitt and Ronald L. Numbers, 3rd ed. (Madison: University of Wisconsin Press, 1997), 284–294.

20. "Sleeping Pill Nightmare," *Time* 79, no. 8 (February 23, 1962): 86. A. A. Allen referenced
the thalidomide tragedy in his ministry magazine and included several pictures of de-
formed babies. *Miracle Magazine* 10, no. 1 (October 1964): 16–17.

21. "By the 1960s and 1970s physicians were complaining not only of a lack of deference,"
writes one historian, "but of lay interference and assaults on professional privileges."
Burnham, "American Medicine's Golden Age," 284–294, quotation 291. For further discussion of the critiques of the medical profession that grew in intensity beginning in the
1950s, and analysis of the surging appeal of alternative medicine, also see Mary Ruggie,
Marginal to Mainstream: Alternative Medicine in America (Cambridge: Cambridge University Press, 2004), 43–74; James C. Whorton, *Nature Cures: The History of Alternative Medicine in America* (New York: Oxford University Press, 2002), 245–251.

22. See for example Christopher Lawrence and George Weisz, "Medical Holism: The Context,"
in *Greater Than the Parts: Holism in Biomedicine, 1920–50*, ed. Christopher Lawrence and
George Weisz (New York: Oxford University Press, 1998), 1–22; Theodore M. Brown,
"George Canby Robinson and 'The Patient as Person,'" in ibid., 135–160; Jack D. Pressman,
"Human Understanding: Psychosomatic Medicine and the Mission of the Rockefeller

Foundation," in ibid., 189–208. George Engel's biopsychosocial model, introduced in the late 1970s, illustrated similar trends.

23. For further discussion of the various forces reshaping Americans' approach to the body and healing during the 1960s and 1970s, see James C. Whorton, *Crusaders for Fitness: The History of American Health Reformers* (Princeton, N.J.: Princeton University Press, 1982), esp. 335–336; Whorton, *Nature Cures*, 245–270; Amanda Porterfield, *The Transformation of American Religion: The Story of a Late-Twentieth-Century Awakening* (New York: Oxford University Press, 2001), 163–201. For further discussion of the surging popularity of highly spiritualized alternative healing approaches in the latter decades of the twentieth century, see esp. Robert C. Fuller, *Alternative Medicine and American Religious Life* (New York: Oxford University Press, 1989), 91–117.

24. David Edwin Harrell, Jr., *Oral Roberts: An American Life* (Bloomington: Indiana University Press, 1985), 457; Oral Roberts, "The Healing of Cancer," *Healing Waters* 2, no. 3 (1949): 2, 14. Years later, when commenting on the holistic trends in mainstream American medicine, Roberts quoted a friend who suggested that "more and more I believe medicine is moving in this direction, toward whole man healing." "Isn't that exciting?" Roberts responded. "Jesus is a restorer of the human being . . . the healer of your whole person . . . *body, mind, and spirit, and* medicine is moving in that direction!" Oral Roberts, "How to See Disease as 'Dis–ease' and Start Learning to Be a Whole Person," *Abundant Life* 30, no. 10 (1976): 4. For a helpful overview of the development of Roberts's thinking regarding "wholeness" and "whole–man healing," as well as a basic time frame for when these ideas germinated in Roberts's mind, see Harrell, *Oral Roberts*, 456–460.

25. Kathryn Kuhlman, "Healing of the Body, Mind and Spirit," (Pittsburgh: Kathryn Kuhlman Foundation, 1960), audio recording, Records of the Kathryn Kuhlman Foundation, Billy Graham Center Archives, Wheaton College, Wheaton, Illinois.

26. Quoted in Harrell, *Oral Roberts*, 458–459. On Tournier's influence among evangelicals more broadly, see David Harrington Watt, *A Transforming Faith: Explorations of Twentieth-Century American Evangelicalism* (New Brunswick, N.J.: Rutgers University Press, 1991), 151.

27. See Norman Cousins, "The Holistic Health Explosion," *Saturday Review* (March 31, 1979): 17–20.

28. Norman Cousins, *Anatomy of an Illness as Perceived by the Patient* (New York: Norton, 1979), 119.

29. Nolen, *Healing: A Doctor in Search of a Miracle*, 14.

30. For discussion of Americans' simultaneous use of both traditional and nontraditional medicine, see Ruggie, *Marginal to Mainstream*, 45–52.

31. Angus Sargeant, "A Call for Healing Honesty," *Logos* 5, no. 2 (1975): 9–11.

32. "Divine Healing: An Integral Part of the Gospel" (Springfield, Mo.: Gospel Publishing House, August 20, 1974).

33. Francis MacNutt, *Healing* (1974; reprint, New York: Bantam Books, 1977), 145–151.

34. Barbara Pursey, "Healing Is for the Whole Person," *Logos* 9, no. 1 (1979): 23.

35. Charles Hunter, "Healing the Sick," *Charisma* 3, no. 4 (1978): 36.

36. Harrell, *All Things Are Possible*, 367.

37. See Harrell, *Oral Roberts*, esp. 207–252, 374–379.

38. Harrell, *All Things Are Possible*, 374–379.

39. Quoted in Yvonne Nance, "Doctor Ron Lamb Says: 'ORU Turned Me On . . . And Turned My Life Around,'" *Abundant Life* 30, no. 2 (February 1976): 23. Also see Harrell, *Oral Roberts*, 392–396.

40. Oral Roberts, "I Believe the Cure for Cancer Has a Spiritual Origin," *Abundant Life* 31, no. 1 (1977): 2.

41. Oral Roberts, "God Still Heals Today—He Is Just Using Different 'Delivery Systems,'" *Abundant Life* 30, no. 1 (1976): 16.

42. Oral Roberts, "The Master Plan God Has Given Me," *Abundant Life* 31, no. 11 (1977): 3–4. For examples of early pentecostal discussions of Luke's relationship to the medical profession, see for example Maria Beulah Woodworth-Etter, *Life and Experience Including*

Sermons and Visions of Mrs. M. B. Woodworth-Etter, rev. ed. (St. Louis, Mo.: Commercial Printing, 1904), 268; J. H. Huggins, "Divine Healing," *Pentecostal Holiness Advocate* 4, no. 4 (May 27, 1920): 4–5; E. N. Bell, "Questions and Answers," *Weekly Evangel*, no. 122 (January 8, 1916): 8–9.

43. Roberts, "God Still Heals Today," 16.

44. Roberts, "I Believe the Cure for Cancer Has a Spiritual Origin," 2.

45. Quoted in Harrell, *Oral Roberts*, 382.

46. As the historians Ronald Numbers and Darrel Amundsen indicate, "most denominationally affiliated hospitals were distinguished more by their names than by their medical practices, admissions policies, or the religious beliefs of their staffs." Ronald L. Numbers and Darrel W. Amundsen, eds., *Caring and Curing: Health and Medicine in the Western Religious Traditions*, 1986, 2–3. Along similar lines, skeptics questioned just how different Roberts's operation would be from that of a more traditional hospital. In 1982 the sociologist Margaret Poloma, for example, briefly acknowledged the attempts by Roberts and others to transform the practice of traditional medicine, but quickly discounted its chances for success. Speaking of Roberts's attempt to build a charismatic hospital, she suggested that a "divine message or vision communicated to Roberts, might spark enthusiasm for the project, but such events are unlikely to be part of its daily operation." *The Charismatic Movement: Is There a New Pentecost?* (Boston: Twayne, 1982), 104–108. For further discussion of religious hospitals that appeared in the history of Christianity see Amanda Porterfield, *Healing in the History of Christianity* (New York: Oxford University Press, 2005), esp. 52–53, 110–112.

47. Roberts, "Master Plan," 7.

48. Roberts, "I Believe the Cure for Cancer Has a Spiritual Origin," 3–4. Roberts had long expressed special interest in the healing of cancer. See Roberts, "Healing of Cancer."

49. Roberts, "Master Plan," 7.

50. Roberts, "I Believe the Cure for Cancer Has a Spiritual Origin," 3–4.

51. Oral Roberts, "Where Prayer and Medical Science Mix for Miracles," *Abundant Life* 31, no. 8 (1977): 12.

52. Charles Francis Hunter, *Handbook for Healing*, (Kingwood, Tex.: Hunter Books, 1987): 20–21, 8–10.

53. Ibid., 104, 101.

54. Though those treated for various illnesses on mission trips received medical care regardless of whether or not they accepted the missionaries' message, evangelism remained a central goal. According to the ministry website, God "equipped [HealthCare Ministries] with the resources to use medical evangelism to reach areas of the world that are untouched by the Gospel." "About Us," www.healthcareministries.org/about-us. Also see Wilson, *Strategy of the Spirit*, 46; Gary B. McGee, *This Gospel Shall Be Preached* (Springfield, Mo.: Gospel Publishing House, 1989), 252–254.

55. Oral Roberts, *Still Doing the Impossible* (Shippensburg, Pa.: Destiny Image, 2002), 148–150.

56. Jay Horning, "The Oral Roberts Appeal," *St. Petersburg Times*, January 20, 1987, 1.

57. "Praise the Lord and Pass the Loot," *Economist*, May 16, 1987, 23.

58. Quoted in Stephen Strang, "Oral Roberts: Victory out of Defeat," *Charisma* 15, no. 5 (1989): 81, 86–87.

59. For a brief history of Operation Blessing, see "History," http://www.ob.org/_about/history.asp. Also see "Flying Hospital," http://l1011.homestead.com/flyinghosp.html.

Chapter Four

1. Phyllis Wells, "My Psychiatrist," *Aglow: For the Spirit Renewed Christian Woman*, no. 35 (1978): 7, 9.

2. On evangelicals' changing relationship with the broader culture, see Joel A. Carpenter, *Revive Us Again: The Reawakening of American Fundamentalism* (New York: Oxford University Press, 1997); George M. Marsden, *Reforming Fundamentalism: Fuller Seminary and the*

New Evangelicalism (Grand Rapids, Mich.: Eerdmans, 1987); Christian Smith, *American Evangelicalism: Embattled and Thriving* (Chicago: University of Chicago Press, 1998). Specifically regarding evangelicals' new-found openness to psychotherapy, see David Harrington Watt, *A Transforming Faith: Explorations of Twentieth-Century American Evangelicalism* (New Brunswick, N.J.: Rutgers University Press, 1991), 137–154. Exemplary titles include James C. Dobson, *Dare to Discipline* (Wheaton, Ill.: Tyndale House, 1970); Paul D. Meier, Frank B. Minirth, and Donald Ratcliff, *Bruised and Broken: Understanding and Healing Psychological Problems* (Grand Rapids, Mich.: Baker, 1992); Frank B. Minirth, *Christian Psychiatry* (Old Tappan, N.J.: Fleming H. Revell, 1977); Paul D. Meier, Frank B. Minirth, and Frank B. Wichern, *Introduction to Psychology and Counseling: Christian Perspectives and Applications* (Grand Rapids, Mich.: Baker, 1982); Frank B. Minirth and Paul D. Meier, *Happiness Is a Choice: A Manual on the Symptoms, Causes, and Cures of Depression* (Grand Rapids, Mich.: Baker, 1978).

3. See Jamie Buckingham, "Lord of the Subconscious," *Logos Journal* 39, no. 10 (1971): 48, 50; Jamie Buckingham, "Making God Lord of the Subconscious," *Charisma* 2, no. 2 (1976): 15–17, 30–33. Also see Jamie Buckingham, *Risky Living: Keys to Inner Healing* (Plainfield, N.J.: Logos International, 1976).

4. T. J. Jackson Lears, "From Salvation to Self–Realization: Advertising and the Therapeutic Roots of the Consumer Culture, 1880–1930," in *The Culture of Consumption: Critical Essays in American History, 1880–1980*, ed. Richard Wightman Fox and T. J. Jackson Lears (New York: Pantheon, 1983), 11.

5. Betty Tapscott, "Healing for the Inner Self," *Charisma* 4, no. 7 (1979): 22.

6. Joyce Landorf, "The Poised Beauty of Self–Acceptance," *Charisma* 4, no. 4 (1979): 63.

7. Bob Mumford, "Mental Fitness," *New Wine* 11, no. 4 (1979): 26–27.

8. Bert Ghezzi, "You Can Stop Feeling Bad about Yourself," *Charisma* 11, no. 3 (1985): 38–42.

9. Derek Prince, "From Rejection to Acceptance," *New Wine* 9, no. 8 (1977): 4–9, 22.

10. David A. Seamands, *Healing for Damaged Emotions* (Wheaton, Ill.: Victor Books, 1981).

11. Rita Bennett, *Emotionally Free* (Old Tappan, N.J.: Fleming H. Revell, 1982).

12. For further discussion of Sanford's influence in the charismatic movement see esp. William L. De Arteaga, "Agnes Sanford: Apostle of Healing, and First Theologian of the Charismatic Renewal," pt. 2, *Pneuma Review* 9, no. 3 (2006): 4–17; William L. De Arteaga, "Agnes Sanford: Apostle of Healing, and First Theologian of the Charismatic Renewal," pt. 1, *Pneuma Review* 9, no. 2 (2006): 6–17.

13. Agnes Sanford, *Sealed Orders* (Plainfield, N.J.: Logos International, 1972), esp. 95–105.

14. Agnes Sanford, *The Healing Light*, rev. ed. (Plainfield, N.J.: Logos International, 1972), 15.

15. Sanford, *Sealed Orders*, 105.

16. Sanford, *The Healing Light*, 27.

17. Ibid., 18–19.

18. At another point she recommends a similar type of practice conducted weekly; see ibid., 103–104, 113.

19. Ibid., 106.

20. Ibid., 123, 126–127.

21. "There is little doubt," William De Arteaga writes, "that in spite of the controversies she generated, Mrs. Sanford was indeed the first theologian [of] the charismatic renewal. *The Healing Light*, issued as a Logos International paperback, became the healing text book of the early charismatic movement. She discipled many of the leadership of the charismatic renewal, including a handsome young priest named Francis MacNutt who met her at a CFO camp and eventually passed on the core of her teaching to the charismatic movement with his vastly influential works on healing." "Agnes Sanford," pt. 2, 16.

22. For biographical information regarding MacNutt, see "About Us," www.christianhealingmin. org/about/. MacNutt discusses his healing ministry as well as his excommunication from the Catholic Church (which was precipitated by his decision to marry, though he and his wife, Judith, eventually received a special dispensation permitting the marriage in 1993), in David Kyle Foster, "Interview: Francis and Judith MacNutt," www.masteringlife.org/ miscellaneous/interview-francis-judith-macnutt.

23. See William L. De Arteaga, "Glenn Clark's Camps Furthest Out: The Schoolhouse of Charismatic Renewal," *Pneuma* 25, no. 2 (2003): 265–288; Glenn Clark, *The Soul's Sincere Desire* (Boston: Little, Brown, 1926).

24. Francis MacNutt, *Healing* (1974; reprint, New York: Bantam Books, 1977), 164–165. A year after hearing Agnes Sanford for the first time, MacNutt also attended a five-day workshop taught by Sanford called the School for Pastoral Care. MacNutt also mentioned the influence of Tommy Tyson, Jo Kimmel, and John Sanford in the early years of his healing ministry; 6–7.

25. MacNutt defined the ministry of inner healing as follows: "Jesus, who is the same yesterday, today, and forever, can take the memories of our past and 1) *Heal* them from the wounds that still remain and affect our present lives; 2) *Fill with his love* all these places in us that have been healed and drained of the poison of past hurts and resentment." Ibid., 164.

26. Ibid., 169.

27. Sherry Andrews, "What's Out of Sight is Not Out of Mind," *Charisma* 2, no. 2 (1976): 13.

28. While Bennett pulled back from a full affirmation of psychology, at another point she drew a parallel between being filled with the Holy Spirit and having a grasp of basic psychological insights. "If parents aren't psychologically aware and/or Spirit-filled and Spirit-led Christians," she wrote, "children get hurt." Bennett, *Emotionally Free*, 36, 19, 51.

29. Like other influential healing figures in the charismatic movement, Stapleton participated in the Camps Farthest Out, and also spoke at the ecumenical 1977 gathering of charismatics for a conference in Kansas City that attracted approximately 50,000 individuals. For an account of her own baptism in the Holy Spirit, see Ruth Carter Stapleton, "Ruth Carter Stapleton: Exclusive Interview," *World Harvest* 17, no. 5 (1979): 8–9.

30. Ruth Carter Stapleton, *The Experience of Inner Healing* (Carmel, N.Y.: Guideposts, 1977), 7–8. Despite Stapleton's defense of psychology, she (like other practitioners of inner healing) denied that she was practicing a form of psychotherapy. Part of the motivation behind this claim may have been a desire to avoid charges of practicing a form of medical care without a license, though it also highlighted the lay character of the inner healing movement. See Ruth Carter Stapleton, *The Gift of Inner Healing* (Carmel, N.Y.: Guideposts, 1976), 45–53.

31. William James, "Is Life Worth Living?," in *Pragmatism and Other Writings*, ed. Giles B. Gunn (New York: Penguin Books, 2000), 236.

32. William James, *The Varieties of Religious Experience: A Study in Human Nature*, ed. Martin E. Marty (1902; reprint, New York: Penguin Books, 1982), 31.

33. Andrew R. Heinze, *Jews and the American Soul: Human Nature in the Twentieth Century* (Princeton, N.J.: Princeton University Press, 2004), esp. 98–102, 165–167. For further discussion of James and his views on the relationship between psychology and religion, see Ann Taves, *Fits, Trances, and Visions: Experiencing Religion and Explaining Experience from Wesley to James* (Princeton, N.J.: Princeton University Press, 1999), esp. 261–307.

34. Sanford, *Healing Light*, 137.

35. Stapleton, *Gift of Inner Healing*, 13, 17. Also see W. Hugh Missildine, *Your Inner Child of the Past* (New York: Simon and Schuster, 1963). Some later practitioners of inner healing, however, would critique the concept of the "inner child." Mark Pearson, a practitioner of inner healing and president of the Institute for Christian Renewal and New Creation Healing Center, for example, cautioned against conceptions of an "inner child" emphasized by figures such as Stapleton and the Bennetts that posited "an innocent, pure core being" in each individual, "someone who could profitably be listened to for guidance and direction." Pearson argued that these ideas undermined reliance on Christ and neglected the biblical doctrine of original sin. Furthermore, quoting another practitioner of inner healing, Leanne Payne, he suggested that "it is important to realize that the way of the wounded 'inner child' is so often the way of the foolish child." Mark A. Pearson, *Christian Healing: A Practical and Comprehensive Guide*, 2nd ed. (Grand Rapids, Mich.: Chosen Books, 1995), 130–131. In 2005, Pearson's book was published by the charismatic publisher Charisma House.

36. As Stapleton explained, "our subconscious memory, a mental computer, records everything. It forgets nothing. The only means we have of revising this emotional record is by the re-creative work of the Holy Spirit. And often the Spirit must redo our earliest recollections." *Experience of Inner Healing*, 21. In her attempt to explain how this could be possible, she quoted Maxwell Maltz, who argued that "something imagined vividly enough and in some detail is as influential on one's emotions as an objective event experience." Stapleton went a step further, however, in claiming that faith imagination "creates an objective experience. It does not approximate or simulate one." *Gift of Inner Healing*, 37. Also see Maxwell Maltz, *Psycho-Cybernetics: A New Way to Get More Living out of Life* (Englewood Cliffs, N.J.: Prentice-Hall, 1960).

37. Bennett, *Emotionally Free*, esp. 79–89.

38. Matthew Linn and Dennis Linn, *Healing Life's Hurts: Healing Memories through Five Stages of Forgiveness* (New York: Paulist Press, 1978), 223.

39. David A. Seamands, *Healing of Memories* (Wheaton, Ill.: Victor Books, 1985), 27.

40. Leanne Payne, *The Broken Image: Restoring Personal Wholeness through Healing Prayer* (1981; reprint, Grand Rapids, Mich.: Baker Books, 1996), 107–108.

41. Stapleton, *Gift of Inner Healing*, 69.

42. An early article on inner healing published in *Charisma*, for example, noted the resistance to Sanford's focus on "healing of the memories" among some practitioners of inner healing: Andrews, "What's Out of Sight Is Not Out of Mind," 14.

43. Stephen Strang, "Important Mental Health Ministry Emerges," *Charisma* 5, no. 3 (1979): 5. Also see "Dr. Richard D. Dobbins Bio," www.drdobbins.com/meet-the-doctor; and "Christian Psychiatric Care Unit Expands," *Charisma* 15 (1990): 20. Also see Margaret M. Poloma, *The Charismatic Movement: Is There a New Pentecost?* (Boston: Twayne, 1982), 106–108; Margaret M. Poloma, *The Assemblies of God at the Crossroads: Charisma and Institutional Dilemmas* (Knoxville: University of Tennessee Press, 1989), 228–229.

44. For further discussion of Gross, see Donald A. Eisner, *The Death of Psychotherapy: From Freud to Alien Abductions* (Westport, Conn.: Praeger, 2000), 168–170. Gross is discussed in connection to Jim Bakker in John Dart, "Denies Takeover Attempt: Swaggart Admits a Role in Going after Bakker," *Los Angeles Times*, March 25, 1987.

45. Bennett, *Emotionally Free*, 149; Payne, *Broken Image*, 11, 47–48; Stapleton, *Experience of Inner Healing*, 111.

46. Rita Bennett quoted in David Hazard, "An Inside Look at Inner Healing," *Charisma* 12, no. 2 (1986): 48. Regarding the female leadership in the inner healing movement, the author of an article on inner healing in *Charisma* briefly mentions the opposition it received due to the prominence of women in the tradition; see Andrews, "What's Out of Sight Is Not Out of Mind," 14.

47. Notable exceptions to these trends include the Global Alliance of Affirming Apostolic Pentecostals and the Apostolic Restoration Mission. See "Our Faith," www.gaaap.net/our-faith.html; and "Homosexuality and the Scripture," www.apostolicrestorationmission.4t.com/id27.htm.

48. "The idea that you can be a committed Christian and still be beset by homosexual urges is very threatening to some people," Comisky continued. Quoted in Davin Seay, "Hope for the Homosexual," *Charisma* 11 (1986): 34–35.

49. Ibid., 35.

50. Stapleton, *Gift of Inner Healing*, 64–72.

51. Roger Dean, "Homosexual Completely Delivered," *Cross and the Switchblade* 11, no. 3 (1973): 5.

52. David Wilkerson, "The 100% Cure," *Cross and the Switchblade* 11, no. 3 (1973): 3.

53. Dave Wimbish, "The Tomczak Ordeal," *Charisma* 7, no. 1 (1981): 26, 31. Also see "Author Wins Judgment for Slander," *New York Times*, September 10, 1983.

54. Andrews, "What's Out of Sight Is Not Out of Mind," 12–14.

55. Hazard, "Inside Look at Inner Healing," 44–49.

56. Jimmy Swaggart, "The Psychologizing of the Church," *Evangelist* 20, no. 1 (1988): 6–10. Jimmy Swaggart, "Psychotherapy," *Evangelist* 25, no. 4 (1992): 6. Also see Martin Bobgan

and Deidre Bobgan, *Psychoheresy: The Pschological Seduction of Christianity* (Santa Barbara, Calif.: EastGate, 1987); Dave Hunt and T. A. McMahon, *The Seduction of Christianity: Spiritual Discernment in the Last Days* (Eugene, Ore.: Harvest House, 1985).

57. Swaggart, "Psychotherapy," 6.

58. Bob Gass, "The Healing of Memory," *Christ for the Nations* 36, no. 6 (1983): 5–6.

59. For discussion of the Word of Faith movement see Milmon F. Harrison, *Righteous Riches: The Word of Faith Movement in Contemporary African American Religion* (New York: Oxford University Press, 2005); David Edwin Harrell, Jr., *All Things Are Possible: The Healing & Charismatic Revivals in Modern America* (Bloomington: Indiana University Press, 1975), esp. 169–172, 185–186, 200–201, 234–235; Grant Wacker, "The Pentecostal Tradition," in *Caring and Curing*, ed. Ronald L. Numbers and Darrel W. Amundsen (New York: Macmillan, 1986), esp. 527–529; Bruce Barron, *The Health and Wealth Gospel: What's Going on Today in a Movement That Has Shaped the Faith of Millions?* (Downers Grove, Ill.: InterVarsity Press, 1987).

60. In his attack on Word of Faith theology, for example, D. R. McConnell lays out significant areas of plagiarism. See D. R. McConnell, *A Different Gospel: A Historical and Biblical Analysis of the Modern Faith Movement* (Peabody, Mass.: Hendrickson, 1988), esp. 6–14. Hagin's defenders, however, deny the charges. See for example "Plagiarism of E. W. Kenyon by Kenneth E. Hagin?," www.kenyons.org/Plagiarism.htm.

61. See Kenneth Hagin, *Seven Things You Should Know about Divine Healing* (Tulsa: Kenneth Hagin Ministries, 1979), 32–35.

62. For further discussion of Word of Faith proponents' use of the term "rhema," see Harrison, *Righteous Riches*, 7–9. A statement made in the "What We Believe" section of Kenneth Copeland's ministry website illustrates the continued importance of direct revelations in the Word of Faith movement: "we are called to reveal the mysteries, the victorious revelations of God's Word, that have been hidden from the ages." "About KCM," www.kcm.org/about/index.php?p=what_we_believe.

63. Smith Wigglesworth, *Faith That Prevails* (1938; reprint, Springfield, Mo.: Gospel Publishing House, 1966), 7.

64. John G. Lake, *The John G. Lake Sermons on Dominion over Demons, Disease and Death*, ed. Gordon Lindsay (Shreveport, La.: Christ for the Nations, 1949), 28.

65. F. M. Britton, *Pentecostal Truth* (Royston, Ga.: Pentecostal Holiness Church, 1919), 90.

66. Harrison, *Righteous Riches*, 11. Robins also provides a helpful summary of Word of Faith teachings in R. G. Robins, *Pentecostalism in America* (Santa Barbara, Calif.: Praeger, 2010), 130–132.

67. Kenneth E. Hagin, *Healing Belongs to Us* (Tulsa: Kenneth Hagin Ministries, n.d.), 27.

68. Kenneth Hagin, Jr., *Seven Hindrances to Healing* (Tulsa: Kenneth Hagin Ministries, 1980), 24.

69. Essek William Kenyon, *The Father and His Family: A Restatement of the Plan of Redemption* (1916; reprint, Joshua, Tex.: Romans VIII Evangelistic Association, 1964), 196.

70. David Edwin Harrell, Jr., *Oral Roberts: An American Life* (Bloomington: Indiana University Press, 1985), 460–463.

71. Daisy Matthews, "God Gave Me a New 1961 Cadillac!," *Miracle Magazine* 6, no. 9 (1961): 9.

72. Kenneth Copeland, "Dominating the Law of Sin and Death," *Believer's Voice of Victory* 13, no. 11 (1985): 5–6.

73. Price never specified what someone's net worth had to be to qualify as "rich," but he did clarify that "God is not opposed to His children being millionaires." Frederick K. C. Price, *High Finance: God's Financial Plan Tithes and Offerings* (Tulsa: Harrison House, 1984), 49.

74. For examples of the types of critiques Word of Faith leaders encountered, see Hunt and McMahon, *Seduction of Christianity*; McConnell, *Different Gospel*.

75. See "The TBN Story," www.tbn.org/index.php/3/18.html. Also see Harrison, *Righteous Riches*, 161–162.

76. Robins, *Pentecostalism in America*, 112.

77. For discussion of the influence of metaphysical traditions in the black community and their contributions to the spread of Word of Faith emphases among black Christians in the

latter decades of the twentieth century see Jonathan L. Walton, *Watch This! The Ethics and Aesthetics of Black Televangelism* (New York: New York University Press, 2009), esp. 47–74; Catherine Bowler, "Blessed Bodies: Healing in the African-American Faith Movement," in *Global Pentecostal and Charismatic Healing*, ed. Candy Gunther Brown (New York: Oxford University Press, 2011), 84–86. Also see Harrison, *Righteous Riches*, 137–141; Stephanie Y. Mitchem, *Name It and Claim It? Prosperity Preaching in the Black Church* (Cleveland: Pilgrim Press, 2007), 68–103.

78. Dollar quoted in Walton, *Watch This*, 151. Also see 145–165, quotation 150.

79. Kenneth Hagin, "True Spiritual Healing," *Word of Faith* 13, no. 5 (1980): 4–5.

80. Kenneth Copeland, "Leaving the Past Behind," *Believer's Voice of Victory* 16, no. 7 (1988): 14.

81. Joyce Meyer, "The Believer's Attitude toward Healing," *Life in the Word* 15, no. 12 (2001): 12. It is telling that Meyer's ministry website included a disclaimer clarifying her relationship to Word of Faith emphases. In answer to a "frequently asked question" as to whether or not her ministry qualifies as "Word of Faith," she responded: "Joyce Meyer Ministries believes in the Word of God. Joyce teaches that God has made promises to us in His Word and as believers, we should trust His promises (see 2 Peter 1:3, 4). However, it can be damaging when people place their faith in faith alone instead of placing their faith in God. Misappropriation of God's promises solely for personal gain is not scripturally supported." "Joyce Meyer Ministries: FAQ," www.joycemeyer.org/AboutUs/faq.aspx.

82. Joyce Meyer, *Straight Talk: Overcoming Emotional Battles with the Power of God's Word* (New York: Faith Words, 2004), 262–267.

83. Joyce Meyer, *Beauty for Ashes: Receiving Emotional Healing* (1994; reprint, New York: Warner Books, 2002), 9.

84. Joyce Meyer, *Beauty For Ashes: Receiving Emotional Healing*, rev. ed. (New York: Faith Words, 2003), 3.

85. T. D. Jakes, *Woman, Thou Art Loosed! Healing the Wounds of the Past* (1993; reprint, Minneapolis: Bethany House, 2004), 84, 126, 119.

86. For further discussion of Jakes's background and message, including his interest in psychology, see Shayne Lee, *T. D. Jakes: America's New Preacher* (New York: New York University Press, 2005), esp. 23, 91–97. Also see Shayne Lee and Phillip Luke Sinitiere, *Holy Mavericks: Evangelical Innovators and the Spiritual Marketplace* (New York: New York University Press, 2009), 53–75.

87. Jakes, *Woman, Thou Art Loosed*, 29, 7, 14, 174.

88. "Bishop T. D. Jakes," www.drphil.com/shows/page/BishopJakes/.

89. Paula White, *You're All That! Understand God's Design for Your Life* (New York: Faith Words, 2007), 175–176, 173. For further discussion of White's ministry, see Lee and Sinitiere, *Holy Mavericks*, 107–128.

90. White, *You're All That*, 137–139.

91. Joel Osteen, *Your Best Life Now: 7 Steps to Living at Your Full Potential* (New York: Warner Faith, 2004), 146–149. Osteen became pastor of the independent charismatic Lakewood Church in Houston when his father, the founding pastor, John Osteen, died in 1999. See "Our History," www.lakewood.cc/pages/new-here/our-history.aspx. Also see Lee and Sinitiere, *Holy Mavericks*, 25–51.

92. These are chapter titles in Joel Osteen, *Become a Better You: 7 Keys to Improving Your Life Every Day* (New York: Free Press, 2007).

Chapter Five

1. "College Criticized for Get-Thin Policy," *New York Times*, December 4, 1977, 31.

2. For an example of the way this issue was treated in the popular press, see "F Is for Fat," *Newsweek*, October 24, 1977. For further discussion of ORU's aerobic exercise program and a useful summary of the controversy surrounding these policies, see David Edwin Harrell, Jr., *Oral Roberts: An American Life* (Bloomington: Indiana University Press, 1985), 362–363.

3. "The Cooking Squad or the Praying Band," *Golden Grain* 6, no. 7 (1931): 15.

4. See James C. Whorton, *Inner Hygiene: Constipation and the Pursuit of Health in Modern Society* (New York: Oxford University Press, 2000), 104–105, 89. For further discussion regarding the intersection of nutritional research, advertising, and manufacture of vitamins, as well as the enthusiastic popular response to the "newer nutrition" in the early decades of the twentieth century, see Rima D. Apple, *Vitamania: Vitamins in American Culture* (New Brunswick, N.J.: Rutgers University Press, 1996), esp. 13–53; James C. Whorton, "Eating to Win: Popular Concepts of Diet, Strength, and Energy in the Early Twentieth Century," in *Fitness in American Culture: Images of Health, Sport, and the Body, 1830–1940*, ed. Kathryn Grover (Amherst: University of Massachusetts Press, 1989), 86–122.

5. Besides a regular pattern of only two meals a day, Dewey recommended extended curative fasts that could last for twenty to thirty days. See Edward Hooker Dewey, *The No-Breakfast Plan and the Fasting-Cure* (Meadville, Pa.: author, 1900); Edward Hooker Dewey, *Experiences of the No-Breakfast Plan and the Fasting-Cure* (Meadville, Pa.: Edward Hooker Dewey, 1902); James C. Whorton, *Crusaders for Fitness: The History of American Health Reformers* (Princeton, N.J.: Princeton University Press, 1982), 262–267; R. Marie Griffith, *Born Again Bodies: Flesh and Spirit in American Christianity* (Berkeley: University of California Press, 2004), 113–115.

6. For more on the career of Bernarr Macfadden, see Griffith, *Born Again Bodies*, 116–119; Whorton, *Crusaders for Fitness*, 296–303.

7. See Upton Sinclair, *The Fasting Cure* (New York: M. Kennerley, 1911); Peter N. Stearns, *Fat History: Bodies and Beauty in the Modern West* (New York: New York University Press, 2002), 35.

8. Stearns, *Fat History*, 36.

9. Heavily influenced by New Thought assumptions, Fletcher popularized his unique approach to diet among a significant proportion of middle- and upper-class Americans. For more on Fletcher see Whorton, *Crusaders for Fitness*, 168–181; Stearns, *Fat History*, 32–35; Griffith, *Born Again Bodies*, 106–107.

10. Stearns discusses the gradual influence of nutritional research on the medical field in Stearns, *Fat History*, 25–47. For more on the history of vitamins and nutritional research more generally, see Apple, *Vitamania*; Elmer Verner McCollum, *A History of Nutrition: The Sequence of Ideas in Nutrition Investigations* (Boston: Houghton Mifflin, 1957), esp. 201–419. For an example of the actuarial studies conducted by life insurance companies in the early twentieth century regarding the connections between excess weight and mortality, see Henry Clapp Sherman, *Chemistry of Food and Nutrition* (New York: Macmillan, 1911), 214–218.

11. Stearns, *Fat History*, 48–68, quotations 54, 56, 59. In establishing the historical context, Stearns also highlights the way the growing number of white-collar jobs led to concern over workers' increasingly sedentary lifestyles, while an emerging professional sports culture added to the focus on physical strength and fitness. Ibid., 11–24, 39, 48–68. Also see Hillel Schwartz, *Never Satisfied: A Cultural History of Diets, Fantasies, and Fat* (New York: Free Press, 1986), esp. 75–187; Peter N. Stearns, "Fat in America," in *Cultures of the Abdomen: Diet, Digestion, and Fat in the Modern World*, ed. Christopher E. Forth and Carden-Coyne Ana (New York: Palgrave Macmillan, 2005), esp. 239–244.

12. Franklin Hall, *The Fasting Prayer* (San Diego, Calif.: Franklin Hall, 1947), 113, 116.

13. Griffith in particular criticizes Stearns' overreliance on a narrative of secularization, *Born Again Bodies*, esp. 12–13.

14. Harrell, *Oral Roberts*, 225, 242. James Whorton discusses the turn to organic foods and to running as manifestations of the broader "holistic health explosion" in Whorton, *Crusaders for Fitness*, 331–349. Exemplary of these trends, in an interview published in the charismatic journal *New Wine*, Cooper cited statistics suggesting that the number of Americans who jogged had risen exponentially from 100,000 in 1968 to as many as 25 million ten years later. Dick Leggatt, "The Healthy Christian: An Exclusive Interview with Dr. Kenneth Cooper," *New Wine* 11, no. 4 (1979): 4–8.

15. See Frank Ford, "Frank Ford on Religion," *Mother Earth News* (September-October 1974), www.motherearthnews.com/Nature-Community/1974-09-01/Interview-With-Frank-Ford.aspx.

16. Advertisement for *The Simpler Life Cookbook* in *Charisma* 3, no. 1 (1977): 3. Lindsey's book was credited as the best-selling nonfiction book of the 1970s by the *New York Times*. See Hal Lindsey and Carole C. Carlson, *The Late Great Planet Earth* (Grand Rapids, Mich.: Zondervan, 1970).

17. See Lindsay Heinsen, "The New Jerusalem," *D Magazine*, May 1978, www.dmagazine.com/Home/1978/05/01/The_New_Jerusalem.aspx; Eric Levin, "A Stern Test of Faith," *People* 20, no. 1 (July 1983), www.people.com/people/archive/article/0,,20085403,00.html.

18. Frances Gardner Hunter, *God's Answer to Fat . . . Loøse It* (Houston: Hunter Ministries, 1975), 85.

19. Dennis Worre, "Fat Christians Can't Run," *Christ for the Nations* 33, no. 10 (1981): 5. The verse Worre quoted was taken from Romans 12:9. Also see Joan Cavanaugh with Pat Forseth, *More of Jesus, Less of Me* (Plainfield, N.J.: Logos International, 1976); Patricia Banta Kreml, *Slim for Him: Biblical Devotions on Diet* (Plainfield, N.J.: Logos International, 1978); Marie Chapian and Neva Coyle, *Free to Be Thin* (Minneapolis: Bethany House, 1979).

20. Ann Thomas, *God's Answer to Overeating: A Study of Scriptural Attitudes* (Edmonds, Wa.: Aglow, 1975), 5.

21. Chapian and Coyle, *Free to Be Thin*, 170.

22. Quoted in Neva Coyle and Marie Chapian, *There's More to Being Thin Than Being Thin* (Minneapolis: Bethany House, 1984), 79, 81.

23. Griffith, *Born Again Bodies*, esp. 160–238. Indicative of pentecostals' and charismatics' influence on the broader Christian diet culture, at several points Griffith discusses or at least mentions a number of individuals tied to the pentecostal-charismatic movement, including Neva Coyle, Frances Hunter, T. D. Jakes, Lisa Bevere, and Pamela Smith.

24. Lona Ann White, "Weighting on the Lord," *Charisma* 7, no. 9 (1982): 41.

25. Alvester Williams, "I Lost over 200 Pounds When I Used God's Reducing Plan," *Miracle Magazine* 6, no. 12 (1961): 3.

26. Hunter, *God's Answer to Fat . . . Loøse It*, 24–25.

27. Kreml, *Slim for Him*, 115.

28. Coyle and Chapian, *There's More to Being Thin*, 31–32.

29. Kreml, *Slim for Him*, 114.

30. Cavanaugh and Forseth, *More of Jesus, Less of Me*, 35.

31. Hunter, *God's Answer to Fat . . . Loøse It*, 69–71.

32. Melba Ward, "Dieting with Jesus," *Aglow: Magazine for Christian Women*, no. 23 (1975): 27.

33. Omartian's testimony can be found at Stormie Omartian, as told to 'Leen Pollinger, "Breaking Down the Door," *Aglow: For the Spirit Renewed Christian Woman* 20, no. 1 (1989): 6–8. An advertisement for Omartian's video appeared in *Aglow* 19, no. 4 (1988): 2.

34. For a broader discussion of the emergence of prominent black charismatics in the United States who gained national attention beginning especially in the 1980s, see Scott Billingsley, *It's a New Day: Race and Gender in the Modern Charismatic Movement* (Tuscaloosa: University of Alabama Press, 2008).

35. T. D. Jakes, *Lay Aside the Weight: Taking Control of It before It Takes Control of You!* (Tulsa: Albury, 1997), 62–63.

36. For a brief bio of Richardson, see "Donna Richardson Joyner," www.donnarichardson.com/bio.html#.

37. Valerie Lowe, "She's the Expert on Fat," *Charisma* 29, no. 12 (2004): 47.

38. Kara Davis, *Spiritual Secrets to Weight Loss* (Lake Mary, Fl.: Siloam Press, 2002), 173–174.

39. "Lee Haney: TotaLee Fit," www.tbn.org/index.php/2/4/p/31.html. Also see www.leehaney.com/.

40. La Vita Weaver, *Fit for God: The 8 Week Plan That Kicks the Devil Out and Invites Health and Healing In* (New York: Doubleday, 2004).

41. Maureen Salaman, *The Diet Bible: The Bible for Dieters* (New York: McGraw-Hill, 1990), 3–4.

42. Ibid., 3–7, 180–188, quotation 4.

43. For background on the major players in the laetrile controversy as well as discussion of key legal developments, see Gerald E. Markle and James C. Petersen, "The Laetrile Phenomenon: An Overview," in *Politics, Science, and Cancer: The Laetrile Phenomenon*, ed. Gerald E. Markle and James C. Petersen (Boulder, Colo.: Westview Press, 1980); Grace Powers Monaco, "The Laetrile Phenomenon: Legal Perspective," in *Politics, Science, and Cancer: The Laetrile Phenomenon*, ed. Gerald E. Markle and James C. Petersen (Boulder, Colo.: Westview Press, 1980), 99–132. For Salaman's version of the controversy, see Salaman, *Diet Bible*, 180–188.

44. Salaman, *Diet Bible*, 184–185.

45. See John Schneider, "The History of KGTT/KGGC/KSAN/KEST San Francisco," www.bayarearadio.org/schneider/kest.shtml; and "A History of Glad Tidings Church San Francisco," http://gtsf.org/a-history-of-glad-tidings/.

46. For an account by Salaman of the significance of Richardson's arrest and her subsequent involvement in various capacities on behalf of "freedom of choice in medical care," including her role at the National Health Federation, see Salaman, *Diet Bible*, 180–188. Also see the National Health Federation website, www.thenhf.com.

47. While a general distrust of government united many of the individuals attracted to the Populist Party, observers also highlight the group's strong ties to white nationalism and the anti-Semitic views espoused by many of its members. For a brief discussion of Salaman's role in the party, see Leonard Zeskind, *Blood and Politics: The History of the White Nationalist Movement from the Margins to the Mainstream* (New York: Farrar, Straus and Giroux, 2009), 111–112.

48. Staff at the Cathedral of Faith in San Jose, California, were able to confirm that Salaman attended the church at least as early as 1986, though it is possible she began attending even earlier.

49. Salaman, *Diet Bible*, 187–188.

50. James Walsh, Joseph Foote, and John Ambrose, *Safeguarding Children's Nerves: A Handbook of Mental Hygiene* (Philadelphia: J. B. Lippincott, 1924), 25.

51. The history of osteopathy in the United States is an especially good example of the professionalization of alternative therapies; see Norman Gevitz, *The DOs: Osteopathic Medicine in America*, 2nd ed. (Baltimore: Johns Hopkins University Press, 2004).

52. In answer to a question regarding his relationship to traditional medicine, Weil portrayed himself as a neutral referee in the competition between various healing paradigms: "I really think I'm in the middle. Sometimes, I'm attacking traditional medicine, sometimes I'm defending it; sometimes I'm defending alternative medicine and sometimes attacking it, so I think I'm pretty even handed in my criticism. I'm unique in that I'm not aligned with any one school of thought." "Interview with Dr. Andrew Weil: Eight Weeks to Optimum Health," www.manyhands.com/innerview/weil.html. Also see Andrew Weil, *Spontaneous Healing: How to Discover and Enhance Your Body's Natural Ability to Maintain and Heal Itself* (New York: Knopf, 1995); Andrew Weil, *Eight Weeks to Optimum Health: A Proven Program for Taking Full Advantage of Your Body's Natural Healing Power* (New York: Knopf, 1997).

53. Bernie S. Siegel, *Love, Medicine, and Miracles: Lessons Learned about Self-Healing from a Surgeon's Experience with Exceptional Patients* (New York: Harper and Row, 1986), 179.

54. Besides these developments, by the late twentieth century a significant number of M.D.s, especially family practitioners, increasingly referred their patients to alternative physicians such as chiropractors for certain ailments. As the title of a recent study indicates, alternative medicine has gone from "marginal to mainstream." See Mary Ruggie, *Marginal to Mainstream: Alternative Medicine in America* (Cambridge: Cambridge University Press, 2004); James C. Whorton, *Nature Cures: The History of Alternative Medicine in America* (New York: Oxford University Press, 2002), 272–295. For a discussion of the mainstreaming of alternative therapies such as chiropractic medicine specifically in the context of evangelical and charismatic Christianity, see Candy Gunther Brown, "Chiropractic and

Christianity: The Power of Pain to Adjust Cultural Alignments," *Church History* 79, no. 1 (2010): 144–181.

55. An archived link for Whitaker's website, which provides a brief bio, can be found at http://web.archive.org/web/19981212023509/http://www.calling-dr-whitaker.com/.

56. Reginald Cherry, *Healing Prayer: God's Divine Intervention in Medicine, Faith, and Prayer* (Carmel, N.Y.: Guideposts, 1999), 21–42. Also see "About Dr. Reginald B. Cherry, M.D.," www.thepathwaytohealing.com/about.

57. Reginald Cherry, *The Bible Cure* (Orlando, Fl.: Creation House, 1998), 56–58.

58. Reginald Cherry, *The Doctor and the Word* (Orlando, Fl.: Creation House, 1996), 102–106.

59. Cherry, *Healing Prayer*, 24–27.

60. Cherry, *Doctor and the Word*, 16. Also see "About Dr. Reginald B. Cherry, M.D.," www.thepathwaytohealing.com/about.

61. A frequent contributor to *Charisma*, Colbert also published columns in magazines and websites associated with the high-profile ministries of John Hagee and Joyce Meyer, among others, and sold widely distributed books (some of which were sold via Wal-Mart) including Don Colbert, *Toxic Relief: Restore Health and Energy through Fasting and Detoxification* (Lake Mary, Fl.: Siloam, 2001); Don Colbert, *What Would Jesus Eat?* (Nashville: Thomas Nelson, 2002); Don Colbert, *The Bible Cure for Cancer* (Lake Mary, Fl.: Charisma House, 1999). Also see www.drcolbert.com.

62. Colbert, *Toxic Relief*, 35.

63. Ibid., 5–28, quotation 6. For discussion of the importance of detoxification in naturopathic prescriptions, see Whorton, *Nature Cures*, esp. 291.

64. See www.biblicalhealthinstitute.com; and Alex Johnson, "And God Said: Let There Be Lite," December 22, 2004, www.msnbc.msn.com/id/6680007/. *The Maker's Diet* was first published by Siloam, an imprint of the charismatic publisher Strang Communications (now Charisma Media).

65. Jordan Rubin, *The Maker's Diet* (Lake Mary, Fl.: Siloam Press, 2004), 33, 38, 40–49.

66. Ibid., 95. Numerous examples expressing similar sentiments can also be found in chapter 2, "The World's Healthiest People"; chapter 4, "Hygiene: The Double–Edged Sword"; chapter 5: "How to Get Sick: A Modern Prescription for Illness"; chapter 6: "The Desperate Search for Health"; and chapter 8, "Return to the Maker's Diet."

67. For an archived link to one of Rubin's websites where he highlighted his training, see "About the Author," http://web.archive.org/web/20060413232524/http://www.makersdiet.com/publicsite/index.aspx?puid=2d7449b3-4514-465d-9167-50e5bd92484f. The nature of Rubin's accreditation led to his vilification on websites such as "Quackwatch.org." See www.quackwatch.org/11Ind/rubin.html.

68. Don VerHulst, *Ten Keys That Cure* (n.p.: author, 2008), 137. Also see back cover.

69. For discussion of Americans' simultaneous use of both traditional and nontraditional medicine, see Ruggie, *Marginal to Mainstream*, 45–52. In many respects, the divergent attitudes toward scientific medicine displayed by Cherry, Colbert, Rubin, and others reflected similar debates among late-twentieth- and early-twenty-first-century proponents of naturopathic medicine in the United States. See Whorton, *Nature Cures*, 288–292.

70. Salaman's biblical references, found in Isaiah 55:2 and Psalm 17:10, appear in Salaman, *Diet Bible*, xvii–xviii, 24, 67.

71. Ibid., 186.

72. Cherry, *Bible Cure*, ix–x, 1.

73. Ibid., 2–8.

74. Colbert, *What Would Jesus Eat*, x.

75. Colbert, *Toxic Relief*, 7, 171–209.

76. Rubin, *Maker's Diet*, esp. 130–193, quotations 130, 133.

77. VerHulst, *Ten Keys That Cure*, 15.

78. See the following archived link containing promotional materials for Broer's "Eat, Drink & Be Healthy: On the Super Natural Plan," http://web.archive.org/web/20030213032040/http://www.healthmasters.com/books/index.shtml#maxenergy. Broer also developed a DVD series offered through the ministry of Rod Parsley, a popular charismatic minister.

For an archived link promoting "Health Beyond Limits," see http://web.archive.org/web/20071110211109/http://www.breakthrough.net/Onlinestore/Scripts/prodView.asp?idproduct=238. Benny Hinn also offered Broer's books via his website.

79. Maureen D. Eha, "He's Got the Cure," *Charisma* 29, no. 4 (2003): 45.

80. Grant Wacker, *Heaven Below: Early Pentecostals and American Culture* (Cambridge, Mass.: Harvard University Press, 2001), 138, 33.

81. Jonathan R. Baer, "Perfectly Empowered Bodies: Divine Healing in Modernizing America" (Ph.D. diss., Yale University, 2002), 3.

82. For more and the concept of "seed–faith" and Oral Roberts's role in popularizing the teaching, see Harrell, *Oral Roberts*, 460–463.

83. For a brief description of Salaman's involvement with MineralRich, see www.maximumliving.com/about-maximum-living.php. An archived copy of Whitaker's website, where he advertised his vitamins, can be found at "Dr. Whitaker," http://web.archive.org/web/19981212023509/http://www.calling-dr-whitaker.com/.

84. An archived copy of Cherry's website can be found at "Reginald B. Cherry, M.D.," http://web.archive.org/web/20060502044112/http://www.drcherry.com/about_cherry.html.

85. For a description of the products associated with "Divine Health Nutritional Products," see www.drcolbert.com. For a time the website displayed a running total of the number of requests since January 2, 2007, at the bottom of the opening page. See for example http://web.archive.org/web/20080911181115/http://www.drcolbert.com/.

86. *Entrepreneur* ranked Garden of Life fifth on their list of fastest growing companies in the United States in 2004; "2004 Hot 100," http://web.archive.org/web/20070108043529/http://www.entrepreneur.com/hot100/2004.html. Also see Alex Johnson, "And God Said: Let There Be Lite," December 22, 2004, www.msnbc.msn.com/id/6680007/. In part due to this success, no doubt, Rubin's products and claims attracted the scrutiny of the FDA as well as the Federal Trade Commission (FTC). In 2004, the FDA ordered Rubin's company to retract unsubstantiated claims regarding the efficacy of its products. See www.fda.gov/ICECI/EnforcementActions/WarningLetters/2004/ucm146392.htm. Then, in 2006, the FTC filed a complaint that led to Rubin's company paying $225,000 as a penalty for making unsupported claims regarding four specific supplements. See "Dietary Supplement Maker Garden of Life Settles FTC Charges," Federal Trade Commission for Consumers, www.ftc.gov/opa/2006/03/gardenoflife.htm.

87. See www.leehaney.com/.

88. Bill Sizemore, "Is Anything Wrong with Pat Robertson Making a Killing? 'Age–Defying' Shake Stirs Questions about Business Practices and Nonprofit Status," *Washington Post*, August 26, 2005.

89. For an archived link to the description of Omega XL as it appeared in promotions for the product in 2006, see http://web.archive.org/web/20061022194632/http://www.omegaxl.com/omegaxl.htm. The product cost $49.95 for a one-month supply; for each bottle sold, the Whites in turn received $5.00. For more regarding Omega XL, see Michael Sasso, "Preachers of Profit," *Tampa Tribune*, May 14, 2006.

90. See "James Robison and TriVita," www.jamesrobison.com/trivita/. Also see Michael Sasso, "Preachers of Profit," *Tampa Tribune*, May 14, 2006.

91. See Renate Wilson, *Pious Traders in Medicine: A German Pharmaceutical Network in Eighteenth-Century North America* (University Park: Pennsylvania State University Press, 2000), esp. 79–87.

92. Lisa Bevere, *You Are Not What You Weigh: Escaping the Lie and Living the Truth* (Orlando, Fl.: Creation House, 1998), 30, 93. It is also worth noting that Neva Coyle eventually repudiated her earlier works. See Neva Coyle, *Loved on a Grander Scale: Affirmation, Acceptance, and Hope for Women Who Struggle with Their Weight* (Ann Arbor, Mich.: Servant Publications, 1998); Griffith, *Born Again Bodies*, 223–224. Griffith also mentions Omartian's emphasis on the "tyranny of contemporary body standards," though noting the way "Omartian's own books display her model–thin body, making her plea for inclusive appreciation rather feeble." "The Promised Land of Weight Loss: Law and Gospel in Christian Dieting," *Christian Century* 114, no. 15 (May 7, 1997): 448–454.

93. See Linda Mintle, *Breaking Free from a Negative Self-Image* (Lake Mary, Fl.: Charisma House, 2002); and Linda Mintle, *Making Peace with Your Thighs: Get Off the Scales and Get On with Your Life* (Franklin, Tenn.: Integrity Publishers, 2006). Also see http://drlindamintle.com/, and "Helping America Get Healthier," www.ag.org/Pentecostal-evangel/Conversations2008/4896_Mintle.cfm.

94. Marty Copeland, "Facing Fat for the Last Time," www.kcm.org/real-help/article/facing-fat-last-time.

95. Jakes, *Lay Aside the Weight*, 18–19.

96. Joyce Meyer, *Eat and Stay Thin: Simple, Spiritual, Satisfying Weight Control* (Tulsa: Harrison House, 1999), 7, 77, 181.

97. Weaver, *Fit for God*, 108–109.

98. See esp. Frank E. Peretti, *This Present Darkness* (Westchester, Ill.: Crossway Books, 1986); Frank E. Peretti, *Piercing the Darkness* (Westchester, Ill.: Crossway Books, 1989).

99. See C. Peter Wagner, *Warfare Prayer: How to Seek God's Power and Protection in the Battle to Build His Kingdom* (Ventura, Calif.: Regal Books, 1992); C. Peter Wagner, *Breaking Strongholds in Your City: How to Use Spiritual Mapping to Make Your Prayers More Strategic, Effective, and Targeted* (Ventura, Calif.: Regal Books, 1993); C. Peter Wagner, *Confronting the Powers: How the New Testament Church Experienced the Power of Strategic-Level Spiritual Warfare* (Ventura, Calif.: Regal Books, 1996).

100. Pamela Smith, "Diet Deliverance," *Charisma* 18, no. 7 (1993): 88; Pamela Smith, "Your Mom Was Right," *Charisma* 19, no. 3 (1993): 120. Griffith briefly discusses Smith in *Born Again Bodies*, 385–386.

101. Kara Davis, "Why Is the Church So Fat?," *Charisma* 29, no. 12 (2004): 47.

102. Davis, *Spiritual Secrets to Weight Loss*, 208–209. Scripture reference taken from Mark 9:14–29, NRSV, and Mark 9:29, AMP.

103. David Hazard, "An Inside Look at Inner Healing," *Charisma* 12, no. 2 (1986): 48–49.

104. See Gwen Shamblin, *The Weigh Down Diet* (New York: Doubleday, 1997); George H. Malkmus, Peter Shockey, and Stowe Shockey, *The Hallelujah Diet: Experience the Optimal Health You Were Meant to Have* (Shippensburg, Pa.: Destiny Image, 2006).

105. See Carol Chapman Stertzer, "Losing Pounds for God," *Charisma* 23, no. 11 (1998): 52–60, 102–104.

106. See Malkmus et al., *Hallelujah Diet*. For references to Malkmus's influence among charismatics, as well as his association with the Oasis of Hope Cancer Hospital, see "Hallelujah Acres' Partner in Health: The Contreras Cancer Care Center—The OASIS of Hope Hospital," http://web.archive.org/web/19971221165844/hacres.com/html/oasis.html; and George Malkmus, "Where Is God in Time of Sickness," pt. 2, http://healthtip.hacres.com/index.php/2011/07/19/where-is-god-in-time-of-sickness-part-2/. Indicative of the Contreras family's own ties to the charismatic movement, Francisco Contreras published numerous books with the charismatic press Siloam, an imprint of Charisma Media (formerly Strang Communications), including *The Hope of Living Cancer Free* (1999) and *The Coming Cancer Cure* (2002). He also served as a columnist for *Charisma*.

107. Robert Andrescik, "When Man Meets His Maker," *Charisma* 30, no. 10 (2005): 37.

108. I borrow the language of "public transcripts" and "hidden transcripts" from James C. Scott, *Domination and the Arts of Resistance: Hidden Transcripts* (New Haven, Conn.: Yale University Press, 1990).

109. Davis, "Why Is the Church So Fat," 47.

110. This reading of the pentecostal-charismatic movement coincides with Candy Gunther Brown's observation that late-twentieth-century pentecostals and charismatics implicitly reinforced consumerism by stressing the fact that divine healing could and should occur "in the marketplace," as opposed to traditional religious contexts such as churches or tents. See Candy Gunther Brown, "From Tent Meetings and Store–Front Healing Rooms to Walmarts and the Internet: Healing Spaces in the United States, the Americas, and the World, 1906–2006," *Church History: Studies in Christianity and Culture* 75 (2006): 638–639.

111. Describing the advent of modern advertising, Alan Trachtenberg highlights the way advertisers sought to "make habitual the identification of products with something else,

with ideas, feelings, status. Advertisement endowed goods with a language of their own, a language of promise radically new in the history of man-made things," Alan Trachtenberg and Eric Foner, *The Incorporation of America: Culture and Society in the Gilded Age* (New York: Hill and Wang, 1982), 135.

112. Leigh Eric Schmidt, *Consumer Rites: The Buying and Selling of American Holidays* (Princeton, N.J.: Princeton University Press, 1995), 297.

Conclusion

1. Frank E. Peretti, *This Present Darkness* (Westchester, Ill.: Crossway Books, 1986), 48.
2. Ibid.
3. Shari Gundlach, "You Can Lead a Kid to Bean Sprouts . . . But You Can't Make Him Eat," *New Wine* 11, no. 4 (1979): 9–11.
4. Adrian Brookes, "A Dark World Down Under," *Charisma* 28, no. 6 (2003): 66.
5. Francisco Contreras, "New Year's Resolutions," *Charisma* 28, no. 6 (2003): 84. Also see www.oasisofhope.com.
6. For a brief discussion of Contreras Senior's role in the laetrile debates, see James Harvey Young, "Laetrile in Historical Perspective," in *Politics, Science, and Cancer: The Laetrile Phenomenon*, ed. Gerald E. Markle and James C. Petersen (Boulder, Colo.: Westview Press, 1980), 22–24. Contreras's role in the distribution of laetrile attracted national attention. See for example "Laetrile Crackdown," *Time* 107, no. 24 (June 7, 1976): 84.
7. "Alternative Cancer Treatments," www.oasisofhope.com/alternative-cancer-treatments.php.
8. See John Leland, "Christian Diets: Fewer Loaves, Lots of Fishes," *New York Times*, April 28, 2005.
9. See "Divine Connection, Divine Call," *Charisma* 29, no. 4 (2003): 48.
10. Linda L. Barnes, "Multiple Meanings of Chinese Healing in the United States," in *Religion and Healing in America*, ed. Linda L. Barnes and Susan S. Sered (New York: Oxford University Press, 2005), 317.
11. I borrow the term "off-modern" from Svetlana Boym, who describes a particular type of nostalgic response to the rapid social and cultural dislocations associated with modernization. Svetlana Boym, *The Future of Nostalgia* (New York: Basic Books, 2001), xvii. My use of the term "off-modern" does not fully mirror Boym's. In her work she distinguishes between a "restorative nostalgia" that is intent on actually reproducing a lost past, and then contrasts that with what she labels a "reflective nostalgia" that understands the irretrievability of the past yet productively uses that sense of loss to reassess present possibilities. For Boym, the off-modern clearly fits best with this reflective nostalgia. The pentecostal and charismatic healers discussed here, not to mention numerous other alternative healers, typically blended the two, combing a focus on present and future possibilities with a restorative nostalgia intent on recovering a lost connection with nature. That said, the basic off-modern dynamic described by Boym remains a very useful tool for describing the way numerous healers on the American scene past and present juxtapose a nostalgic concern for a lost past with a tempered optimism for the present.
12. Courtney Bender, *The New Metaphysicals: Spirituality and the American Religious Imagination* (Chicago: University of Chicago Press, 2010), 30. Some of the other expressions of metaphysical religion that often do not focus as much on physical healing include groups and individuals who stress dream interpretation, mystical encounters with the divine, communication with the dead or other spirits, etc.
13. The "professionalization" of alternative healing is especially evident in the history of osteopathic medicine. See for example Norman Gevitz, *The DOs: Osteopathic Medicine in America*, 2nd ed. (Baltimore: Johns Hopkins University Press, 2004); James C. Whorton, *Nature Cures: The History of Alternative Medicine in America* (New York: Oxford University Press, 2002), 221–243, 271–295.
14. Oral Roberts, "The Master Plan God Has Given Me," *Abundant Life* 31, no. 11 (1977): 7.

15. Oral Roberts, "I Believe the Cure for Cancer Has a Spiritual Origin," *Abundant Life* 31, no. 1 (1977): 2.
16. Oral Roberts, "God Still Heals Today—He Is Just Using Different 'Delivery Systems,'" *Abundant Life* 30, no. 1 (1976): 16.
17. William Standish Reed, "Is It Time for a New Medicine?," *Logos* 9 (1979): 12–13.
18. Don VerHulst, *Ten Keys That Cure* (n.p.: author, 2008), 15.
19. Jordan Rubin, *The Maker's Diet* (Lake Mary, Fl.: Siloam Press, 2004).
20. Ruth Carter Stapleton, *The Experience of Inner Healing* (Carmel, N.Y.: Guideposts, 1977), 7–8.
21. David Hazard, "An Inside Look at Inner Healing," *Charisma* 12, no. 2 (1986): 48.
22. "Christian Psychiatric Care Unit Expands," *Charisma* 15 (1990): 20.
23. Gary Ferngren, for example, includes Stapleton as an example of healing trends in evangelical and fundamentalist circles. Gary B. Ferngren, "The Evangelical-Fundamentalist Tradition," in *Caring and Curing*, ed. Ronald L. Numbers and Darrel W. Amundsen (New York: Macmillan, 1986), 501.
24. Ken Walker, "Houston Church Reaches Homosexuals," *Charisma* 22, no. 10 (1997): 30.
25. See Leanne Payne, *Restoring the Christian Soul: Overcoming Barriers to Completion in Christ through Healing Prayer* (Grand Rapids, Mich.: Baker Books, 1996).
26. R. G. Robins, *Pentecostalism in America* (Santa Barbara, Calif.: Praeger, 2010), 106. Beginning especially in the early 1980s, other observers of the convergence of the pentecostal-charismatic movement with key aspects of evangelicalism began to talk of a "Third Wave" of renewal. Coined by C. Peter Wagner, the term was meant to highlight individuals in evangelical and mainstream churches who affirmed the validity of the charismatic gifts mentioned in scripture, including divine healing, prophecy, speaking in tongues, and so forth, but did not identify themselves with the traditional pentecostal denominations (the so-called First Wave) or with the Charismatic Renewal in the Roman Catholic Church and in mainline Protestant churches (the so-called Second Wave). See C. Peter Wagner, *The Third Wave of the Holy Spirit: Encountering the Power of Signs and Wonders Today* (Ann Arbor, Mich.: Servant, 1988).
27. Harvey, for example, interviewed Haney as part of his morning radio show. Also see Denene Millner, "Success Story: Steve Harvey," www.mensfitness.com/fitness/success-stories/success-story-steve-harvey.
28. See Cary McMullen, "Florida Outpouring: Internet Draws Thousands to Lakeland Revival," *Ledger*, May 18, 2008, www.theledger.com/article/20080518/NEWS/805180341/1004; Cary McMullen, "Faith-Healing 'Outpouring' Overflows Venue," *Ledger*, April 25, 2008, www.theledger.com/article/20080425/NEWS/804250386; Paul Steven Ghiringhelli, "Lakeland Outpouring Reaches 50-Day Milestone," May 22, 2008, www.charismamag.com/index.php/news-old/19600; and J. Lee Grady, "A Holy Ghost Outbreak in Florida," April 23, 2008, www.fireinmybones.com/Columns/042308.html.
29. For discussion of pentecostals and charismatics who were troubled by aspects of Bentley's ministry, see Cary McMullen, "Florida Outpouring Revival Concerns Pentecostal Leaders," *Ledger*, June 22, 2008, www.theledger.com/article/20080622/NEWS/806220412; J. Lee Grady, "Honest Questions about the Lakeland Revival," May 14, 2008, www.charismamag.com/fireinmybones/Columns/051408.html.
30. A recording of the testimony is available online. See "Benny Hinn—Miracle Healing—Tumor Disappeared," www.youtube.com/watch?v=7pf-XUe_z-8, Flower Pentecostal Heritage Center, Springfield, Missouri. For a similar description of a 1997 Nashville crusade conducted by Hinn, see Stephen Jackson Pullum, *"Foul Demons, Come Out!" The Rhetoric of Twentieth-Century American Faith Healing* (Westport, Conn.: Praeger, 1999), 134–139.
31. These comments were made by Stephen Strader, pastor of Ignited Church in Lakeland, Florida, during one of Bentley's services on July 20, 2008. Recordings of the services previously were accessible at www.god.tv/.
32. Todd Bentley, "My Personal Journey into the Healing Ministry," pt. 3, www.freshfireusa.com/index.php/articles/view/195.
33. Todd Bentley, "The Reality of the Supernatural World, Part 2," www.freshfireusa.com/index.php/articles/view/137.

34. See for example "Diabetes and Healthy Eating," www.bennyhinn.org/articles/1368/diabetes-and-healthy-eating; "Vitamin E May Keep Your Memory Sharp," www.bennyhinn.org/articles/2478/vitamin-e-may-keep-your-memory-sharp.
35. "Divine Connection, Divine Call," 48.
36. See Maureen D. Eha, "He's Got the Cure," *Charisma* 29, no. 4 (2003): esp. 44–45.
37. "Mobbed 'Healer' Asks Court's Aid," *New York Times*, August 7, 1907, 5. Late-nineteenth-century evangelical healers fended off accusations of mesmerism and hypnotism as well. See Heather D. Curtis, *Faith in the Great Physician: Suffering and Divine Healing in American Culture, 1860–1900* (Baltimore: Johns Hopkins University Press, 2007), 122–130.
38. Francis MacNutt, *Healing* (1974; reprint, New York: Bantam Books, 1977), 50.

Epilogue

1. Ogbu Kalu, *African Pentecostalism: An Introduction* (New York: Oxford University Press, 2008), 263. For extended analysis of the significance of healing in the global spread of pentecostalism, see the various essays collected in Candy Gunther Brown, ed., *Global Pentecostal and Charismatic Healing* (New York: Oxford University Press, 2011).
2. Quoted in Philip Jenkins, *The Next Christendom: The Coming of Global Christianity* (New York: Oxford University Press, 2002), 126.
3. Allan Anderson, *An Introduction to Pentecostalism: Global Charismatic Christianity* (Cambridge: Cambridge University Press, 2004), 211, 283.
4. For discussion of the relationship between pentecostal healing and Hindu demonology, see Michael Bergunder, "Miracle Healing and Exorcism in South Indian Pentecostalism," in *Global Pentecostal and Charismatic Healing*, 287–306. In terms of pentecostal healing in South Korea, scholars such as Sean C. Kim warn against simplistic depictions of the relationship between pentecostalism in the country and key aspects of shamanism. While he acknowledges "basic, largely surface similarities" linking the two traditions, he concludes that pentecostal healing in Korea "cannot simply be reduced to shamanization. Rather, it is part of a broader process of indigenization." Kim, "Reenchanted: Divine Healing in Korean Protestantism," in Brown, *Global Pentecostal and Charismatic Healing*, 267–285, esp. 278–282. Also see Anderson, *Introduction to Pentecostalism*, 237–238.
5. Grant Wacker, for example, explores numerous ways early pentecostals cultivated a strong pragmatism characterized by a "realism," "practicality," and accommodation to the "limits of everyday life" that functioned alongside their better known primitivist impulse. Grant Wacker, *Heaven Below: Early Pentecostals and American Culture* (Cambridge, Mass.: Harvard University Press, 2001), 13. Along similar lines, Wallace Best's study of black religion in Chicago during the Great Migration of African Americans to the North highlights pentecostal figures such as Lucy Smith of All Nations Pentecostal Church who merged the otherworldly sensibilities prominent among southern migrants with technological innovations, business acumen, and social outreach. Wallace D. Best, *Passionately Human, No Less Divine: Religion and Culture in Black Chicago, 1915–1952* (Princeton, N.J.: Princeton University Press, 2005), esp. 147–180. In his biography of the early pentecostal leader A. J. Tomlinson, R. G. Robins details the ways the saints shared with other Americans the "celebration of innovation and change; cultural optimism; the glorification of science, technology, and power; a dialectic relationship with urbanization; the blurring of regional boundaries; and a social ethic that undermined traditional assumptions about race and gender." R. G. Robins, *A. J. Tomlinson: Plainfolk Modernist* (New York: Oxford University Press, 2004), esp. 9–62, quotation 37. Robins provides the most sustained argument to date for pentecostals' affinities to modern U.S. culture.
6. Jenkins, *Next Christendom*, 126.

INDEX